Wildlife Rehabilitation

Wildlife Rehabilitation

Volume 5

Selected papers presented at
the Fifth Symposium of the
National Wildlife Rehabilitators Association,
Boston, Massachusetts, February 19-23, 1986
Hosted by the New England Wildlife Center

Edited by Paul Beaver, Ph.D.
and
Daniel James Mackey

FIRST EDITION

Copyright © 1986 by National Wildlife Rehabilitators Association

All rights reserved. No part of this book may be reproduced, in whole or part, in any form or by any means, electronic or mechanical, including photocopying, recording, or by any information storage and retrieval system without permission in writing from the National Wildlife Rehabilitators Association.

Printed in the United States of America

Published on behalf of NWRA by
Daniel James Mackey
2201 Northwest 40th Terrace
Coconut Creek, Florida 33066

CONTENTS

PREFACE   vii

VETERINARY ASPECTS

Scaling Drug Dosages for Animals of Diverse Body Sizes   3
Charles J. Sedgwick, Alison Haskell, and Mark A. Pokras

Poisoning of Birds by Cholinesterase Inhibitor Pesticides   12
Ward B. Stone and Peter B. Gradoni

Wound Treatment   29
Mark A. Pokras

Avian Parasites: Potential Pathogens in Times of Stress   38
William Threlfall

Oiled Bird Rehabilitation: Fact and Fallacy   68
Lynne Frink and Betsy Jones

Common Problems Among Reptiles Presented to Rehabilitation Centers   80
Stephen L. Barten

A Technique for the Repair of Chelonian Shell Fractures, with a Historical Review of Shell Fracture Repair   86
George Heinrich and Donna Heinrich

REARING ORPHANS

The Use of Bird Skin Puppets in Rearing Orphaned Birds   101
Paul Beaver, Denise Steenblock, Ruth Iannazzi, and Mike Ayers

Hand-rearing Chimney Swifts   103
Paul Kyle and Georgean Kyle

Hand-rearing Carolina and Bewick's Wrens   114
Paul Kyle and Georgean Kyle

PROGRAMS FOR PARTICULAR SPECIES

Conservation Program for the Golden Lion Tamarin: Captive Research and Management, Ecological Studies, Educational Strategies and Reintroduction   123
*Devra G. Kleiman, Benjamin B. Beck,
James M. Dietz, Lou Ann Dietz, Jonathan D. Ballou,
and Adelman F. Coimbra-Filho*

The Conservation and Rehabilitation of the Common Barn Owl   146
Terry A. Schulz

ADMINISTRATIVE ASPECTS

The Value of Centralized Wildlife Rehabilitation　　169
Betsy Lewis

A New Approach to Records Analysis in a Wild Bird
　　　　Rehabilitation Center　　177
Lynne Frink and John Frink

PUBLIC EDUCATION

Producing an Effective Presentation　　193
Stephen L. Barten

Sharing Your Nuggets of Knowledge　　199
Lou Strobhar

PREFACE

This book marks a milestone in the history of a young National Wildlife Rehabilitators Association, as it is the fifth volume in as many years of annual National Wildlife Rehabilitation symposiums.

Members and non-members alike can take pride in the body of work they have contributed to science and the world's wildlife in those five years.

Volume V demonstrates that the exchange of information across the boundaries of traditional fields of science can benefit everyone. Veterinarians, rehabilitators, government biologists and pathologists, educators, researchers, wildlife officers, public institutions, and even private citizens acting alone, are merely a few categories of people who, when working together, can make a difference.

As Lynne and John Frink point out to fellow rehabilitators in their paper, "A New Approach To Record Analysis In A Wild Bird Rehabilitation Center":

> "Records can be kept by anyone who has a ballpoint pen. Good records help insure continuity and quality of care. The better our records are, the more we will learn from our successes and our mistakes, and the more we can share with others. The more we learn, the better will be our understanding of what is happening to the wild creatures who depend on us for their continued survival."

Readers wishing to correspond with the National Wildlife Rehabilitators Association may do so by writing to: NWRA, RR 1, Box 125E, Brighton, Illinois 62012.

D.J.M.

Veterinary Aspects

SCALING DRUG DOSAGES FOR ANIMALS OF DIVERSE BODY SIZES

Charles J. Sedgwick, D.V.M., Alison Haskell and Mark A. Pokras, D.V.M.

Tufts University
School of Veterinary Medicine
Wildlife Clinic
200 Westboro Road
North Grafton, MA 01536

INTRODUCTION

Veterinary clinicians have little controlled data for evaluating drug dosage efficacy in the many unfamiliar species and for the potentially vast diversity of body sizes that comprise the wildlife group of animals. Controlled evaluations of drug pharmicokinetics and therapeutic efficacies done for the human or some domestic animals have been carried out for only a few wildlife species.

Unless a drug is an anesthetic, a veterinarian usually cannot immediately appraise the result of a treatment. Therefore, some drug treatments for wildlife species may be effective; some may be ineffective; while others that have inadvertently been overdosed, can prove harmful. Dosages for wildlife species of antimicrobials, anthelmintics and the other therapeutic agents, including nutrients, must be extrapolated from a nebulous array of serendipitous experience and, occasionally, unorthodox clinical philosophies. These may be applied in ways that are inconsistent with physiological and pharmicological principle. The problem is a great one in wildlife veterinary practice.

The purpose of this discussion is to suggest a uniform approach to the practice of drug dosage extrapolation between animals of widely disparate body size, from domestic animal and human practice, to wildlife practice.

The procedure described here will base drug dosages upon energy utilization at rest, or minimum energy cost, or basal metabolism in kilocalories (kcal) per day. The procedure can be applied to any animal among five groups of vertebrates, i.e. passerine birds, non-passerine birds, placental mammals and marsupial mammals. It can also be applied to reptiles when the latter are maintained at their preferred optimal environmental temperature.

The groups are segregated on the basis of their different core body temperature ranges with their discrete set-points regulated by the hypothalamus (Hainsworth 1981). Basing dosages on energy units (kilocalories) is different from expressing them in terms of body size (weight.). Dosages based upon body weight (mg of drug/kg of body weight) plotted on a graph, describe a curved regression line, while those based upon energy utilization (mg of drug/kcal of energy utilization at basal conditions) describe a linear regression line (see figure 1).

Figure 1. Comparison of Gentamicin Dosages. (a) mg/kg at various weight levels (b) mg/kcal/day at various MEC levels.

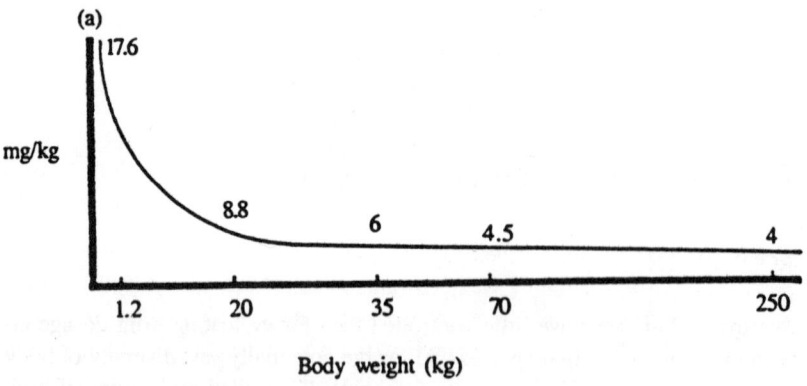

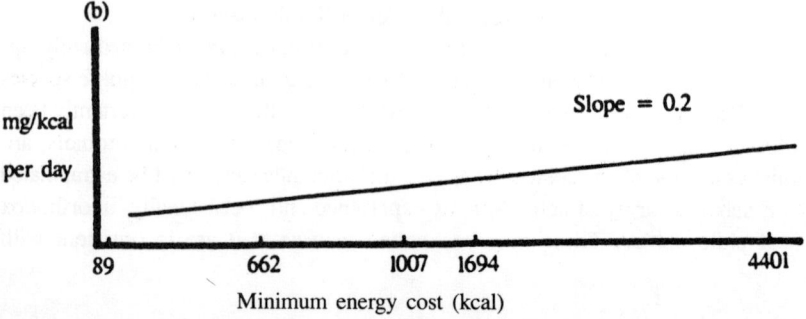

With any given animal subject, if we can assume that there are no unique individual or species susceptibilities to a drug causing that animal to respond to the drug in drastically different ways from most other animals, the problem of dosage extrapolation then becomes one of scaling or comparing animals in terms of their *metabolic size*. Metabolic size is usually represented by the formula: Body weight (W) in kilograms (kg) taken to the three quarters power ($W_{kg}^{0.75}$) (McCullough 1969).

For morphologically similar groups of animals at metabolic rest, sometimes referred to as MEC or basal metabolism, a sixteen-fold variation in body weight (kg) generally represents about a two-fold variation in energy expenditure, expressed as kcal. This observation has long been used by some veterinary clinicians to extrapolate drug dosages from familiar species to species with an unfamiliar history of clinical treatment. For example, it was suggested as a rule of thumb by J.E. Cooper (1985) that extrapolating dosages (mg/kg) from the dog, to much smaller mammals or birds, should require doubling the dog's dosage rates when applying them to the smaller species. This is the correct approach to the procedure, but it is a very imprecise one because there could be significant disagreement about the weight of a "standard-sized" *domestic dog* (there being a sixty-fold difference between the weights of a tea-cup sized Pekingese and an Irish Wolfhound, for example).

In the circles of most current clinical practices, drug dosages are still prescribed in terms of units of drug per unit of animal body weight. However, this is a custom which ignores the principle that disposition of drugs through the vascular network is determined by a pressure head. This pressure head, provided by the pumping heart, is metabolically and not mass (weight) dependent.

MATERIALS AND METHODS

Ideally, any subjects to receive drug treatment by the method of metabolic extrapolation would be accurately weighed (and weight expressed in metric units).

MEC or basal metabolism is calculated as the body weight of any animal in kilograms carried to the three quarter power which is its metabolic size and multiplied by a constant (K) that is based upon the core body temperature set-point range for any of the five discrete animal energy groups, i.e.:

$$\text{MEC} = K^a \times W_{kg}^{0.75}$$

[a] K-factors for each of the five animal energy groups (Hainsworth 1981):

passerine birds	129
non-passerine birds	78
placental mammals	70
marsupial mammals	49
reptiles (at 37°C)	10

These have been determined by measuring the minimum energy cost or basal metabolism for a one kg animal in each of the 5 groups of animals (see figure 2).

Figure 2.

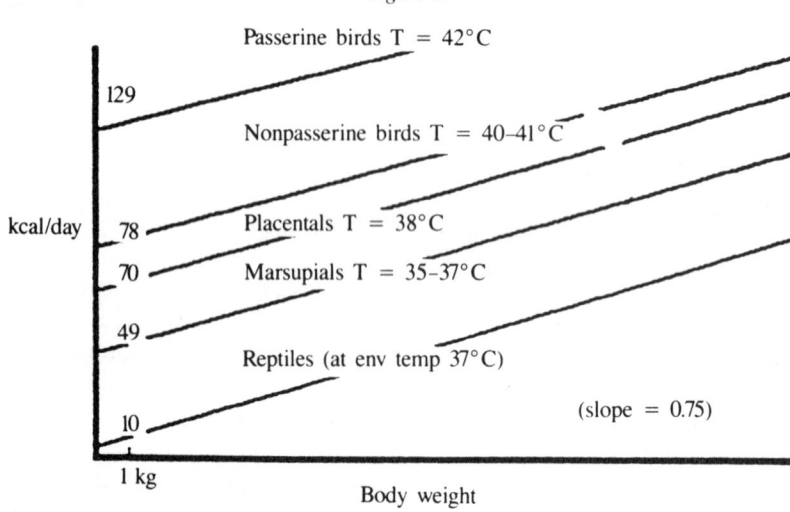

First, calculate a MEC-dosage:
1. An "animal model" for extrapolation of a particular drug is selected. Such an animal model would ideally come from pharmacological research literature where drug dosages have been arrived at via controlled trials, providing drug serum level measurements, where appropriate, and information from meticulous record keeping on clinical response. MEC is then calculated for the model animal. If the model animal is the human one, total dosages are often given as total mg of drug for a child or total mg of drug for an adult and it is useful to know that in the practice of human medicine the weight for an adult is assumed to be 60–70 kg and the child, 30 kg. Therefore, the dosage rates may be computed by dividing total dosages by the appropriate weight of an adult or child.
2. The total daily dosage (mg/24 hours) for the model animal is calculated. Total dosage for the model animal is divided by its MEC to give the MEC-dosage in mg/kcal (this is a universal dosage that can be used to calculate the total daily dosage of the subject animal).
3. MEC for the subject (unfamiliar) animal is then calculated from its weight (kcal/day) and multiplied by the MEC-dosage that was derived from the model animal. This gives the total dosage (24 hrs.) for the subject animal.

Second, extrapolate the treatment regimens (dosing periodicity per 24 hours):
1. The basal metabolic rates (BMR) (kcal/kg) are calculated for both the model and subject animals, i.e.:

$$BMR = K \times W_{kg}^{-0.25} \text{ or } MEC/W_{kg}$$

2. Calculating the dosing periodicity or the way in which the total dosage will be administered in a 24 hour period:

$$\left(\frac{BMR\ (subject)}{BMR\ (model) \cdot period.\ (model)}\right)^{-1} = \text{dosing periodicity (subject)}$$

RESULTS

Scaling a dosage and treatment regimen of Amphotericin B from an adult human model to a non-passerine bird subject can be a worthy exercise in applying scaling principles.

Amphotericen B (AMB) remains one of the most potent broad spectrum agents available for treating deep seated fungal infections and it can be used for mammals or birds. Although its use may be life-saving, it is also one of the most toxic therapeutic agents to be employed by the clinician. It is damaging to the endothelial lining of blood vessels and must be given intravenously at a maximum concentration of 0.1 mg/ml.

The rate of administration of AMB in an aqueous solution of 5% dextrose (D_5W) must be precisely controlled to avoid cardiac arrhythmias (ventricular fibrillation) and the treatment periods during the day must be carefully restricted within definite, short-term schedules to allow long recovery periods for renal function that is disrupted by this drug.

Here is the accepted treatment regimen for AMB based upon a 70 kg human (placental) model (Ginsberg et al. 1980).

1. The total dosage per day for a human adult is 50 mg AMB. Concentration is not to exceed 0.1 mg/ml in D_5W.
2. There will be one treatment period of exactly 4 hours per 24 hour day.

The problem is: Convert the human prescription for administering AMB to one for a non-passerine bird weighing 500 grams (g).

First, calculate a MEC-dosage for AMB:

1. The weight of the model animal (placental) is 70 kg and the total (24 hr) dosage of AMB is 50 mg (0.7 mg/kg).

$$\begin{aligned} MEC &= 70 \times W_{kg}^{0.75} \\ &= 70 \times 70^{0.75} \\ &= 1694 \text{ kcal/day} \end{aligned}$$

2. The total daily dosage of 50 mg AMB for the model animal was given.

50 mg AMB/1694 kcal (1 day) = *0.03* mg/kcal is the MEC-dosage

3. MEC for the subject animal, a 0.5 kg non-passerine bird is:

$$\begin{aligned} MEC &= 78 \times W_{kg}^{0.75} \\ &= 78 \times 0.5^{0.75} \\ &= 46.3 \text{ kcal/day} \end{aligned}$$

The total dosage (subject) is 46.3 kcal × 0.03 mg/kcal = *1.4* mg AMB. Second, extrapolate the treatment regimens (dosing periodicities per 24 hours of drug dosage):

1. Calculate the BMR for both the model and subject animals (BMR = K × $W_{kg}^{-0.25}$ or MEC/W_{kg}):

$$\text{Model's BMR} = 24.2 \text{ kcal/kg}$$
$$\text{Subject's BMR} = 92.7 \text{ kcal/kg}$$

2. Calculate the periodicities of administration. The model animal receives a treatment every day (24 hrs) lasting 240 minutes. What period would be comparable for the subject animal?

$$\left(\frac{\text{BMR (subject)}}{\text{BMR (model)}} \cdot \text{period. (model)} \right)^{-1} = \text{periodicity (subject)}$$

$$\left(\frac{92.7 \text{ kcal/kg}}{24.2 \text{ kcal/kg}} \cdot 24 \text{ hours} \right)^{-1} = 6 \text{ hrs.}$$

The total dosage of AMB for the subject will be divided by 4 and administered once every 6 hours, (i.e. 1.4 mg AMB/4 = *0.35* mg every 6 hours). If the AMB adminstration time is 4 hours (240 min.) for the model animal what will it be for the subject animal?

$$\left(\frac{92.7}{24.2} \cdot 240 \right)^{-1} = 63 \text{ minutes}$$

To summarize: The model animal would receive a total dosage of 50 mg AMB each day in a 0.01% solution during one 240 minute period. This would require 500 ml of 0.1 mg/ml solution or about 30 drops per minutes for the 4 hour administration period.

The subject animal would receive 1.4 mg AMB in a 0.01% solution per day, but divided into 4 treatments (0.35 mg) and each treatment given in 60 minutes every 6 hours. This would require 3.5 ml of 0.1 mg/ml solution or ≤1 drop per minute for a 60 minute administration.

The dosage rate of AMB for the model animal is its total dosage of 50 mg/70 kg = 0.7 mg/kg. The dosage rate for the subject animal is 1.4 mg/0.5 = 2.8 mg/kg. The dosage rate (mg/kg) for the smaller subject animal is much higher than that for the larger model animal, it must be administrered in a highly modified (tamed) manner to prevent its toxicity from damaging the smaller subject animal.

DISCUSSION

Certain classes of drugs are scale-independent, i.e. dosages can not be extrapolated from one species to another based upon metabolic size. The opioids seem to fall into this category where, for example, the effective canine dosages can not be extrapolated to the cats, horses, birds and some individuals within species, but must be greatly reduced if they are to be used at all. The opioids interact with stereospecific and saturable binding sites in the brain that are the receptors for several endogenous ligands. It may be that the narcotic analgesics activate some of the feline and equine opioid receptor sites in ways that the group's own endogenous opioids do not.

Before endeavoring to scale a drug dosage from a model animal to an unfamiliar subject, it is necessary to assume that the drug is scale-dependent. It so, absorption, distribution and elimination of the drug is dependent upon cardiac output; the heart, acting as a pump creates a pressure head. Cardiac output is scale-dependent on metabolic size (Schmidt-Nielsen 1984). Therefore, drug uptake, distribution and elimination are ultimately dependent upon metabolic size.

Minimum energy cost or MEC is a term that has been used in recent literature synonymously with basal metabolism (Hainsworth 1981). It is the rate of energy use, alternatively considered as oxygen consumption, equivalent to that measured in the laboratory for animals deprived of food long enough for them to start using fat as an energy substrate (Respiratory quotient = 0.7, inactive and at a standardized environmental temperature and given photoperiod). It is the energy needed merely for circulatory, ventilatory and digestive functions, etc., in the resting animal. Actual measured basal metabolic rates correlate with calculated MEC by a variation of less than 6% or a goodness of fit of nearly 95% in a very large, diverse sampling of test subject species that have included many nondomestic ones (Abram 1968).

Conventional drug dosages (mg/kg) are usually simply published *for birds or reptiles,* without indicating that consideration should be given to whether the subject animal is an eight gram canary or a one hundred fifty kilogram ostrich, a tiny fence lizard or a very large crocodile. The differences in size between such animals can be of an order of magnitude more than one hundred twenty five thousand-fold.

As with AMB, many drugs are potentially toxic at dosages that are only moderately higher than those required to obtain therapeutic levels, for example, the aminoglycosides. It is obvious that clinicans practicing in a field like zoological medicine, occupied by groups of animals with great variation in mass, must make allowance for this by changing the drug dosage scale (mg/kg) when using this method or by scaling dosages to metabolic size instead. Physicians change scales for most antimicrobials and other drugs when the weight of one class of patient doubles or halves that of another, e.g., going from the adult (70 kg) to the child (35 kg) to the infant (15 kg) (Ginsberg 1980).

The problems of effectively scaling drug dosages in wildlife practice is further complicated by the need to consider homeotherms (mammals and birds) that undergo torpor or hibernation, and poikilotherms (mammals and others) that are partially or totally dependent upon environmental temperature for setting the level of metabolism which, in turn, governs cardiac output and drug disposition. Drug dosage rates in poikilotherms should be adjusted when a subject is not at its preferred optimal temperature zone (POTZ) (Madar et al. 1986).

Figure 2 illustrates the metabolic relationships of the five energy classes of animals in relation to their core body temperature set-points.

Figure 1 illustrates gentamicin dosages for a 1.2 kg (89 kcal) red-tailed hawk; a 20 kg (662 kcal) dog; a 35 kg (1007 kcal) child; a 70 kg (1694 kcal) human adult; and a 250 kg (4401 kcal) bovine. In regression curve 1(a) notice that as mass increases, dosage as mg/kg decreases. The regression line is not rectilineal. The total daily hawk's dosage (17.7 mg/kg) is twice that of the dog's and more than four-fold that of the steer.

Hypothetically, if we knew no dosage for gentamicin in the dog or the steer, but had only a hawk dosage (17.6 mg/kg), we would overdose the dog by two-fold and the steer by four-fold. This would, no doubt, injure the kidneys of the dog and the steer. Conversely, when we take a known dog dosage for gentamicin and multiply it by the weights of smaller, metabolically more active animals, we underdose them. However, when we scale dosage rates down, from a larger model animal to a smaller subject, we must be careful to scale down the treatment periodicity lest we damage the subject with an inappropriately high rate.

Figure 3. The biological energy/weight relationship.

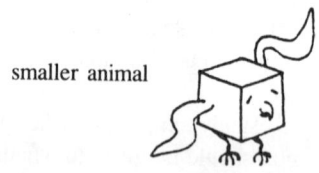

smaller animal

6 square centimeters/gram.

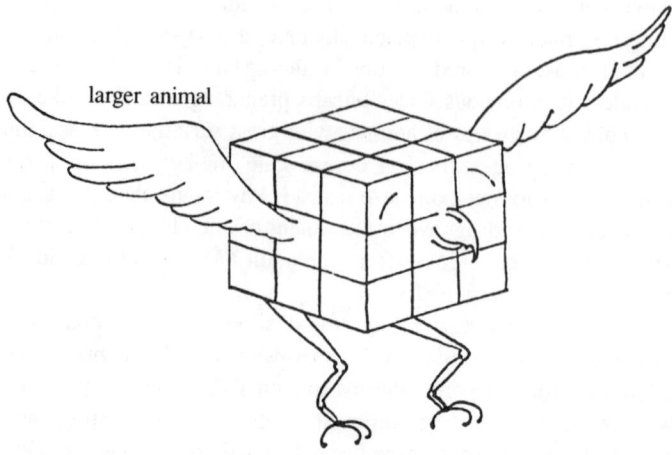

larger animal

2 square centimeters/gram.

Figure 1(b) illustrates that the mg/kcal dosage of 0.2 mg gentamicin/kcal is universal and rectilineal when plotted against the minimum energy cost.

Figure 3 illustrates why smaller animals have greater surface area per unit of mass than larger ones. One cube of the larger animal is the same size as the single cube of the small animal. The small animal has a surface to mass ratio of 6/1. The large animal has a surface to mass ratio of but 2/1 (54/27). If both animals have the same core body temperature range then the smaller animal potentially loses heat three times faster than the large animal and must have an appropriately higher metabolic rate to maintain its core body temperature. This is the basis for increasing mg/kg dosages (or changing the range) when extrapolating dosages from large model animals to smaller subjects.

A drug formulary can be developed for MEC-dosages, and because MEC-dosages tend to be universal, would be much more cognizant of the physiological bases for drug dosimetry.

REFERENCES

Abrams, J.T. (1968) Fundamental Approach to the Nutrition of the Captive Wild Herbivore. *In* Symposia of The Zoological Society of London Number 21. *Comparative Nutrition of Wild Animals*, pp. 44–49. New York, N.Y.: Academic Press.

Cooper, J.E., Hutchison, M.F., Jackson, O.F., and Maurice, R.J. (1985) Manual of Exotic Pets. p. 10. British Small Animal Veterinary Association. Pub. KCO, Worthington West Sussex, England.

Ginsberg, M., and Tager, I. (1980) *Practical Guide to Antimicrobial Agents.* pp. 110–114. Baltimore, William and Wilkins.

Hainsworth, F.R. (1981) *Animal Physiology, Adaptations in Function*, pp. 160–167. Reading, Massachusetts: Addison-Wesley Pub. Co.

Mader, D.R., Conzelman, G.M. and Baggot, J.D. (1985) Effects of Ambient Temperature on the Half-life and Dosage regimen of Amikacin the the Gopher Snake. *J.A.V.M.A.* 187:1134–1136.

McCullough, M.E. (1969) *Optimum Feeding of Dairy Animals.* p. 15. Athens: University of Georgia Press.

Schmidt-Nielsen, K. (1984) *Scaling, Why Is Animal Size So Important?*, pp. 126–134. New York: Cambridge University Press.

POISONING OF BIRDS BY CHOLINESTERASE INHIBITOR PESTICIDES

Ward B. Stone and Peter B. Gradoni

Wildlife Pathology Unit
New York State Department of
Environmental Conservation
Wildlife Resources Center
Delmar, NY 12054-9767

ABSTRACT

Ten cases are reported in which birds were killed by exposure to cholinesterase inhibitor pesticides. Diazinon was the primary or sole toxicant in five cases, isofenphos in two cases. Chlorpyrifos, phorate and carbofuran were each associated with one of the remaining three incidents. Four cases involved pesticide applications to turfgrass (three home lawns, one golf course), while one involved an application to an agricultural field. The source of the toxicant was not determined in five cases, although two of these are believed to be intentional poisonings. Guidelines are given for investigation of potential wildlife poisoning incidents, and for care and treatment of poisoned animals.

INTRODUCTION

Over the past two decades organochlorine pesticides such as DDT, dieldrin and chlordane have been largely replaced in the United States by organophosphate and carbamate compounds. Although far less environmentally persistent than their predecessors, some of these compounds are much more acutely toxic, particularly to birds. Their toxicity derives from their ability to inhibit the action of acetylcholinesterase (AChE), an enzyme which breaks down the neurotransmitter acetylcholine at nerve junctions. Inhibition of acetylcholinesterase results in a buildup of acetylcholine, which disrupts the normal transmission of nerve impulses. In severe cases, this can produce paralysis, convulsions, coma, and respiratory difficulties leading to respiratory arrest (Davis et al. 1971; Dreisbach 1974). Other signs exhibited by affected animals include tremors, dyspnea, ataxia, pupil constriction, excessive salivation, and decreased heart rate.

Poisoning of birds, both wild and domestic, by cholinesterase inhibitor pesticides has been previously documented in the scientific literature (e.g. Akinyemi and Iyoha

1983; Anderson 1985; Balcom 1983; Balcom et al. 1984; Dougherty 1957; Egyed et al. 1974; Grue et al. 1983; Hill and Fleming 1982; Littrell 1986; Stone 1979, 1980; Stone and Gradoni 1985a, 1985b; Stone and Knoch 1982; Stone et al. 1984; Zinkl et al. 1978). The reported incidents have included accidental poisonings, as well as deliberate misuse for the purpose of killing birds perceived as pests. Although some accidental poisonings have resulted from pesticide misapplication, others appear to have occurred in spite of application according to label directions.

Reported poisoning incidents frequently involve large, conspicuous birds, such as waterfowl, dying in areas visible to the general public. Although mortalities of smaller birds under less obvious circumstances (e.g. songbirds on home lawns) are less often documented, they may simply be under-reported.

Wildlife researchers attempting to monitor the occurrence of pesticide-related morbidity and mortality rely heavily on reports from the general public to alert them to potential poisonings. Unfortunately, many persons are unaware of the toxicity of cholinesterase inhibitors to non-target organisms and may not associate sick or dead animals with the application of a pesticide.

Wildlife rehabilitators are usually widely distributed in states, are knowledgeable in zoology, often work with a variety of species, and have extensive contact with the public. This makes them an ideal group to work with state and federal wildlife agencies as an integral part of monitoring activities for toxics-caused morbidity and mortality of wildlife.

The following recent cases documented by the New York State Department of Environmental Conservation (DEC) Wildlife Pathology Unit serve to illustrate the variety of chemicals and circumstances which may be encountered in situations of this sort.

METHODS

Field investigations, postmortem examination of specimens, and handling of tissues for analysis were conducted according to Stone (1979), and Stone and Gradoni (1986). Brains were saved for determination of AChE activity, although control values were not always available for comparison. A depression of at least 50% in brain AChE activity compared to controls of the same species is indicative of death due to poisoning by a cholinesterase inhibitor (Hill and Fleming 1982).

Chemical analyses were performed by Hazleton Laboratories America, Inc., Madison, Wisconsin, unless otherwise indicated. Methods of analysis are referenced in Stone and Gradoni (1986). Brain AChE values are reported by Hazleton in International Units (I.U.), which are mmol (thiocholine liberated)/ml (brain homogenate)/minute/gram of brain tissue (net weight) at 25 degrees Celsius.

Some brain AChE analyses for Case 8 were performed by the University of Illinois Veterinary Diagnostic Laboratory at Urbana-Champaign, using a modification of the method by Ellman et al. (1961). Some pesticide residue analyses for Case 8, and all such analyses for Case 9, were performed by the Illinois Department of Agriculture Animal Disease Laboratory at Centralia. Organochlorine and organophosphate residues were measured by gas chromatography, utilizing electron capture and nitrogen-phosphorus detectors, respectively. Sample preparation, extraction and cleanup were conducted according to AOAC (1984). Carbamates were analyzed by an in-house method using high performance liquid chromatography. Results of analyses performed by these alternate laboratories are designated in the text by an "(I)."

Results of all chemical analyses are given on a wet weight basis.

CASE 1: DOMESTIC DUCKS KILLED BY DIAZINON

On 8 April 1986, the Department of Environmental Conservation (DEC) received a complaint concerning some free-ranging domestic ducks that had died in the Town of Waterford, Saratoga County, New York. Residents reported that the ducks had been fine that morning, until they swam down a canal toward a nearby cooperage. When the ducks returned, two fell dead on a lawn, and a third appeared to be ill. Department personnel on the scene noted heavy solvent fumes emanating from the cooperage, but an investigation did not reveal any discharge of toxic materials that would have likely resulted in the death of birds.

Upon necropsy, both ducks (muscovies, *Cairina moschata*) were found to be adult females, in breeding condition, in good to very good flesh. There was no notable gross pathology. The crop of one bird contained a foul-smelling fluid and a large number of earthworms. The esophagus contents of the other bird included a smaller number of earthworms, some brown fluid, grass-like vegetation, and several large seeds. An organophosphate screen of the crop contents of the first bird revealed 421 ppm wet weight of diazinon (0,0-diethyl 0-[2-isopropyl-4-methyl-6-pyrimidinyl] phosphorothioate), an insecticide widely used on turfgrass, ornamentals, and agricultural crops. This represents the highest level of diazinon we have yet recorded in the ingesta of a bird. Although no controls were analyzed, the brain AChE activity of this bird (1015 I.U.) appears, at least qualitatively, to have been significantly depressed compared to levels measured in other waterfowl species diagnosed as dying from other than cholinesterase inhibitor poisoning (see Cases 3 and 5). In any case, the history, results of the postmortem examination, and the finding of a high level of diazinon in the ingesta justify a diagnosis of diazinon poisoning.

The source of the diazinon in this case remains undetermined, although a baseball field and lawns to which the pesticide may have been applied were near the cooperage.

CASE 2: DOMESTIC DUCKS KILLED BY DIAZINON APPLIED TO A HOME LAWN

On 20 April 1986 a homeowner in the Town of Greece, Monroe County, New York, reportedly applied a granular diazinon product (5% active ingredient) to his lawn at a rate of 2 lbs./1,000 ft.^{2} (5.4 lbs. active ingredient/acre). He did not water in the product, since it reportedly began to rain immediately following the application (National Weather Service data collected at the Rochester-Monroe County Airport nine miles to the south show 0.35 inches of precipitation on 20 April, followed by 0.02 inches on each of the following two days; National Oceanic and Atmospheric Administration [NOAA] 1986).

On 22 April, seven free-ranging domestic ducks (white pekins, pekin crosses, and one muscovy) were found dead in a creek near the treated area. The ducks had been known to feed on the lawn in question, and duck feces were found on the treated area during an investigation of the incident. Post-mortem examination showed all of the ducks to be in good flesh, with obvious fat deposits. All were in breeding condition, with the ovaries of the females containing many large, developing ova. The males all had prolapsed penises. With the exception of one bird, which had a broken neck, there was no evidence of trauma.

Nematodes of the genus *Tetrameres* were found in the proventriculus walls of most birds. All but one duck had brownish fluid in the esophagus, and pieces of earthworms were found in the esophagi of two ducks. Earthworm pieces were also found in the proventriculi of three ducks, with yellowish mucous in others. The gizzards generally contained grit and small amounts of vegetation. The intestines contained a blood-tinged brown fluid.

Organophosphate screens of the upper alimentary canal contents of four ducks showed levels of diazinon varying from 13 to 63 ppm (ave. 38 ppm), along with small amounts (<0.02–0.25 ppm) of chlorpyrifos (0,0-diethyl 0-[3,5,6-trichloro-2-pyridyl]-phosphorothioate), another commonly used turfgrass insecticide. Although no controls were analyzed, brain AChE levels of the six birds tested (767–1413 I.U., ave. 938 I.U.) appeared to be significantly depressed compared to levels measured in waterfowl diagnosed as dying from other than cholinesterase inhibitor poisoning (see Cases 3 and 5). The brain of a seventh duck analyzed for chlorinated hydrocarbons showed only a trace (0.003 ppm) of DDE. A soil sample from the lawn contained 0.03 ppm of diazinon, and 0.04 ppm chlorpyrifos. Although both diazinon and chlorpyrifos were detected in the ingesta of the ducks and in soil from the lawn, the preponderance of diazinon in the ingesta points to this compound as the primary toxicant. The reason for the detection of chlorpyrifos in the absence of a history of chlorpyrifos application is not known.

CASE 3: CANADA GEESE KILLED BY DIAZINON

On 3 May 1986, two Canada geese (*Branta canadensis*) were found dead on a pond in the Town of Pound Ridge, Westchester County, New York. The birds had reportedly been seen alive the previous day. One was submitted to the Wildlife Pathology Unit for examination.

This bird was found to be an adult male in good flesh, with no sign of trauma. An excessive amount of saliva was found in the mouth and upper esophagus (one sign of cholinesterase inhibitor poisoning), and the proventriculus and gizzard were filled with fresh grass and clover. The intestines were inflamed, with blood-tinged contents, and the vent was stained with feces. A culture of the feces for *Salmonella* sp. was negative.

An organophosphate screen of the proventriculus contents detected 30 ppm of diazinon. Although no concurrent controls were analyzed, the brain AChE activity of 1022 I.U. appeared significantly depressed (ave. 79%) compared to values measured four months later in three Canada geese (2324–7343 I.U., ave. 4760 I.U.) that had been shot (legal case). The source of the diazinon was not determined, although the grass and clover gizzard contents indicate a probable turfgrass source.

CASE 4: PROBABLE INTENTIONAL POISONING OF ROCK DOVES WITH DIAZINON

On 14 May 1986 seven rock doves (common pigeon, *Columba livia*) were found dead in the City of Watervliet, Albany County, in the vicinity of a pigeon coop where a flock of approximately 100 rock doves were regularly fed. Two additional dead birds, and one debilitated bird, were also found over the next two days.

Most of the dead birds were adult females in fair-to-good flesh. Crop and gizzard contents included what appeared to be a commercial "birdseed" mix, corn, and in one case bread. All birds exhibited a purple area of hemorrhage in the subcutaneous tissue overlying the crop. The lungs were moderately congested with blood. Intestinal hemorrhage varying from a slight to severe was also present.

A pool of the contents of two crops screened for organophosphates contained 3500 ppm diazinon, 0.14 ppm methyl parathion, 0.15 ppm malathion, and 0.75 ppm chlorpyrifos. A second pool of the contents of two crops contained 21 ppm diazinon and 0.05 ppm chlorpyrifos. Cholinesterase activity of three brains averaged 964 I.U. (extremes 865–1065 I.U.). No controls were analyzed; however, the levels appear to be significantly depressed, compared to those measured in a variety of other avian species. A fourth brain analyzed for chlorinated hydrocarbons contained only 0.012 ppm dieldrin and 0.005 ppm oxychlordane, well below the threshold of lethality for these compounds.

The exceptionally high level of diazinon found in one pool of crop contents, and the types of food items found in the alimentary canals, strongly suggest a purposeful poisoning, although the source of the diazinon was not determined in this case.

CASE 5: MALLARDS KILLED BY DIAZINON APPLICATION TO A HOME LAWN

On 19 May 1986, three mallard (*Anas platyrhyncos*) ducklings were observed dying on a home lawn in the Town of Greece, Monroe County, New York. They were reportedly part of a brood of eight ten-day-old ducklings (accompanied by a pair of adults) which had been observed on the property for ten days prior to the incident. During this time they had been fed fresh bread. Prior to their deaths, the ducklings were observed laying down and falling on their bills.

At necropsy, all of the ducklings (two females, one male) were found to be in good flesh, and not anemic. All had congested lungs, but there was no gross pathology suggestive of trauma or disease. The upper alimentary canals were full of earthworms.

An organochlorine screen of one brain showed none of the compounds analyzed for to be near levels expected to be lethal. Acetylcholinesterase activity of a pool of two brains (624 I.U.) appeared to be significantly depressed (ave. 81%) compared to levels measured four months later in seven hatch-year mallards (2044-7149 I.U., ave. 3314 I.U.) diagnosed as dying from a nematode (*Echinura uncinata*) infection. An organophosphate screen of the gizzard and crop contents of one bird revealed 227 ppm of diazinon, and 0.10 ppm of isofenphos (Amaze®, Oftanol®; (1-methylethyl 2-{{ethoxy} [1-methylethyl] amino} phosphinothioyl}oxy} benzoate). Those of a second bird contained 62 ppm diazinon and 0.14 ppm isofenphos. This led to a diagnosis of organophosphate poisoning, primarily by diazinon.

The lawn in question had been treated by a lawn care company on 17 April 1986 with an application of Lesco® Pre-M 60 DG herbicide (pre-emergent weed control), Trimec® 992 Broadleaf Herbicide, and Oftanol® 2 Insecticide. The same chemicals were also applied to six other lawns on the same street during the period from 17 April to 24 April. Another lawn on the street had been treated by a different lawn care company on 14 May; and the property owner reported that his children occasionally fed ducks bread on the lawn. Lawn care company records indicated that the application consisted of Betasan® 4E (pre-emergence herbicide), Dursban® 4E insecticide, and Lesco® herbicide.

Finally, it was discovered that a neighbor had recently applied a granular product containing 2.1% diazinon (Premium Grub Out Insect Control Plus Fertilizer® 22-5-9 with Diazinon) to his lawn to control white grubs. The product was applied with a Prize Lawn PSB drop spreader, using the Scotts® drop spreader setting rate given on the pesticide label. Label directions for control of white grubs state that the product should be applied at a rate of 6 lbs./1,000 ft.^{2} (5.5 lbs. active ingredient/acre), and the bag used contained a total of 30 lbs.

At this rate the bag should have covered 5,000 ft.^{2} Given a reported total application area of 4,500 ft.,^{2} and the fact that approximately three pounds of product were left unused, it appears that the application rate was reasonably correct. One half of a criss-cross pattern was applied to the front lawn on approximately 7 May, followed by one hour of watering with a perforated ribbon type "sprinkler hose." The criss-cross pattern was completed in the front yard, and a full criss-cross pattern was applied to the fenced-in back yard on approximately 15 May. The front yard was then watered again, and the back yard was partially watered and finished the next day. Watering time was about two hours. The reported watering would not appear to be inconsistent with the rather unspecific label directions to "water lawn thoroughly after application."

CASE 6: RED-WINGED BLACKBIRDS POISONED BY ISOFENPHOS

On the morning of 24 August 1985, approximately 100 red-winged blackbirds (*Agelaius phoeniceus*) began to drop the trees in two yards in Fairport, Town of Perinton, Monroe County, New York. Most of the birds had died by the time a conservation officer arrived on the scene six hours later. Those that were still alive were unable to stand or fly. All had tightly clenched claws and had defecated on themselves. Some remained stuck among tree branches where they had fallen. Thousands of various birds were observed feeding in a large lot of field corn across the street, but nothing suspicious was noted. A neighbor reported that a commercial lawn care company had applied pesticides to his property the previous morning, and that he had observed "hundreds" of "small brown birds" feeding on his lawn and in his shrubs on the morning of the incident. He and other neighbors also reported a strong chemical odor following the application and during the time the birds were dying. Fourteen birds were collected and frozen on 24 August, with additional specimens collected on 27 August from an area where they had been discarded on the 24th.

All 14 birds collected on 24 August proved to be hatch-year individuals (13 males, 1 female), in good flesh. All had congested lungs. Fragments of corn kernels were found in the gizzards of eight birds, with insect parts noted in at least four gizzards. No food remains were found in two gizzards. The birds in the second sample were grossly similar to those in the first group, except for expected decomposition.

An organophosphate screen (which did not include isofenphos) of seven gizzards and their contents from the first group of birds was negative. An additional organophosphate screen (I) of a second set of seven gizzards and contents (first group of birds) revealed 22.1 ppm isofenphos; organochlorine and carbamate screens were negative. Although no controls were analyzed, the brain cholinesterase values of six birds from the first group (457–747 I.U., ave. 593 I.U.) appear to be significantly depressed compared to those measured in two other icterids (common grackles, *Quiscalus quiscula*) diagnosed as dying from other than cholinesterase inhibitor poisoning (4860, 6541 I.U., ave. 5700 I.U.). An organochlorine screen of the brain of one blackbird showed only 0.033 ppm DDE, 0.061 ppm dieldrin, and 0.501 ppm hexachlorobenzene, none of which would be expected to result in mortality of birds at these levels.

The available data clearly supported a diagnosis of isofenphos poisoning.

In an effort to determine the source of the isofenphos, a pesticides specialist questioned the farmer who owned the nearby cornfield. The farmer reported that he had not applied any insecticides to the field, but had hired a commercial applicator. An inspection of the applicator's records indicated that Amaze® had not been applied to the field. The records of five commercial lawn care companies operating in the area were also inspected, including those of the company that had reportedly applied pesticides to the aforementioned neighbor's property. The records showed that Sevin® (carbaryl) and Kelthane® (dicofol) had been applied to trees on the property. In addition, a different company had applied Oftanol® to the lawn during the first week of July. It was also determined that, during the six weeks preceding the incident, one company had applied approximately 90 tons of granular fertilizer impregnated with 1½% Oftanol® to lawns in the Rochester area, with an estimated 10 tons applied in the Fairport area. Although the source of the isofenphos that killed the birds is still not certain, the foregoing information implicates a lawn application of Oftanol®.

CASE 7: BRANT KILLED BY ISOFENPHOS

On 13 May 1986, four brant (*Branta bernicla*) were found dead in a bayside park in the Town of Hempstead, Nassau County, New York. An additional two brant, one dead and one debilitated, were found later in the day during an investigation of the incident by a DEC technician. Park personnel reported that no pesticides had been applied to the grass in recent weeks; however, two sod samples were obtained from a golf course located across the bay less than one-half mile from the park. No dead brant were found on the golf course.

Necropsies conducted that evening showed all of the birds to have been in good or excellent flesh. Most had congested lungs. The upper alimentary canals were generally empty except for sand in the gizzards. The gizzard of one bird also contained short pieces of grass. There were varying degrees of hemorrhage in the small intestines, with a particularly severe case in one bird.

A culture of this bird's feces for *Salmonella* sp. was negative. Tapeworms and *Tetrameres* sp. nematodes were noted in the alimentary canals of three birds, but there was no evidence that these parasites were responsible for the mortalities. No protozoan parasites were noted microscopically in the feces.

An organophosphate screen of the gizzard contents of one bird, and the gizzard and small intestine contents of another, revealed 0.86 ppm and 0.07 ppm isofenphos, respectively. One of the golf course sod samples was also screened for organophosphates and was found to contain 3.9 ppm isofenphos. An analysis for bendiocarb in the gizzard and small intestine contents of one bird was negative.

Brain AChE activity of five birds varied from 523 to 1144 I.U. (ave. 808 I.U.). Although there was no concurrent analysis of controls, these values appear to be significantly depressed compared to those observed in the congeneric Canada goose for birds diagnosed as dying from other than cholinesterase inhibitor poisoning (see Case 3). A screen of a sixth brain for chlorinated hydrocarbons detected only a very low level of DDE (0.26 ppm); traces of dieldrin (0.011 ppm) and heptachlor epoxide (0.006 ppm) were found in a chlorinated hydrocarbon screen of one liver.

Based on the postmortem examination and the results of the chemical analyses, the birds were diagnosed as dying from poisoning by isofenphos.

Further investigation of the incident by a DEC pesticide specialist disclosed that, according to the Certified Commercial Applicator Record of Pesticide Purchase and Use maintained by the golf course superintendent, Oftanol® insecticide was applied on 12 May 1986. Twenty-four gallons of concentrate were applied to the fairways at the label rate of one gallon/acre (2 lbs. active ingredient/acre), for control of Japanese beetle grubs and *Hyperodes* sp. weevils.

The golf course superintendent further reported that, prior to application with a 200-gallon boom sprayer, the concentrate was diluted with sufficient water to produce an application of 1.25 gallons of diluted insecticide per 1,000 ft.^{2} (54.5 gallons/acre). The golf course sprinklers were turned on for approximately 30 minutes immediately following the application. After several hours the sprinklers were turned on for a second 30 minute interval. This procedure was followed in order to avoid puddling. According to the superintendent's estimate, 184 pairs of sprinklers were operating at an output of 70 gallons/minute/pair. This would produce a volume of 386,400 gallons (or approximately 0.6 inch distributed over the 24 acre treatment area) of water per 30 minute interval. This would appear to be ample to wet the soil to a depth of one to one-and-one-half inches, as specified on the label.

The pesticide specialist also questioned the park supervisor, who reported that no pesticides had been applied in the park for several years. Although it cannot be definitely proven, it is most likely that the brant were exposed to isofenphos on the Oftanol®-treated fairways of the golf course.

CASE 8: ROBINS KILLED BY CHLORPYRIFOS ON A HOME LAWN

On approximately 7 April 1986 a homeowner in the Town of Henrietta, Monroe County, New York, applied Grub-out® Fertilizer (10-6-4) and Insect Control (EPA Reg. 228-161-28003, EPA Est. 28003-IN-1) to his lawn with a Scott's® Conventional lawn spreader set at 4.5. This granular product contains 0.70% chlorpyrifos. A total of four, 33 lb. bags were reportedly applied to a lawn area of approximately 20,000 ft.^{2} (2 lbs. active ingredient/acre). As each bag was intended to cover 5,000 ft.^{2} (for control of grubs and *Hyperodes* sp. weevils), the application rate appears to have been correct. The lawn was not watered according to label directions following application. However, the homeowner reported that it rained the following day. (National Weather Service data from the Rochester-Monroe County Airport six miles to the north-northwest show 0.18 inches of precipitation on 7 April, 0.02 inches on 8 April, 0.08 inches on 9 April, and 0.04 inches on 10 April and on 11 April; NOAA 1986).

On 13 April, one dead American robin (*Turdus migratorius*) was found on the lawn. A DEC pesticide specialist investigating the incident on 14 April found another dead robin in the yard.

Two neighbors stated that they had also applied granular grub killers to their lawns during the period from 5 April to 8 April. The products used contained diazinon at concentrations from 3.6% to 5.8%. Another neighbor reported an application of fertilizer and pre-emergent crabgrass control by a commercial lawn care company. Sod samples were obtained from these lawns, as well as from the lawn on which the dead birds were found.

Both robins were adult males in good flesh; one had a worm in its mouth. There were no signs of trauma, and no other notable gross pathology.

An organophosphate screen showed 18 ppm chlorpyrifos, and 0.82 ppm diazinon, in the gizzard contents of one bird; 12 ppm chlorpyrifos and 0.10 ppm diazinon were found in the gizzard contents of the other. Organophosphate screens of sod samples from the treated areas generally verified the reported pesticide applications: 13 ppm chlorpyrifos and 0.07 ppm diazinon from the lawn where the dead birds were found, diazinon (7.8 and 5.7 pm) and a trace of chlorpyrifos (0.06 ppm in first sample) from the two lawns reportedly treated with diazinon, and a trace (0.07 ppm) of diazinon from the commercially treated lawn. It is not known why traces of diazinon and chlorpyrifos were found in sod samples from lawns not reportedly treated with these compounds.

Brain AChE activities of the robins were 2136 and 1821 I.U., respectively. Although no controls were analyzed at the time, these activities are depressed more than 50% compared to values measured nine months earlier (6066–6721 I.U., ave. 6336 I.U.) in three brain samples from robins diagnosed as dying from causes other than cholinesterase inhibitor poisoning. It was therefore concluded that the birds in question died from organophosphate poisoning, with chlorpyrifos the primary toxicant.

CASE 9: CANADA GEESE POISONED BY PHORATE MISAPPLICATION

Near the end of March 1986, approximately 60 Canada geese were found dead in a farmer's field in the Town of Batavia, Genesee County, New York. The birds were located in a low, wet area where moldy corn silage had been spread, leading to speculation that they had died from infection by the fungus *Aspergillus*.

Over the next several weeks additional dead geese were found in various stages of decomposition at the original kill site and at several other locations nearby, bringing the total mortality to approximately 140 birds. Samples of corn kernels, soil, and dead earthworms were collected from the original kill site on 9 April; additional soil samples were obtained from the other kill sites and from several control areas on 2 May.

Twenty geese examined by the Pathology Unit were in good flesh, with little notable gross pathology. In particular, there was no indication of *Aspergillus* infection. Microscopic examination of blood (two birds), feces (one bird), and small intestine contents (one bird) did not reveal any parasites or other pathogens that would have caused the mortalities. The upper alimentary canals contained varying amounts of greenish-brown fluid and "sludge," corn, grit, and occasional green vegetation.

Organophosphate screens of the gizzard contents of two geese revealed 109 ppm and 36 ppm phorate (Thimate®; 0,0-diethyl S-{[ethylthio]methyl} phosphorodithioate), a restricted use pesticide used to control insects on a variety of agricultural crops. Additional organophosphate screens (I) of the gizzard contents of a third bird, and the upper alimentary canal contents of a fourth also detected phorate at levels of 0.89 ppm and 8.18 ppm, respectively. Two samples of corn kernels from the original kill site contained 37 and 439 ppm phorate, 0.12 and 0.59 ppm diazinon, and 0.04 and 0.14 ppm ronnel. The presence of phorate was also confirmed by gas chromatography/mass spectrometry (Schrader Analytical and Consulting Laboratories, Inc., Detroit, Michigan) in the extract of the second corn sample (91.5 μg/ml); no diazinon was detected by this analysis. Dead earthworms collected with the second corn sample contained 4.0 ppm phorate. Of two soil samples collected from the original kill site, one contained 0.589 ppm phorate, while the second did not contain detectable levels of any of the organophosphates in the screen. Likewise, three additional soil samples from the other kill sites, and one from a control site where no dead geese had been found, did not contain detectable levels of organophosphates.

Brain AChE activities in the first two geese were 467 I.U. and 447 I.U., respectively. These values appear significantly depressed (ave. approximately 90%) compared to those of Canada geese diagnosed as dying from other than cholinesterase inhibitor poisoning (see Case 3). Brain cholinesterase analyses (I) of the third and fourth geese showed 0.36 μM/g/min. and 0.16 μM/g/min., respectively. These values were characterized by the lab as indicating "almost a complete loss of normal brain cholinesterase values" compared to typical avian brain cholinesterase of 5-12 μM/min/g.

One brain screened for organochlorines contained only 0.005 ppm DDE, a level far below that expected to be lethal.

The above findings strongly support a diagnosis of death due to poisoning by phorate.

Although the events leading up to the kill were never fully elucidated, it appears that the pesticide was placed into a manure spreader along with fertilizer and the moldy silage, and then applied to the farmer's field. Such an application was inconsistent with label directions on several counts; in particular, the pesticide is to be applied at planting time, and incorporated into the soil. This would reduce, although not necessarily eliminate, exposure of non-target species. Obviously, surface application in conjunction with corn silage creates a hazardous situation for feeding birds.

In addition to a stipulated payment of $500 for misapplication of the pesticide, the farmer also agreed to donate $3,000 to the New York State Conservation Fund/Migratory Bird Account, which is used to fund waterfowl management and habitat acquisition.

CASE 10. AMERICAN CROW AND RED-TAILED HAWK POISONED WITH CARBOFURAN

On 9 February 1986, several American crows (*Corvus brachyrhyncos*), a red-tailed hawk (*Buteo jamaicensis*), and a number of European starlings (*Sturnus vulgaris*) were found dead along a fencerow in a harvested cornfield in the Manheim area of northern Lancaster County, Pennsylvania. The starlings had been partially scavenged. A second red-tailed hawk, alive but partially paralyzed, was found at the same location. This bird was taken into captivity, where it recovered almost fully within two days, and was released within a week. One crow and the dead red-tailed hawk were submitted to the Pathology Unit for examination.

The crow proved to be a greater-than-one-year-old male, in fair-to-good flesh. There was little notable gross pathology other than an enlarged spleen and congested lungs. The stomach contained corn, as well as bird flesh, feathers and bones. A carbamate pesticide screen (I) of the stomach contents detected 425 ppm carbofuran (2,3-dihydro-2-dimethyl-7-benzofuranyl methylcarbamate) a restricted use carbamate pesticide highly toxic to birds. Organochlorine and organophosphate screens were negative. The presence of carbofuran in this sample was also confirmed by gas chromatography/mass spectrometry (National Veterinary Service Laboratory, Ames, Iowa).

The red-tailed hawk was a less-than-one-year-old female in very good flesh, with a large amount of fat. The gross pathology was limited to slightly congested lungs, and a small, ulcerated lesion on the inner lining of the stomach. The esophagus contained a starling, with more starling parts and small mammal remains in the stomach. A carbamate pesticide screen (I) of the starling's gizzard and contents showed 67.2 ppm carbofuran; organophosphate and organochlorine screens were negative.

Brain cholinesterase activities of the crow and hawk were determined to be 1628 and 3331 I.U., respectively. Interpretation of these values is complicated by a lack of comparable controls. Although not as low as those we have usually observed in cases of cholinesterase inhibitor poisoning, this may be a result of postmortem reactivation of brain AChE, which may occur in cases of carbamate poisoning (Hill and Fleming 1982).

Taken together, the available data point to carbofuran poisoning as the most likely cause of death of these birds.

Carbofuran is used to control insects, nematodes and mites on a variety of agricultural crops. The timing of this incident indicates a misapplication of the chemical, since carbofuran is intended to be applied and incorporated into the soil during the growing season.

An intentional poisoning of starlings by a farmer is most probable, especially in view of other bird poisonings reported (Hubley 1986) in Lancaster County during the same winter. The red-tailed hawk then became a victim of secondary poisoning when it consumed carbofuran-contaminated starlings. Balcomb (1983) has described similar secondary poisoning of red-shouldered hawks (*Buteo lineatus*) related to carbofuran application at corn planting. The crow may have been exposed to the toxicant directly in carbofuran-laced corn, or from scavenging poisoned starlings or other birds.

DISCUSSION

Half of the cases involved the organophosphate insecticide diazinon. At the time of this writing, the U.S. Environmental Protection Agency had recently decided to cancel the registration of diazinon for use on golf courses and sod farms, due to its high avian toxicity and a long history of associated bird kills on large, grassy areas (U.S. Environmental Protection Agency 1985).

However, Cases 2 and 5, and other reports (Anderson 1985; Stone and Gradoni 1985a, b) document the occurrence of diazinon-related bird mortality associated with other turfgrass areas such as home lawns. Monitoring of wildlife mortality due to turfgrass applications of diazinon and other pesticides on such areas would provide important data on which to base future regulatory decisions.

In contrast to the cases involving diazinon, the isofenphos poisonings described in Cases 6 and 7 are, to our knowledge, the first documented wildlife mortalities attributed to this compound. The isofenphos-related mortality of brant documented in Case 7 follows five other brant poisoning incidents documented in the same township during the previous seven years (Stone and Gradoni 1985a, b). All the previous cases were related to diazinon, which in four cases was known to have been recently applied to a golf course at or near the scene of the mortalities.

The chlorpyrifos-related mortality of robins documented in Case 8 is the fourth case of bird mortality that we have documented in relation to turfgrass application of this chemical (Stone and Gradoni 1985a, and unpublished data). Two of the previous cases involved golf courses where diazinon had also been applied, although chlorpyrifos poisoning was judged to be a primary or contributory factor in the mortalities. The third case involved at least one American robin, and possibly several other passerine birds, that died in a yard following a spray application of chlorpyrifos by a commercial lawn care company.

Cases 2 and 8 involve the application of granular pesticides to turfgrass, with failure to "water in" the granules according to label directions. Although these are technically misapplications, it is questionable whether watering according to the label would have prevented the mortalities. Stone and Gradoni (1985) have noted that such watering can actually increase the risk to non-target species. Birds (e.g. geese) may be killed by ingesting grass to which pesticides have spread during watering. If puddles form, birds may then be poisoned by drinking pesticide-contaminated water, absorbing the pesticide through their skin as they stand in water, or ingesting floating pesticide granules mistaken for food items.

It is also noteworthy that in Cases 1, 2, 5 and 8, earthworms were found in the pesticide-contaminated ingesta of the poisoned birds. In another case reported by Stone and Gradoni (1985b), earthworms from a diazinon-treated lawn were also found to contain diazinon. Although a direct cause-and-effect relationship has not been established, it is possible that birds may be poisoned by pesticide-contaminated earthworms (or other invertebrates) even after the chemical has been irrigated or "watered" by rainfall. Furthermore, the watering itself may stimulate earthworms to come to the surface where they may attract feeding birds, and pesticide-intoxicated earthworms may also be more easily captured.

Case 8 is also illustrative of some of the practical difficulties of watering according to label directions on some turfgrass pesticides. The label directions on the product in question state that it should be watered at a rate of 30 gallons/1,000 ft.^{2} immediately following application, with an additional one inch of water applied two to three days later (rainfall during this period may be counted toward the total). One inch of water applied to the 20,000 ft.^{2} lawn involved in this case equals a volume of approximately 12,468 gallons. Assuming a home lawn sprinkler output of 5–6 gallons/minute, it would take approximately 35–42 hours of watering to achieve the necessary volume.

Aside from the possible expense of using such large volumes of water, such high consumption may be prohibited by local authorities in order to conserve water supplies. Furthermore, a single sprinkler would probably have to be moved many times in order to evenly distribute the water over the lawn. Finally, the time and effort involved in determining sprinkler output, calculating lawn areas, and measuring the amount of water applied would probably be enough to discourage most people from scrupulous adherence to the label directions. Alternatively, watering directions on some pesticide labels may be so vague (e.g. as in Case 5, "water lawn thoroughly") as to make a determination of compliance impossible. Any of the above-mentioned difficulties may contribute to a homeowner's decision to let rain suffice to water the lawn following a pesticide application.

Cases 4 (diazinon poisoning of rock doves) and 10 (carbofuran poisoning of a red-tailed hawk and American crow) both involved probable intentional poisonings. Stone (1979) and Stone et al. (1984) have documented similar intentional bird poisonings using cholinesterase inhibitor pesticides not intended for bird control. It should be noted, however, that although such use is illegal, a number of pesticides (e.g. Avitrol®[1], Starlicide®[1], and the organophosphate fenthion) *are* registered for use by certified applicators to control certain birds such as rock doves, starlings, grackles, blackbirds, crows, and magpies. Such control efforts generally involve the protection of agricultural crops or the control of large roosting flocks. More research is needed on the incidence of both direct and secondary poisoning of non-target species resulting from such legal control efforts.

As wildlife rehabilitators may well be faced with poisoning cases involving cholinesterase inhibitors, the following guidelines (modified from Stone 1979) are offered for investigating suspected poisoning incidents and caring for affected animals.

Time is of the essence when cholinesterase inhibitors may be involved. The relatively rapid breakdown which makes these compounds less likely to accumulate in the environment, also makes detection more difficult. This is particularly true of pesticide residues in decaying animal carcasses. A delay of even a day or two may be critical during warm weather. General postmortem examination is also much more difficult when specimens have been allowed to decompose. Therefore, if an

---

[1] Not a cholinesterase inhibitor.

accurate diagnosis is to be made, any specimens of dead wildlife involved should be collected and preserved as soon as possible.

However, before entering areas that have been sprayed with pesticides one should be sure that it is safe to do so. Cholinesterase inhibitors may be inhaled or absorbed directly through the skin, and some, such as parathion, are highly toxic to humans as well as to wildlife. Protective clothing (e.g. rubber boots, gloves), and in some cases even a respirator, may be necessary to avoid excessive exposure. Depending on the route of exposure, animals may be externally contaminated with a pesticide, and thus should not be handled without gloves. This of course is a good precaution when handling any dead animal, especially if the cause of death is not certain.

Specimens for analysis should be packaged in plastic bags and labelled with species, location, date, and other pertinent information. Ideally, one representative group of specimens should be frozen (the best way to preserve pesticide residues), while another group should be refrigerated above freezing to better preserve the cell structure of tissues for microscopic examination. If possible and appropriate, samples of soil, water, vegetation, grain or other materials that may be contaminated with a pesticide should be placed in clean, labelled glass jars and frozen.

The specimens and other samples should be submitted as soon as possible to a wildlife pathologist or other qualified individual. Unfortunately, most states do not employ wildlife pathologists. Federal fish and wildlife agents, or state wildlife departments, may be of help in locating the proper person or laboratory (appropriate environmental law enforcement personnel should of course be contacted if possible legal action is anticipated). Faculty of various institutions of higher education may also have an interest and be willing to cooperate in the investigation, examination of specimens and chemical analyses.

Along with specimens, it is important to provide as complete a written history as can be obtained. Important details would include the date and location of the incident; amounts and types of pesticide applied (including E.P.A. or other pesticide registration numbers, if possible); reason for the application; method and timing of application; clinical signs exhibited by affected animals; and names, addresses and telephone numbers of persons involved.

Apart from obtaining specimens for analysis, it is important that all dead wildlife be collected and removed from the site to avoid possible secondary poisoning. Carcasses should be buried deeply or incinerated. Further poisonings may also be prevented by removing and safely disposing of pesticide-contaminated material, plowing or raking it under, or washing it into the soil. Wildlife may also be temporarily scared away from a contaminated area using various mechanical noise-making devices or human volunteers.

Wildlife debilitated but not killed by pesticides are more likely to suffer injuries or be killed by predators. Pesticide-intoxicated waterfowl may drown in their uncoordinated condition if they are unable to hold their heads out of the water (Stone 1979). Such animals can be placed in cages or well-ventilated boxes out of the sun, where they may recover within a few hours. Intramuscular injections of atropine sulfate, and intravenous administration of Protopam (pyridine-2-aldoxime methochloride) may also be useful in treating organophosphate poisoning; however, Dreisbach (1974) reported that Protopam might be harmful in cases of carbamate poisoning.

Veterinarians may be able to provide advice or assistance in this regard, although it should not be assumed that all such persons will be familiar with diagnosis and treatment of cholinesterase inhibitor poisoning. Observations on the effectiveness of various treatments could prove to be a valuable addition to the scientific literature.

Although pesticides must undergo a number of standard toxicity tests prior to registration, it is impossible to completely predict their environmental impact given the variety of circumstances and non-target species that may be encountered in actual use. If, after a pesticide has been registered and in use, problems occur which demonstrate an unreasonable threat to human health or the environment, its registration may be reviewed, and then restricted or cancelled. Continued monitoring and reporting of the environmental effects of currently registered pesticides is thus essential for informed decision-making relative to their safety and continued use. All wildlife rehabilitators are encouraged to assume an active role in this effort.

ACKNOWLEDGEMENTS

We would like to acknowledge the field investigation work of the following DEC personnel: David Baker, Laura Bigler, Dan Carroll, Scott Florence, Floyd Knowlton, Greg Lindenfelser, Gail Mortimer, Nancy Robson, and Mike Scheibel. We also thank *Pennsylvania Wildlife and Outdoor Digest* editor, Jack Hubley, for submitting the crow and red-tailed hawk described in Case 10.

Partial funding for this research was provided by New York State's Return A Gift To Wildlife program (Project No. W-4).

REFERENCES

Akinyemi, J.O., and Iyoha, M.O. 1983. A case of suspected poisoning of West African crowned cranes *Balearica pavonina pavonina* with diazinon, an organophosphate insecticide. Zool. Garten N.F., Jena 53: 317–319.

Anderson, J.F. 1985. Diazinon poisoning of brown-headed cowbirds. J. Field Ornithol. 56(4): 407–408.

Association of Official Analytical Chemists. 1984. Official methods of analysis, 14th ed. AOAC, Washington, D.C.

Balcomb, R. 1983. Secondary poisoning of red-shouldered hawks with carbofuran. J. Wildl. Manage. 47(4): 1129–1132.

Balcomb, R., Bowen, C.A., II, Wright, D., and Law, M. 1984. Effects on wildlife of at-planting corn applications of granular carbofuran. J. Wildl. Manage. 48(4): 1353–1359.

Davis, J.W., Anderson, R.C., Karstad, L., and Trainer, D.O. 1971. Infectious and parasitic diseases of wild birds. Iowa State Univ. Press, Ames, Iowa. 344 pp.

Dougherty, E., III. 1957. Thiophosphate poisoning in White Pekin ducks. Avian Dis. 1: 127–130.

Dreisbach, R.H. 1974. Handbook of poisoning: diagnosis and treatment. Lange Medical Publ., Los Altos, CA. 517 pp.

Egyed, M.N., Malkinson, M., Eilat, A., and Schlosberg, A. 1974. Basudin (diazinon) poisoning in goslings. Refu. Vet. 31: 83–86.

Grue, C.E., Fleming, W.J., Busby, D.G., and Hill, E.F. 1983. Assessing hazards of organophosphate pesticides to wildlife. N. Am. Wildl. Nat. Res. conf., Trans. 48: 200–220.

Hill, E.F., and Fleming, W.J. 1982. Anticholinesterase poisoning of birds: field monitoring and diagnosis of acute poisoning. Environ. Toxicol. Chem. 1: 27–38.

Hubley, J. 1986. The ultimate pest. Pennsylvania Wildlife 7(2): 16–20.

Littrell, E.E. 1986. Mortality of American wigeon on a golf course treated with the organophosphate, diazinon. Calif. Fish and Game 72(2): 117–126.

National Oceanic and Atmospheric Administration. 1986. Climatological Data: New York. Vol. 98, No. 4, pp. 13–14.

Stone, W.B. 1979. Poisoning of wild birds by organophosphate and carbamate pesticides. N.Y. Fish Game J. 26: 37–47.

———. 1980. Bird deaths caused by pesticides used on turfgrass. N.Y.S. Turfgrass Conf., Proc. 4:58–62.

Stone, W.B., and Gradoni, P.B. 1985a. Wildlife mortality related to use of the pesticide diazinon. Northeastern Env. Sci. 4(1): 30–38.

———. 1985b. Recent poisonings of wild birds by diazinon and carbofuran. Northeastern Env. Sci. 4(3/4): 160–164.

Stone, W.B., and Knoch, H. 1982. American brant killed on golf courses by diazinon. N.Y. Fish Game J. 29: 95–96.

Stone, W.B., Overmann, S.R., and Okoniewski, J.C. 1984. Intentional poisoning of birds with parathion. Condor 86: 333–336.

U.S. Environmental Protection Agency. 1985. Diazinon support document. Washington, D.C.

Zinkl, J.G., Rathert, J., and Hudson, R.R. 1978. Diazinon poisoning in wild Canada geese. J. Wildl. Manage. 42: 406–408.

WOUND TREATMENT

Mark A. Pokras, D.V.M.

Tufts University
School of Veterinary Medicine
Department of Environmental Studies
200 Westboro Road
North Grafton, MA 01536

As rehabilitators, we are faced every day with wounded animals. Even though most of us will never be surgeons, it is very important to remember that the way we initially treat wounded animals will make a vast difference in determining how their wounds eventually heal.

All of you have had instances where an animal comes in with apparently devastating wounds, you treat them in your normal way, and they close absolutely beautifully in just a couple of weeks. On the other hand, you've probably also had instances where tiny, insignificant-looking wounds don't heal. They may smolder on, getting slowly worse for weeks and weeks, and you end up having to euthanize the animal.

This paper will present some of what veterinarians and human physicians understand to be taking place during wound healing. Hopefully you will gain an improved grasp of some of the complex factors that contribute to wound healing, and how improved patient care and handling of the wounds by rehabilitators can significantly alter the clinical outcome.

When an animal comes to your rehabilitation center with a traumatic injury, the first feeling that everyone has is, "Oh my gosh, we've got to do something!" Sometimes you have to stop, back off a minute, and remember that the first principle of medicine is DO NO HARM. If the wound you're dealing with isn't immediately life-threatening, it may be best to just put the animal someplace quiet and dark, and give yourself and the animal some time to relax. Think carefully about what you're going to do next.

Let's review some of the kinds of wounds you may be dealing with. One common kind of wound is called an *abrasion*. An abrasion is caused by friction against a rough surface...like when you fall and slide on an asphalt street. Abrasion-type wounds are very sensitive and heal more slowly than most other kinds of wounds. Another kind of wound is a *laceration*. A laceration is a cutting or tearing sort of a wound where the edges are torn and irregular. If treated correctly, they frequently heal very well. A third kind of wound is a *penetrating* wound like a bullet wound, or a bite or claw wound. Penetrating wounds tend to have small openings on the outside, but can be very deceptive. They frequently go much deeper than you expect and have more destruction of deep tissue than is apparent from the surface. These wounds are very likely to get infected and must often be handled surgically to avoid complications. The last term I wanted to cover is *contusion*. A contusion is a bruising wound from blunt impact. There may be rupture and tearing of tissue but frequently the surface tissue is intact so you can't see the damage beneath. Contusions may frequently hide broken bones, so they must be examined very carefully.

Before discussing the practical aspects of treating wounds, I think it's important for you to have a basic understanding of the stages of healing in an "ideal" wound.

Wound healing can be broken down into four stages. The first is usually called the "inflammatory stage." Immediately after the wound occurs there is a short period of vasoconstriction. This is when little blood vessels around the wound contract, clots form in those blood vessels, and bleeding stops. Vasoconstriction doesn't last very long—only about 5 or 10 minutes. After that, there is actually an enlargement in the size of blood vessels in the area of the wound and an increase in blood flow to the area. This phase of increased blood flow will help to bring inflammatory cells into the wound. Especially important are various kinds of white blood cells that will help with the healing later on.

The second stage of wound healing is called the "debridement phase." This take place starting about 6 hours after the injury. The white cells that came into the wound during the inflammatory stage are the important players at this point. They perform a couple of crucial functions. First, they ingest and destroy bacteria that may be in the wound; and, second, they take care of getting rid of any dead tissues that are around the wound from the injury. While the white cells are working, another kind of cell, called a fibroblast, begins to come into the wound site. Fibroblasts are going to be very important later in wound healing in making a substance called collagen which contributes to the strength of the wound, but they come into the wound during the debridement phase. Quantities of white cells coming in, ingesting bacteria, and dying during the debridement phase are called pus when you see them in a wound. Seeing pus doesn't necessarily mean that infection is present. Even if there were no bacteria present, the white cells coming in and eliminating dead cells and tissues could form pus. But pus does interfere with healing and should be kept to a minimum.

The third phase of wound healing is called the "repair phase." The fibroblasts that came into the wound during the debridement phase begin to make collagen and this will give structural strength to the scar which closes to the wound. Collagen formation is not fast. Even in an ideal wound there is really no significant strength in the wound from the collagen until the fifth or sixth day after the injury. Another important part of the repair phase is an ingrowth of capillaries. New capillaries grow into the area of injury, increasing the blood flow into the area and nourishing the new, growing tissue. The third part of the repair phase is a multiplication of the cells of the epithelium on the edges of the wound. These cells multiply and are going to migrate over the surface of the wound in a layer. Given time, depending on the size of the wound, they will cover the surface of the wound in a process called epithelialization. Before the epithelium can cover the wound, activity of the fibroblasts and the proliferation of the capillary loops underneath forms what is called granulation tissue. Granulation tissue on the wound surface is moist, red, and kind of nubbly-looking. It protects the healing wound, and is resistant to infection. It is also crucial to have this moist surface tissue to encourage the new epithelium to grow in from the edges. There is quite a bit of evidence that granulation tissue is also important in causing large wounds to contract and get smaller as they get older.

Collagen continues to be added to the wound for roughly the first three weeks of healing. After that, no new collagen is added and we enter what is called the final phase of wound healing or "maturation." During the maturation phase, the collagen is remodeled into a stronger orientation. It's a slow process. In large wounds it can actually take years for a wounded area to reach full strength. And even after this time, wounded tissue only becomes about 80% as strong as the normal tissue around it.

All wounds heal in basically the same way. There are new cells formed from pre-existing cells. If a clean, surgical wound is sutured back together, there is minimal space that needs to be occupied by granulation tissue. The growing fibers can cross directly from one side of normal tissue to the other side of normal tissue in a process called "healing by first intention." On the other hand, if you've got a wound where there's a big gap, the wound has to first fill in with a blood clot and then with granulation tissue that will eventually epithelialize. This is known as "healing by second intention." Many, if not most, of the wounds that rehabilitators handle will have to be allowed to heal by second intention.

If you've got a wounded animal that has just come in for treatment, how do you make the decision whether or not the wound can be sutured and allowed to heal by primary healing or whether this needs to be left open and allowed to heal by second intention?

There are three factors that one needs to consider in making this decision. How old is the wound, how contaminated (dirty) is the wound, and how big is the wound?

Surgeons talk about the so-called "golden period" of wound healing. If a clean wound is between four and twelve hours old, you can probably remove most of the bacterial contamination on the surface simply by cleaning it well with an appropriate lavage solution. Once you get past that roughly twelve-hour point, bacteria have invaded into the tissue enough so that no amount of washing will get them out. The second factor is contamination. If a wound is grossly contaminated, if it was caused by a rusty fish-hook, or if it has soil in it or feces, you certainly can't close that wound by primary intention. In fact, you may want to open it wider to allow for drainage and to lavage it. The third factor is size. Sometimes a wound is so large that even if it's clean and less than six hours old there's not enough viable tissue left to pull together and close that wound. Looking at these three factors, many of the wounds presented to rehabilitators certainly shouldn't be closed by first intention.

Now that we've discussed a little bit about the nature of wounds, let's begin our discussion of practical things you can do to improve your handling of wounds.

There are three factors affecting wound healing over which you have some control. These are: (1) number of bacteria, (2) host defense mechanisms, and (3) the wound environment. Clearly your goals are to minimize bacterial populations, help the host defenses in any way possible, and remove anything from the wound environment that will interfere with healing. These goals can be reached by judicious lavage, debridement, bandaging, and by paying careful attention to the animal's nutrition and medication.

LAVAGE

One of the most useful things you can do with a contaminated wound is to lavage it—wash it out. There is a lot of discussion in the medical literature about what techniques and materials are best. The main principle in effectively cleaning out wounds is to use as much fluid as possible. There is a direct correlation between the amount of fluid used, and percent of bacteria that are washed out of wounds. One of the questions that is frequently discussed in the veterinary literature is whether or not pressure lavage should be used. The use of syringes to spray lavage fluid over the wound or a Water Pik® to give pulses of pressure to lavage out a wound is recommended by many experts. A stated disadvantage of using pressure lavage is that it may wash bacteria into crevices in the wound and increase infection later on. But in most people's minds, the advantages outweigh the disadvantages.

When you are going to lavage a wound, what fluids should you use to do it? Well, a lot depends on what you have available. If you're going with the principle that you want to use a large volume of fluid, then you want to go with something relatively cheap. For grossly contaminated wounds, tap water can be used for the first several washes. Tap water does cause some osmotic changes in the tissues, but these tend not to be severe problems. Then for the last lavage or two you can go to more physiologically balanced solutions like normal saline. If the wounds are smaller, saline should be used for the entire lavage process.

What are you going to put in these fluids to try to kill bacteria and clean the wound? There are some things you definitely *don't* want to use. One is any kind of soap. Soaps and detergents have been shown to be very destructive to the sensitive tissues in wounds, so avoid using them. Another thing you should *not* use in an open wound (although people probably still do) is hydrogen peroxide. Hydrogen peroxide, although effective for killing bacteria, also kills a lot of cells in the wound, so avoid it if at all possible.

There are a number of antiseptics that you can add to your lavage fluids that are less harmful and really will help a great deal in controlling infection. One that a lot of people have on hand is Betadine® solution (*not scrub*—the betadine scrub has detergent in it that you *don't* want to use in wounds). The solution doesn't contain detergent, and when diluted 50:50 with saline, is a very good lavage for wounds. Betadine solution has been shown to increase the growth of granulation tissue as well as killing bacteria.

Another solution that some like better than Betadine is Nolvasan® (a solution of chlorhexadine). It comes in about a 2 percent solution. You want to dilute that down by about a factor of twenty so that you're using one-tenth of one percent solution to lavage wounds. Nolvasan is very good for killing bacteria and it's very, very safe on the tissues.

There are a lot of other fluids that are occasionally used for cleaning out wounds—but if you stick to tap water or saline with Betadine® or Nolvasan®, you're going to be very safe and very effective. You should talk with your local veterinarian and see what they have to say about their particular preference.

DEBRIDEMENT

Debridement is the process of removing dead, non-viable, or grossly contaminated tissue from the area of the wound so that the wound can be closed. There are a number of different ways of approaching debridement. Certainly one of the earliest forms of debridement was cautery with a hot iron. I hope that we have come quite a way since then.

From our point of view, there are three basic forms of debridement. These are surgical, enzymatic, and debridement through bandaging techniques.

One of the keys to debridement is asepsis—keeping the area clean. A lot of the infected wounds that are seen in hospitals or rehabilitation centers are caused by infections coming from those people who are trying to help. Human hands and breath contain many different kinds of micro-organisms that can cause problems in wounds. *Any time you are dealing with wounded tissue, even just for physical exam, you should wear disposable gloves (and masks if possible).*

In surgical debridement the devitalized tissue is cut out of the area of the wound. Doing this will cause the animal pain and will take time, so anesthesia is certainly needed. If the animal is badly injured, is a bad surgical risk, or if you don't have the capability of anesthestizing the animal, surgical debridement probably isn't practical. Surgical debridement for most wounds is probably best left to the veterinarian. Few rehabilitation centers are equipped to handle this sort of procedure and its attendant complications. Wounds needing surgical debridement should be carefully bandaged until your veterinarian can treat them.

The next form of debridement is enzymatic debridement. This technique involves the use of various kinds of enzymes or chemicals that will kill bacteria and actually digest dead, devitalized tissue without removing good tissue. It is particularly useful if the patient is a poor surgical risk or if you're going to have a hard time telling the devitalized tissue from the healthy tissue and you don't want to remove too much. In addition, it doesn't disturb granulation tissue.

There are some disadvantages to it, though. One is that it is relatively expensive. Another is that it is slow—it takes many days to enzymatically debride a wound.

And last, if there is really ground-in debris or extensive tissue damage, enzymatic tissue debridement may not be completely effective.

There are many different products, both powders and ointments, that are used for enzymatic debridement. Three that many people may be familiar with are Kymar®, Elase®, and Granulex®. Although their actions are a bit different, their objectives are the same. They liquify the devitalized tissue and thereby increase the drainage from the wound. Increased damage means that more attention will have to be paid to the wound and that bandages will have to be changed more frequently. This is going to be difficult with some animals and it is going to be more costly in terms of your staff time. These factors should be considered carefully if you are going to utilize enzymatic debridement.

BANDAGING

When you're considering bandaging a wound, you need to carefully consider the goal of your bandaging. Bandages can be used to debride wounds, to encourage granulation tissue, to compress wounds so hematomas won't form or to protect and stabilize damaged tissues. Once you have decided on your goal(s) for bandaging, you can select the appropriate materials and techniques.

You should envision bandages as having three layers—a contact layer that actually touches the wound, a middle layer and an outer layer. The contact layer is in many ways the most important. Because it is touching the damaged tissue, it is crucial that this layer be sterile. The two major decisions you must make are whether you want this contact layer to be wet or dry, and whether or not you want the bandage to stick to the wound. If you've got a wound with a lot of fluid coming out of it (serum, pus, or foreign material) and you are certain you need to debride that wound, you should probably use an adherent contact layer. This will stick to the surface, so that when it is peeled off, it will take with it all the debris from the wound surface.

On the other hand, if you have healing epithelium, a burn, granulation tissue, or a clean surgical wound, you don't want that bandage sticking to the wound, and you need to use a non-adherent surface layer. There are a number of products you can use for this purpose—Telfa® or Adaptic® pads are excellent. Another good non-adherent surface layer is a small mesh cotton gauze, sterile of course, that has been very lightly impregnated with a petroleum jelly product. This will be both non-adherent and will help to keep the wound surface moist.

Once again, you should talk to your veterinarian about his/her particular preferences. But the general rule is that you want to dry wounds that are very moist and oozing, and moisten wounds that are very dry.

The intermediate layer of the bandage (usually squares of gauze) can either be wet or dry. Dry bandage material has a great absorptive capacity, so if you have a wound that is going to be oozing a lot of fluid or necrotic debris, you probably want a bandage that has an intermediate layer that is dry. If you're using a bandage with a wet intermediate layer, you are using what is called a wet-to-dry application.

In this case, the bandage is applied warm and wet and allowed to dry before being removed. This wet-to-dry application is useful if you've got a viscous exudate from the wound (like pus), and you want to thin it out and debride the wound. You can also use what is called a wet-to-dry bandage. The bandage is put on wet and kept moist during the entire time. This kind of bandage does not have much capacity for debriding a wound, however it keeps a nice, moist environment, encourages granulation tissue and is good when you have a dry, relatively clean wound.

This type of bandage is not often used for animals because of two drawbacks. First, you will need to handle the animal more frequently to moisten the bandage. And second, there is a tendency for the tissues to stay too wet and become macerated if the bandage is not carefully watched.

I can't stress enough that any time a moist bandage is applied to a wound it should be sterile and should be warmed to body temperature. A warm dressing will cause dilation of blood vessels in the area and increase the inflammatory response which will help the wound heal faster.

The outer layer of the bandage serves to hold the first two layers in place against the wound, and to protect those layers from becoming contaminated. You can use gauze or products such as Vetwrap® or Elasticon®. It is important that you choose something that is the right size and the right tension for the animal that you are going to be bandaging. It is also important that you allow for any swelling that might take place. You don't want this bandage to be too tight.

On the other hand, if it is too loose, the animal is going to have a much easier time tearing it off. You must try to predict what you think that animal will be doing. In most cases, you will want this outermost layer to be porous so that the fluid absorbed from the wound in the first two layers can evaporate and so that oxygen can penetrate the deeper layers of the bandage. If you have an animal that is going to be getting into the water and there is a chance of contamination from the outside, you should think about putting a non-porous, occlusive or waterproof material on the outside. This may necessitate changing the bandage more frequently.

Recently, new biocompatible bandaging materials have become available to veterinarians. These products (such as Dermaheal® and Tegaderm®) are self-adhesive, simplify the bandaging process, and may be better tolerated by animals than traditional bandages. At present, they are rather expensive, and like other bandages, must be monitored carefully (tissues beneath may remain too moist). The Tufts Wildlife Clinic has been using such products extensively on mammals and birds for the last six months, and we find ourselves relying increasingly on them. Once again, talk to your own veterinarian about his/her experience with this bandaging option.

There is a great deal of controversy over whether a wound should be immobilized or allowed to move around in order to best promote healing. At this time, it looks as though the data favor immobility for encouraging the best possible healing. So it is probably preferable to use a bandage that restricts movement somewhat, as long as it doesn't put so much pressure on the wound that the circulation is compromised.

MEDICATION AND NUTRITION

There are several factors under the control of the rehabilitator or veterinarian that can markedly affect the odds for wound healing. Elevated levels of corticosteroid hormones have been clearly shown to slow healing. High steroid levels can come about in two ways: from administration of steroid drugs (exogenous route), or from the animals own adrenal glands when it is stressed (endogenous route). Obviously, anything you can do to decrease the stress to which an animal is subject will help it to heal faster. Additionally, the use of any long-term corticosteroid drugs should be avoided. An initial dose of steroids for shock won't affect healing. But keeping that animal on steroids for more than a couple of days will noticeably slow healing.

The use of systemic antibiotics should be considered in all wildlife trauma cases. Since the philosophy of administration and availability of specific drugs will vary from veterinarian to veterinarian, I strongly recommend that rehabilitators work closely with their local veterinary practitioners to develop a rational approach for trauma cases.

In the absence of specific culture and sensitivity results, broad-spectrum, relatively non-toxic antibiotics are advisable. Aminoglycosides (like gentamycin) or other reasonably toxic drugs should be avoided unless the animals' organ system functions are being monitored. Because of the stress of handling in wildlife cases, it is usually best to choose an oral antibiotic that can be given in the food rather than having to give IM or IV injections several times a day. Remember that there are always exceptions...you may not want to use oral drugs in rabbits...IV antibiotics may be needed for a severe infection. So, once again, discuss your particulr case with your veterinarian.

One of the easiest ways to encourage wound healing is to optimize an animal's nutrition. After an injury, the body's requirements for total energy and for protein increase markedly. In part, this increase serves to fuel the repair processes of the body. Additionally, for reasons not well understood, animals lose protein at an abnormally rapid pace after being injured (the so-called catabolism of trauma). More severe injuries are associated with an increased magnitude and duration of this protein loss. To compensate, you should provide 2-3 times the normal caloric intake and utilize easily digestible, high protein sources of food.

Supplementation of specific nutrients may speed the repair process. All the B vitamins are necessary for tissue repair and are cheaply and easily provided. Vitamin C is clearly important for adequate collagen formation. Although many animals can make their own vitamin C under normal conditions, it is advisable to supplement the diet during wound healing.

Vitamin A is of particular interest because it has been shown to off-set some of the impaired wound healing caused by endogenous or exogenous steroids. Thus it may be of particular value in treating wildlife which experience high stress levels simply from being near people. Since vitamin A is fat soluble, large doses can be toxic. For dogs, doses of 400 I.U. per kilogram per day are considered safe. A MED dose of 300 I.U. per 100 Kcals of minimum energy per day has been recommended (Sedgwick, personal communication).

Zinc deficiency has been well documented to retard wound healing. It is unlikely that any of us are providing zinc deficient diets. However, the calcium supplements that many people add to diets can make zinc physiologically unavailable. Since the requirements for zinc are not well documented, it is difficult to recommend a precise dose, but 0.01 mg per Kcal of minimum energy required per day should be adequate.

CONCLUSION

In summary, there are many things that rehabilitators can do to optimize wound healing in their patients. There is no magic secret—but there are a few important ideas to remember:

- evaluate the wound carefully the first time
- plan your treatment carefully; think before doing
- whatever you do, be as gentle, quiet, and sterile as possible
- keep reading, learning and asking questions...there are always better ways.

RECOMMENDED FOR FURTHER READING

Bojrab, M.J. 1981. A handbook of veterinary wound management. College of Veterinary Medicine, University of Missouri, Columbia.

Dall, J.A. 1979. Wounds and injuries. *In* Cooper, J.W. and Eley, J.T. First aid and care of wild birds. David and Charles Publishers, N. Pomfret, VT.

Hunt, T.K. and Dunphy, J.E. (eds.). 1971. Fundamentals of wound management. Appleton-Century-Crofts, New York, NY.

Hunt, T.K. 1983. Wound healing. *In* Way, L.W. Current surgical diagnosis and therapy (6th ed.). Lange Publishing Company. Los Altos, CA.

Johnston, D.E. 1981. Skin and subcutaneous tissue. *In* Bojrab, M.J. (ed.). Pathophysiology in small animal surgery. Pp. 405-419.

Peyton, L.C. 1984. Wound healing: the management of wounds and blemishes in the horse—part 1. Comp. Cont. Educ. for the Pract. Vet. 6(2): S111-S117.

Probst, C.W. et al. 1984. The surgical management of a large thermal burn in a dog. J. Am. Anim. Hosp. Assoc. 20(1): 45-49.

Sedgwick, C. Associate Professor. Tufts School of Veterinary Medicine, North Grafton, MA.

Swaim, S.F. 1980. Surgery of traumatized skin. W.B. Saunders Co. Philadelphia.

Swaim, S.F. and Wilhalf, D. 1985. The physics, physiology and chemistry of bandaging open wounds. Comp. Cont. Educ. for the Pract. Vet. 7(2): 146-156.

Smeak, D.D. and Olmstead, M.L. 1984. Infections in clean wounds. Comp. Cont. Educ. for the Pract. Vet. 6(7): 629-633.

AVIAN PARASITES: POTENTIAL PATHOGENS IN TIMES OF STRESS

William Threlfall

Department of Biology
Memorial University of Newfoundland
St. John's, Newfoundland, Canada A1B 3X9

Birds are host to numerous species of parasites, ranging from protozoa, flukes, tapeworms, roundworms, spiny-headed worms to arthropods. The parasites may live externally (extoparasites) or internally (endoparasites). And all damage the host to varying degrees. The damage done by parasites, clinical signs and symptoms of infestation/infection, diagnosis and treatment vary according to the species of parasite. Selected examples are described and discussed.

The rehabilitator must decide whether to treat birds in his/her facility, and should strive to prevent the animals from becoming infested/infected while in captivity. The key to preventing parasite-related problems is good husbandry, and the adage "Prevention is better than the cure" is particularly apt in the case of parasites. Life-cycles are shown to be simple (one-host), complex (two or more hosts), or involve a vector (e.g. mosquito, midge, louse fly, blackfly).

People with access to large numbers of common birds, or small numbers of rare, or exotic birds can help to advance our knowledge of bird parasites if they are willing to cooperate with researchers by collecting parasites, or by submitting dead wildlife specimens for necropsy.

Techniques for collecting, relaxing and fixing parasites will be discussed in this paper.

In nature, no animal or plant lives in isolation. Each organism interacts with members of its own species and with other species. The relationships may be of several kinds, with some being casual (e.g. one plant shading another), or more intimate, as seen in the predator-prey relationship. The most intimate associations are those where two organisms live together in a symbiotic relationship (Dogiel 1962; Read 1970; Schmidt and Roberts 1981).

The term symbiosis is derived from the Greek (*sym* [*syn*]—together, with: *biosis*—manner of life), means "living together," and was first used by DeBary (1879) to cover a wide range of associations (Hertig et al. 1937). In some cases, one organism may live on, or in, another organism and cause it no damage. In this case we are looking at a commensal and its host, as exemplified by the ectocommensal pilot fish (*Naucrates ductor*) and sharksucker (*Echeneis naucrates*), that are usually associated with sharks (Brandes 1974). *Entamoeba gingivalis*, an amoeba, is an endocommensal that inhabits the human mouth (Levine 1973).

Termites eat wood but are unable to digest the cellulose that comprises the bulk of the food, this task being undertaken by flagellate protozoans that live in the gut of the termite. The flagellates produce a cellulase that breaks down the cellulose into a form (simpler carbohydrates or sugars) that can be used by the termites. In this instance both partners derive benefit from the association and neither can survive without the other (Rietschel and Rohde 1974; Ernst 1975; Borror et al. 1976). This relationship is an obligate one and is called mutualism, with the principals being mutuals. A further interesting type of mutually beneficial activity is that known as cleaning symbiosis, where one animal cleans another. Many small reef fishes and shrimps will set up station in quiet water where fishes congregate and when other fishes pass they make their presence known. If a fish wishes to be cleaned

All animals serve as hosts for parasites at some time in their life. Birds present a series of habitats, differing in structure, and chemical and physical parameters, on/in which communities of parasites may become established. (a) Adult and (b) Great black-backed gull chick (*Larus marinus*), (c) Black-legged kittiwake (*Rissa tridactyla*) chicks, (d) Atlantic puffin (*Fratercula arctica*) adult, with capelin (*Mallotus villosus*) in its beak.

of parasites, necrotic tissue and other external abnormalities it will stop and wait to be examined and then groomed by the small cleaner fish or shrimp (Limbaugh 1961).

Terrestrial examples are seen in the case of the Egyptian plover (*Pluvianus aegyptius*) that removes leeches and other debris from the mouth of crocodiles (Benson 1972), and the tick birds (Buphagus spp.) that remove parasites from the skin of various African game animals (Benson 1973).

Not all such relationships are neutral or beneficial in nature. In many cases, a small organism may take up residence on or in another animal that is larger and stronger than itself and will cause harm to that organism. In this instance the relationship is a parasitic one, with the parasite living at the expense of the host and relinquishing some of its basic physiological attributes to the host. Each parasite is subject to two environments during its life-cycle, namely the environment on/in

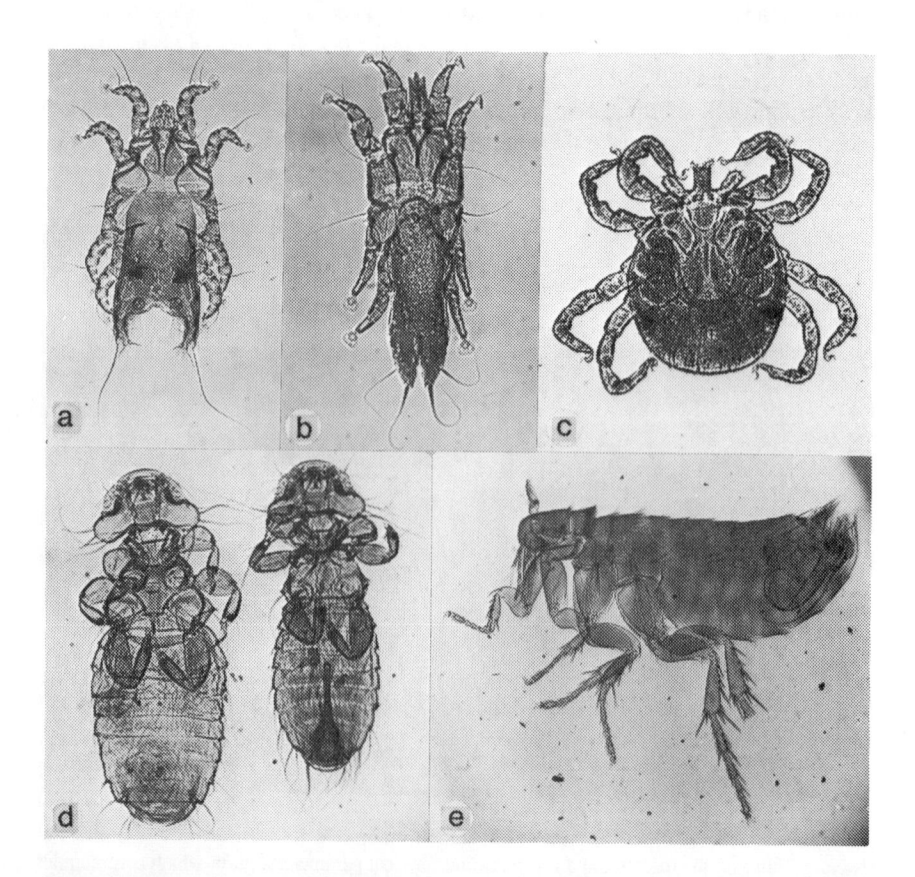

Figure 1. Ectoparasites live on the outside of the bird and may often be found in large numbers. (a), (b) feather mites (Acarina), (c) tick (*Ixodes uriae*: Acarina), (d) feather lice (Mallophaga), (e) adult flea (Siphonaptera). Specimens are not all to the same scale.

the host (microenvironment) and the environment of the host (macroenvironment) (Pavlovski 1934), and must possess adaptations to survive in both.

Parasites may be found living on/in almost every part of a bird (Rothschild and Clay 1952). Lice, fleas, ticks and mites that normally live on external surfaces are ectoparasites, while many protozoa, flukes, tapeworms, roundworms and spiny-headed worms (endoparasites) inhabit the internal organs (Figures 1, 2, 3, 4). The

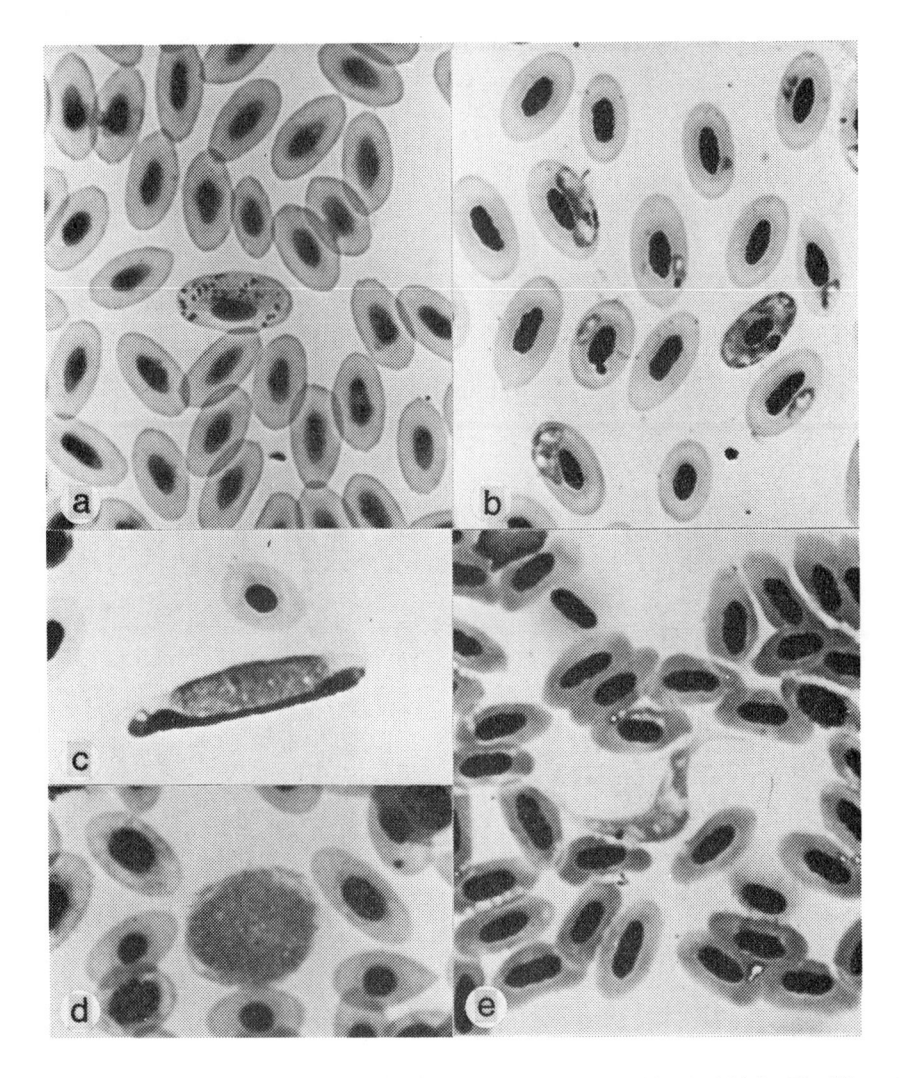

Figure 2. Protozoan parasites are commonly found living in the blood of birds. The life-cycle of these haematozoa usually involves a vector (e.g. mosquito, midge, blackfly, or louse fly.) (a) *Haemoproteus nettionis,* (b) *Plasmodium circumflexum,* (c) *Leucocytozoon simondi,* (d) *Akiba caulleryi,* (e) *Trypanosoma bouffardi.* (Photographs courtesy of G.F. Bennett.)

endoparasites may live in the intestine and its associated organs, or within the viscera in such places as the muscles, blood, and vessels of the circulatory and lymphatic systems.

Ectoparasites are acquired by contact between organisms or directly from the environment, whereas endoparasites gain entry to the host through ingestion of contaminated food, feces and bedding, or directly through the integument with or without the aid of a vector. A vector is an organism, usually an arthropod, that transmits a parasite from one host organism to another (Figure 5). In situations where an organism is held in captivity, certain factors no encountered in the wild become

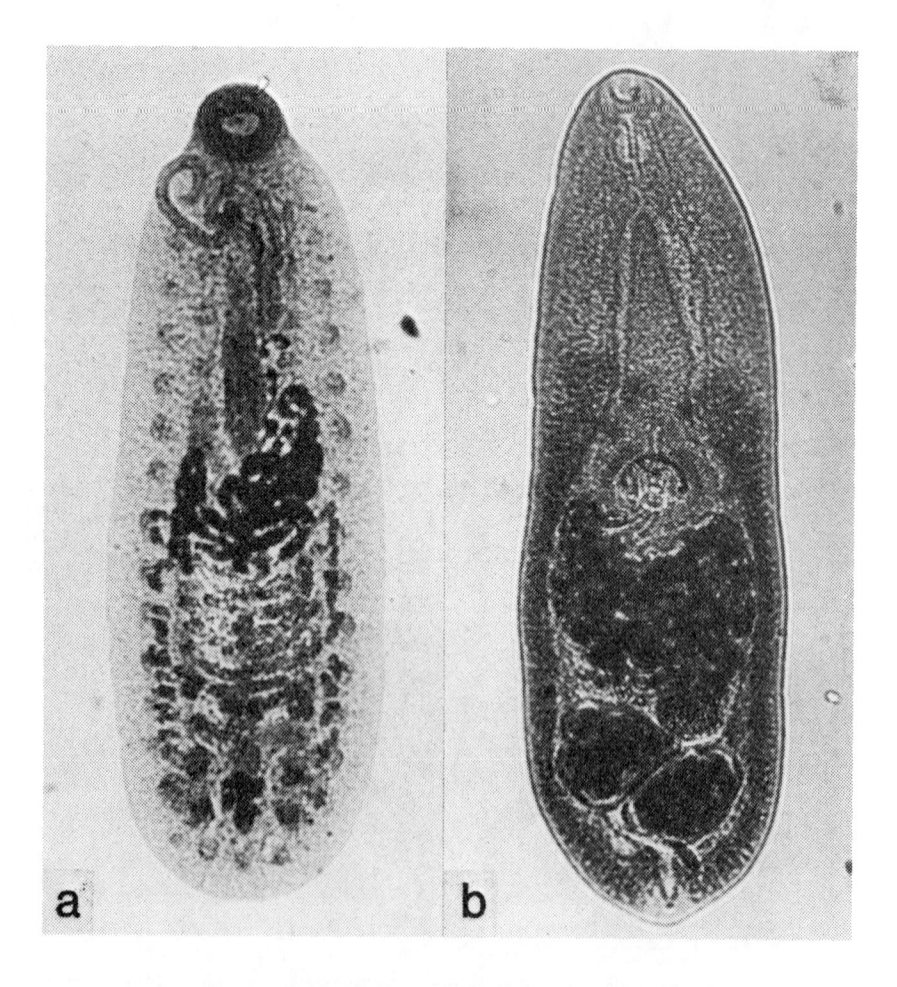

Figure 3. Flukes are common endoparasites of all classes of vertebrates, with some groups such as the notocotylids (a) being found in both birds and mammals. *Cryptocotyle lingua* (b) is widespread among aquatic fish-eating birds, and is usually located in the anterior region of the small intestine.

important such as contaminated bedding. Indeed, the following six factors should be monitored closely when concerns arise about parasites in birds that are being raised and/or maintained in captivity: food, feces, flies, filth, fingers, fomites.

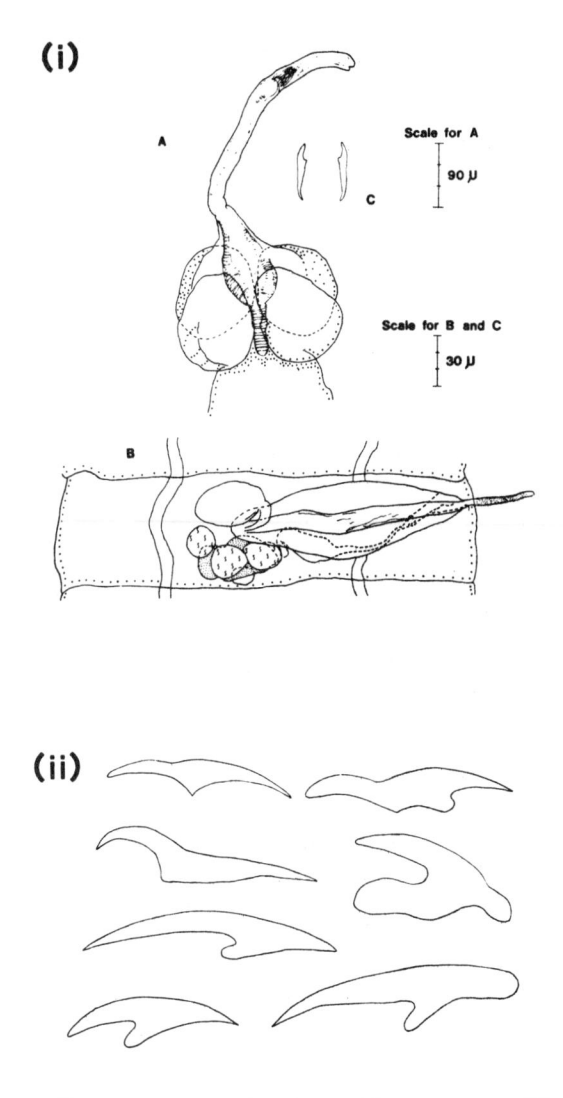

Figure 4. (i) *Hymenolepis (Microsomacanthus) formosoides*, a tapeworm of the common eider duck (*Somateria mollissima*). All tapeworms consist of a scolex, or attachment organ (A), bearing suckers and hooks (C), and a body composed of numerous proglottids (B) ("segments") containing male and female reproductive organs. (ii) Hooks are usually borne on a muscular rostellum, and vary in number, size, and shape according to the species being examined. The hooks shown are not all to the same scale and vary in length from 24 to 286 micrometers.

Endoparasites have developed a wide range of life-cycle strategies, ranging from simple to complex. In direct (one-host) life-cycles protozoan cysts or worm eggs pass out in the feces, infective stages develop within the cyst or egg and are then ingested directly by another definitive host (Figure 6). A definitive host is the host in which the sexually-reproducing stage of the parasite resides. A larva may hatch out of some roundworm eggs and live freely in the environment for a period of time before becoming infective (Figure 7). These larvae may be ingested or they may penetrate the integument of the host to gain entry into the body. Roundworm larvae may mature directly on reaching their preferred site within the host (e.g. *Ascaridia* spp.), or a migration through the body may occur before maturation (e.g. *Syngamus trachea* (the gapeworm). Other parasites have life-cycles that involve more

DEFINITIVE HOST

VECTOR

DEFINITIVE HOST

Figure 5. The life-cycle of many parasites may involve a vector which transmits the organism directly from one host to another (e.g. avian malaris (*Plasmodium* spp.)/mosquito.)

DEFINITIVE HOST

EGG/LARVA   (DIRECT)   EGG/LARVA

DEFINITIVE HOST

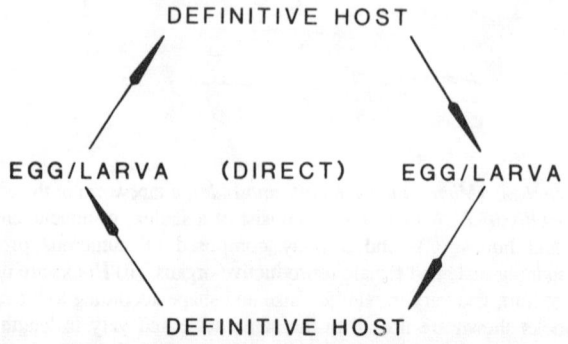

Figure 6. Direct life-cycle (e.g. many roundworms).

than one host (Figure 8a, b). In many of these complex life-cycles, in addition to the parasite producing thousands of eggs asexual reproduction may occur at various points during the cycle, ensuring the passage from one definitive host to another, and ultimately the survival of the species. This is best seen in the flukes where a snail, in which asexual reproduction occurs, is always involved in the life-cycle.

Little has been written on the pathogenic effects (Bennet et al. 1976; page 1976), or mortality, of wild organisms as a result of parasitic infections. This is in large part due to our lack of knowledge, and it may well be that in the future parasites may be shown to have important impacts on wildlife populations.

Cornwall (1963) observed waterfowl mortality in Manitoba as a result of infections with the roundworm *Echinuria uncinata*, while Anderson (1976) discussed the impact of three helminth diseases on populations of wild ungulates [parelaphostrongylosis and elaeophorosis in cervids; lungworm pneumonia in bighorn sheep (*Ovis canadensis*)]. Anderson (op. cit.) concluded that these worms do impact seriously on certain ungulate species in North America. If die-offs result from parasitic infections they are usually explicable in a number of ways. In some cases the birds were under some form of stress. [(e.g. *Trichostrongylus pergracilis* killing red grouse (*Lagopus lagopus*)] in Scotland and northern England when food is scarce in the spring (Leslie 1912). Herman and Wehr (1954), Herman et al. (1955) and Herman (1969) discuss mortality among Canada geese (*Branta canadensis*) induced by the presence of large numbers of the roundworm *Amidostomum anseris* that caused damage to the host gizzards, and a lack of quality food at certain times in the Pea Island National Wildlife Refuge, North Carolina.

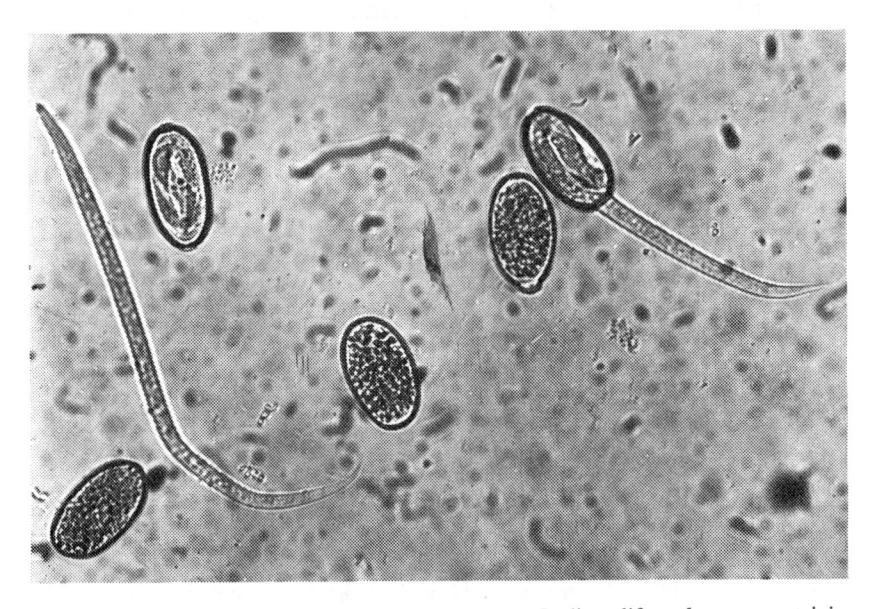

Figure 7. Cyathostoma lari (Nematoda) eggs and larvae. In direct life-cycles eggs containing infective larvae, or the larvae themselves, are ingested or burrow through the integument.

If birds are introduced to a new area, or managed intensively, they may be susceptible to infection by various endemic parasites, as was seen in the Seney National Wildlife Refuge, Michigan where Canada geese succumbed to heavy infections of *Leucocytozoon simondi* (Herman et al. 1975). Finally, if parasitized birds are introduced into an area the parasites may be transmissible and highly pathogenic to the endemic fauna, as was found in the case of the bird malaria *Plasmodium relictum* that depleted the drepanidad (Honey-creeper) population when it was introduced to the Hawaiian Islands (Warner 1968). It is of interest to note that when wild animals die and no cause can be established for the mortality that parasites often become the scapegoats and receive the blame, despite the fact that the parasite burden of the birds is often low (Cowan 1946; Clark et al. 1958) when compared with the burden in normal, apparently healthy animals (e.g. Bishop and Threlfall 1974). This does not mean to imply that parasites do not on occasion cause death. Kulachkova (1953, 1954, 1957, 1958) reported mortality in common eider (*Somateria mollissima*) chicks associated with massive infections with flukes in the Kandalaksha State Preserve, U.S.S.R. Individual chicks had burdens of up to 646,300 flukes representing five species.

When birds are admitted to a rehabilitation facility it is likely that the majority will already be parasitized, and due to the stress imposed by captivity, many will

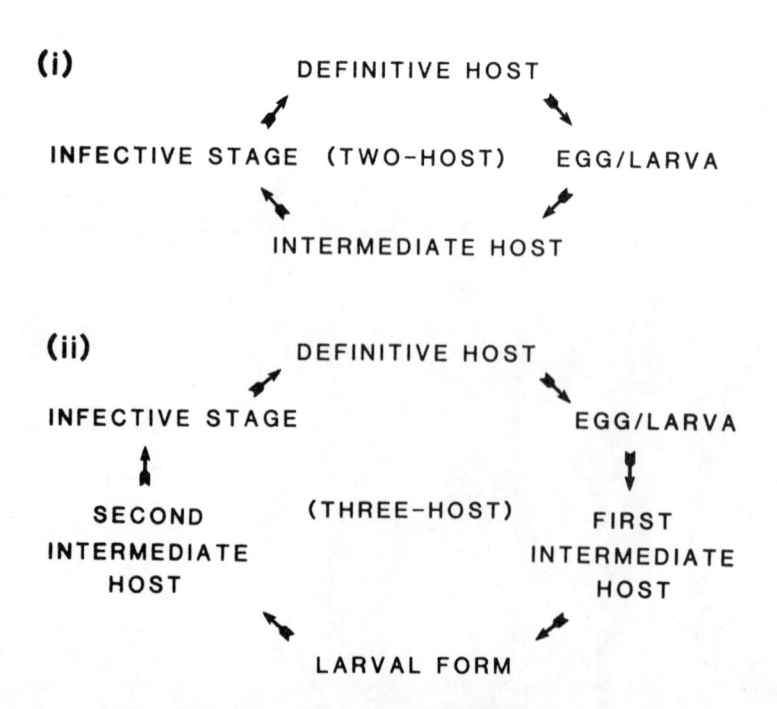

Figure 8. Parasite life-cycles may be complicated and involve more than one kind of host. (i) The two-host life-cycle is typical of the tapeworms and some flukes. (ii) The three-host life-cycle is seen in many flukes and some of the roundworms.

start to show the effects of their parasite burden. In a small number of cases the animals will initially be parasite-free but acquire parasites while in the facility. The most likely candidates for acquisition are ectoparasites and those organisms with a direct (one-host) life-cycle [e.g. many of the roundworms (Nematoda)]. The parasites will be transmitted during contact or through feces and contaminated bedding. Many mites are particularly difficult to eradicate due to their living in cracks and crevices in the housing during the day and only emerging at night to feed. The birds may also become infected via contaminated food, e.g. by feeding gulls fish that bear infective larvae (metacercariae) of flukes (Digenea) (Figure 9), or feeding double-crested cormorants (*Phalacrocorax auritus*) bluegills (*Lepomis macrochirus*)

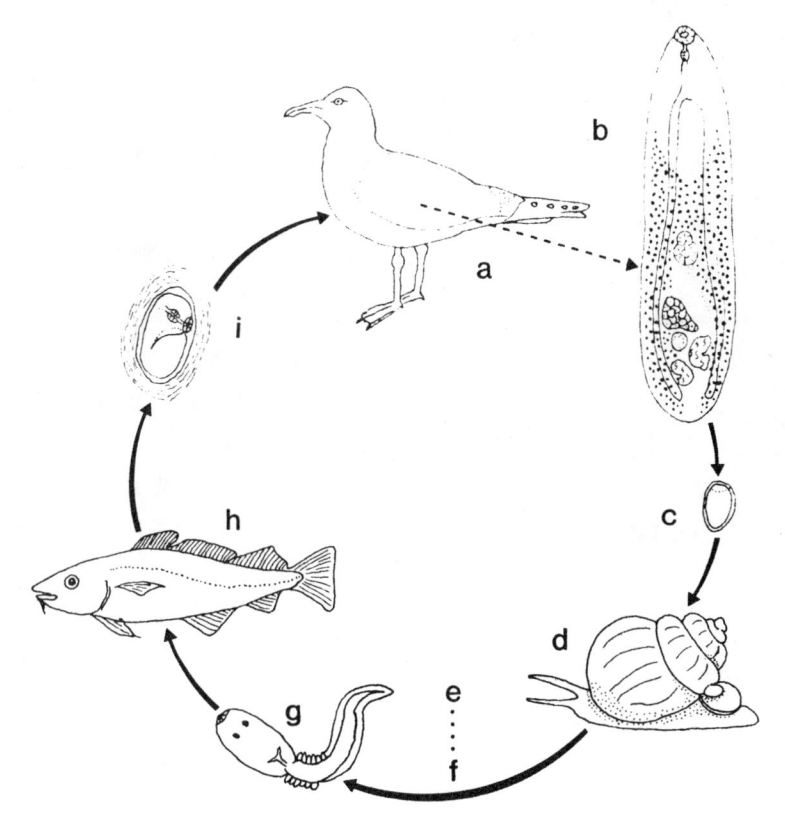

Figure 9. Life-cycle of *Cryptocotyle lingua.* This fluke is found in the small intestine of a variety of fish-eating birds, such as gulls (a). The adult fluke (b) produces eggs (c) that are passed out with the bird's feces. The egg hatches when it is ingested by a marine snail (e.g. *Littorina littorea*) (d). In the snail asexual reproduction occurs with two larval forms being seen, namely the sporocyst (e) followed by the redia (f). Each redia produces numerous cercariae (g) that burrow their way out of the snail and swim around until they encounter a fish that is a suitable second intermediate host (h). Many species of marine fishes may act in this way. The cercariae penetrate the skin if the fish, losing their tail, and become encysted as metacercariae (i). The fish reacts to their presence by depositing melanin around them. Birds become infected when they eat fish that carry infective metacercariae.

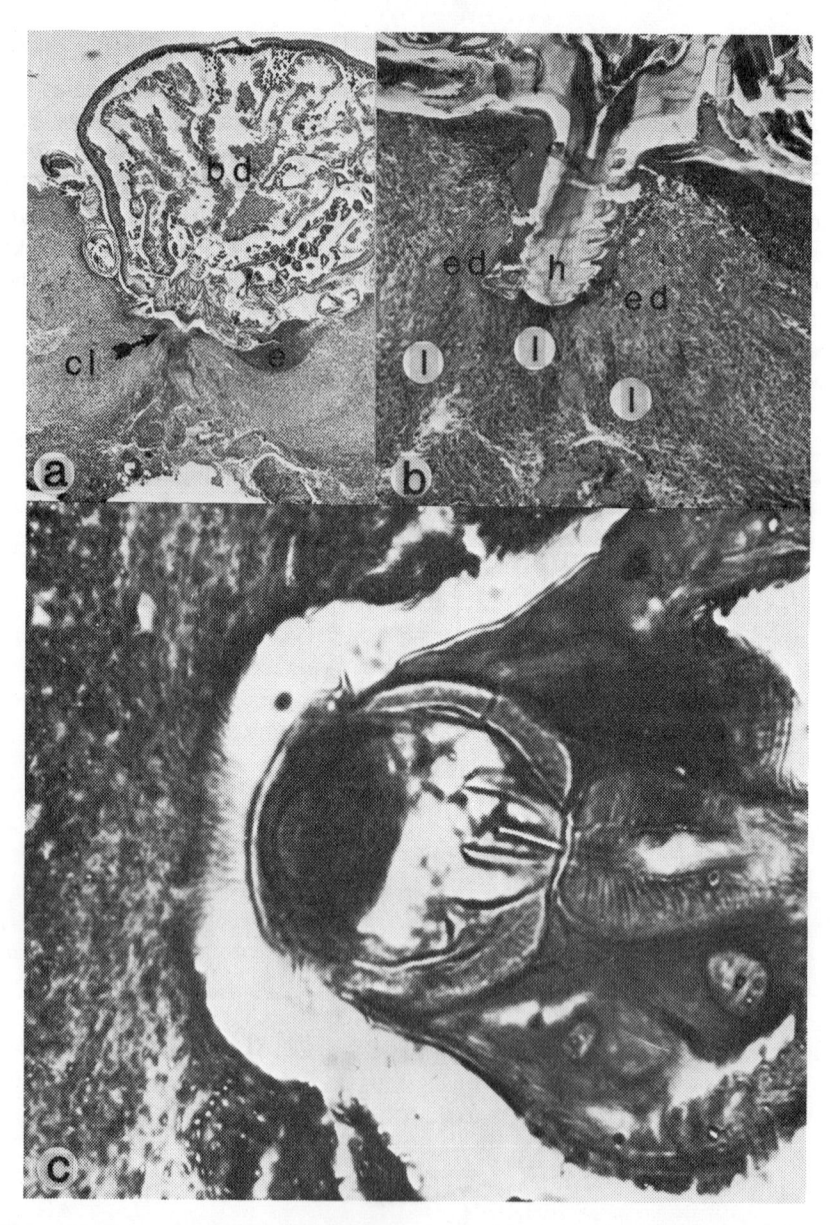

Figure 10. Some parasites remove blood from the host to the extent that the host becomes anemic. (a) Section of the seabird tick *Ixodes uriae* feeding on a chicken. The mouthparts are deeply embedded in the skin and mouthparts. bd: body of tick; cl: cement layer around mouthparts; e: eosinophilic reaction; ed: edematous tissue; h: hypostome (part of mouthparts) of tick; l: leucocyte (white blood cell) infiltration. (c) Section of *Cyathostoma lari* (Nematoda) attached to the mucosa lining the nasal sinuses of a herring gull (*Larus argentatus*). Note the plug of host tissue inside the buccal capsule of the worm, and the large cutting teeth.

containing infective larvae of the roundworm *Contracaecum spiculigerum*.

As noted earlier parasites establish a physiological relationship with the host and cause it some harm, the degree of damage inflicted varying with the species of parasite, its numbers and preferred site on or in the body. The type of damage done falls into four main classes, namely mechanical damage, withdrawal of metabolites, toxic effects, and predisposing the host to secondary infection (Cheng 1964).

Mechanical damage may be done when infective larvae penetrate the integument, or when the larvae migrate around the body before maturing. Visceral parasites (both adult and larval stages) may put pressure on vital organs impairing their functions, or they may completely block, or occlude, blood and lymph vessels. The digestive tract may also become blocked by parasites. Withdrawal of metabolites may be viewed in several ways. In some cases the parasite uses the host's food, while in others it may show a predilection for a particular substance that is essential for the well-being of the host, and a lack of which results in disease. Some parasites ingest blood so that an infestation may cause the host to become anemic (Figure 10). The parasites may secrete substances or produce toxins that have either local or more generalized effects throughout the body, and often stimulate a host reaction. Finally, parasites may damage various tissues, such as the skin, allowing the entry of viruses, bacteria or fungi into the body where they may induce secondary infections.

It is not possible in a work such as this to discuss all the parasites known to live on and in birds. Each major group of parasites will be discussed, and specific examples will be utilized to illustrate germane points.

Two excellent general works concerned with the diseases and parasites of birds are Arnall and Keymer (1975) and Keymer (1981), while Wobeser (1981) deals exclusively with waterfowl. Cooper and Eley (1979) cover a wide variety of subjects, including diagnosis of disease, infectious diseases and parasites in their work on first aid and care of wild birds.

The most frequently seen ectoparasites on birds are dorso-ventrally flattened biting-lice (Mallophaga: Figure 1) that normally feed on feathers and skin debris. In heavy infestations the feathers are damaged and being to lack their normal lustre, giving the bird a "moth-eaten" look. In addition large numbers of eggs, so-called nits, may be seen attached to the feathers usually near the shaft. When present in small numbers the lice present no problem, and may even be picked off by hand. Insecticide sprays may be used in heavy infestations, but great care should be taken in choosing an appropriate agent.

Many man-made products are extremely toxic to birds and persistent. Natural substances such as the pyrethrums are good parasiticides and relatively non-toxic. As the life-cycle of these parasites is direct and transmission occurs mainly through contact heavily contaminated birds should be quarantined, and their quarters thoroughly cleaned after use. If birds are kept in crowded conditions and their cages are not kept scrupulously clean, a serious build-up of ectoparasites may result. The principle of *"Prevention is better than the cure"* is a golden rule with regard to parasite infestations/infections.

The majority of birds are host to a wide range of feather mites, many of which occur in large numbers and seem to cause few problems. Some species, however, do cause damage by sucking blood or body fluids. Feeding causes irritation and restlessness in the bird host and occasionally anemia.

Mites of the genus *Knemidocoptes* may cause feather loss, or the base of the beak, legs and feet may become swollen and distorted (see Arnall and Keymer, op. cit). Heavy infestations cause the skin to thicken and become knobbly. A crusty covering composed of an exudate produced by the bird and skin debris resulting from the burrowing activity of the mites covers the area. Infected regions become honey-combed with burrows. In this latter group the parasites spend their whole life on the bird and treatment consists of the application of various acaricides such as benzyl benzoate and bromocyclen in an oil or spirit base. In its early stages an infestation may be controlled by the application of liquid paraffin, but in advanced situations the crusty layer is first softened with liquid paraffin and then an acaricide is applied.

The red mite (*Dermanyssus gallinae*), on the other hand, is a periodic visitor usually feeding on the birds at night and then retreating to cracks and crevices in the bird's cage during the day. Treatment in this case involves not only the bird but much more importantly, the living quarters. The cages and perches should be painted regularly with an acaricide-containing paint, or they should be steam-cleaned.

Ticks (Figure 1) are much larger than mites and are blood-feeders that transmit a number of diseases. They visit a bird to feed, remaining attached for a period of time ranging from a few minutes to several days. When engorged they drop off only to visit a bird at a later date for another meal. Some tick life-cycles may take as long as five years to become egg-mature adults (see Eveleigh and Threlfall 1974). Normally only small numbers of these parasites will be found on a given bird and they may be picked off after applying methyl or isopropyl (rubbing) alcohol to the parasite's body. Care must be taken to ensure the removal of the mouthparts of the parasite that are embedded in the host skin (Figure 10) or a secondary infection may occur. Heavy infestations may result in irritation, dermatitis and anemia.

Adult fleas are laterally-flattened ectoparasites that are frequently found on a wide variety of birds (Holland 1949), but are more closely associated with birds nests. A single nest may contain very large numbers of these organisms (e.g. I have removed well over 500 fleas from one House Sparrow (*Passer domesticus*) nest). The adults are blood feeders that cause little harm, other than being an irritant, in small numbers. Large numbers, however, may cause severe blood loss, anemia and even death in nestlings. Control is quite difficult as they only feed on the bird and their life-cycle is completed to a large extent off the host. Eggs are laid in the nesting/bedding material and the larva that emerges from the egg feeds on organic detritus (e.g. sloughed-off epidermal scales and bits of feathers).

When it is fully mature the larva spins a cocoon and then pupates. After some time (from a week to a year) a hungry adult emerges from the cocoon. The larvae and pupae will live in cracks and crevices in the bird's pen or cage making them difficult to reach. The application of a suitable insecticide may be used to break the life-cycle this stage.

When handling live wild birds one or two large fly-like creatures may often be seen scurrying about in the feathers. These are louse flies, or hippoboscids. Rothschild and Clay (1952) likened the presence of two louse flies on a small bird to a man having two large shore crabs running around in his underclothes.

Some species have reduced wings but are capable of limited flight, while other species are wingless. They have a somewhat dorso-ventrally flattened body that allows them to move easily through the feathers. Their feet and legs are enlarged, enabling them to grasp firmly onto the birds feathers or skin. They are blood-feeders that transmit a variety of disease-causing organisms, including haematozoan parasites (e.g. *Haemoproteus* spp.). They are rarely a problem but their numbers may build up to pest proportions if conditions in a bird-holding facility are suitable.

Numerous species of flies are known to bite and feed on birds including mosquitoes (*Aedes* spp., *Anopheles* spp., *Culex* spp.), midges (*Culicoides* spp.), and blackflies (*Simulium* spp.), and many are responsible for the transmission of disease-causing agents ranging from viruses to roundworms. Although blood-loss caused by these animals may cause little inconvenience they may act as a considerable irritant. Once again the rehabilitator may prevent problems by fly-proofing cages and pens with mosquito netting. If sick birds have open lesions action should be taken to ensure that they do not become fly-blown. Several species of blowflies (Family Calliphoridae) are attracted to open wounds and may deposit eggs or larvae on the living and dead tissue. The maggots then eat the flesh of the bird causing a condition known as myiasis. Affected wounds are susceptible to secondary infection. Maggots may be removed manually and the wound should be cleaned and dressed.

Many species of protozoans, including amoebae, flagellates, ciliates and sporozoans, are parasitic in birds. Only a small number are known to be pathogenic in wild birds despite the fact that two of the most important domestic bird diseases, coccidiosis and histomoniasis, are caused by protozoa. The signs and symptoms of aprotozoan-induced disease will depend on the parasite species, level of infection, location within the host and the parasite's life-style. *Plasmodium* spp. cause bird malaria (Figure 2) with the parasites attacking and destroying red blood cells (erythrocytes), and endothelial cells. This parasite seems to cause little harm under normal conditions, but heavy infections may cause a febrile disease. The birds will become depressed and incoordinated, and the feathers become ruffled. Diagnosis is by the demonstration of pigmented parasites in the erythrocytes. Antimalarial drugs such as mepacrine hydrochloride may be used to treat infected animals. *Plasmodium* spp. are extremely widespread in a large number of bird species (Bennett et al. 1982), usually occurring at low levels in much of the population and causing little apparent harm. Once again, prevention is the best policy. The life-cycle involves a vector in the form of a mosquito and it is at this stage that measures should be taken to interrupt the cycle. Mosquito-proofing the rehabilitation facility, pens and cages would allow for the control of this parasite and several others that

Figure 11. Fish may act as the second intermediate host in the life-cycle of many flukes, as in the case of the cunner (*Tautogolabrus adspersus*) and the fluke *Cryptocotyle lingua*. (a) Uninfected gill of a cunner. (b) Gill of a cunner heavily infected with *C. lingua* metacercariae. Note the numerous cysts. (c) Cunner fins showing different degrees of infection. (d) Cunner scales showing different degrees of infection with *C. lingua* metacercariae. In (c) and (d) each parasite cyst is surrounded by a layer of the black pigment melanin. This causes a condition known as "black-spot disease" that is frequently seen in both freshwater and marine fishes.

utilize vectors (e.g. *Haemoproteus* spp./*louse flies*, *Leucocytozoon* spp./blackflies, and *Akiba* spp./midges). Prophylactic actions for the latter are similar to those for the malarias (*Plasmodium* spp.) although the drugs utilized for their control and their preferred sites/cells within the host may differ.

Intestinal protozoans, such as coccidia of the genera *Eimeria* and *Isospora* cause quite different damage than that produced by the haematozoa. The life-cycle of these parasites is direct and the birds ingest oocysts containing infective sporozoites. The sporozoites released when the cyst walls are digested penetrate intestinal cells and undergo asexual reproduction. The newly developed parasites are released and enter more cells where the process is repeated. This cycle quickly leads to the destruction of enormous numbers of intestinal mucosa cells. Eventually, after several asexual cycles two specialized cell-types will be formed, small microgametes and large macrogametes. A microgamete enters and fertilizes a macrogamete to form a zygote that secretes a resistant cyst wall, becoming in the process an oocyst. The oocysts are passed to the outside in the bird's feces where they mature by the formation of sporocysts containing infective sporozoites within the cyst wall. Infection occurs when this stage is ingested.

Low or moderate levels of infection with coccidia may result in immunity to re-infection. The clinical signs of coccidiosis are numerous but will depend to a large extent on the species of birds and coccidian involved, as well as the age and health of the host. The intestine wall will show inflammation of varying degrees of severity. The birds will generally become unthrifty, anemic, emaciated and diarrhoeic. The diarrhoea may be green, watery and slimy, or bloody. The disease itself may be mild and chronic resulting in few deaths, or it may be acute and rapidly produce much mortality. Diagnosis is by demonstration of oocysts in the faeces. The most efficacious drugs in treatment of this condition are the sulphonamides.

This parasite is easily spread and the number of oocysts builds up rapidly where birds are overcrowded and where food and water may become contaminated with feces. Good husbandry is the key to controlling this organism. It is of interest to note that with coccidia the most desirable situation is one where light infections may develop, thus stimulating immunity, rather than trying to attain a coccidia-free environment.

Several thousand species of flukes (Digenea) are known parasites of birds, yet few are pathogenic. Our knowledge of the pathogenicity of this group is limited but in heavy infections with certain species the birds will show, among other signs, a general malaise, lack of appetite, anemia and diarrhoea. In most cases the presence of these parasites is only discovered at necropsy, or when fecal analyses are performed. Once a bird is in captivity there is little chance that it will acquire flukes, except in the case of aquatic birds that are being fed fresh fish that may act as second intermediate hosts for various flukes (Figures 3, 9, 11).

Tapeworms (Cestoda) are extremely common in birds but little work has been performed on their pathogenic effects. One of the first signs of these parasites is the presence of proglottids ("segments") in the feces (Figure 12). Clinical signs of infection are dull plumage, poor appetite (resulting in weight loss), anemia and thirst. Grain and seed eating birds are less likely to become infected than invertebrate or flesh-eating birds as the life-cycle of these parasites involves an intermediate host in which an infective larva develops. The larva is usually a cysticerioid (in invertebrates) or a cysticercus (bladderworm; in vertebrates). Avian cestodes appear resistant to most anthelmintics, and many widely used drugs are toxic to birds.

It is essential that the whole worm be removed when a bird is treated and the feces should be examined to make sure that the scolex ("head"; Figure 12), neck and strobila ("body," chain of proglottids) have been passed. Many drugs cause destrobilation with only the strobila being evacuated and the scolex and neck remaining in the bird. The neck will then start to produce a new strobila. Dichlorophen appears to be one of the more effective drugs in the control of tapeworms.

Good hygiene will prevent or reduce the chances of birds acquiring tapeworms. In some instances birds may carry a burden of several thousand worms and show no ill-effects, while other tapeworms in small numbers may have a marked effect. The rehabilitator or veterinarian must once again decide whether or not to treat a given host, realizing that the treatment may have more deleterious effects than the infection. Further, in outdoor aviaries where earthworms and other invertebrates that act as intermediate host are available, a choice must be made between the benefits accruing from the consumption of these creatures and the ultimate effects of the tapeworms they may carry.

The most common parasites of vertebrates are roundworms (Nematoda) that can be found in a variety of sites throughout the body. Their pathgenicity will depend on the species being investigated, location within the body, and the numbers present, as well as the age and general health of the host. Roundworms are usually small thread-like creatures from a few millimeters to a few centimeters in length, and most have a direct life-cycle. A few species utilize an intermediate host, while others have a direct life-cycle but whose infective larvae may be found in a variety of invertebrates (e.g. earthworms, beetles, ants) that are called paratenic hosts.

One of the most widespread roundworms, in terms of both host species and geographical distribution, is the gapeworm (*Syngamus trachea*). This worm is acquired by eating eggs containing infective larvae, or paratenic hosts such as earthworms and snails. Larvae released in the digestive tract of the host migrate through the body and eventually reach the upper respiratory tract (trachea) where they mature. The female worm becomes attached to the epithelial lining of the trachea. The smaller male is permanently attached, *in copulo*, to the female about one third of the way from her anterior end. Eggs are passed in the feces and develop to the infective stage in the soil, or bedding.

The presence of these worms in the trachea causes irritation, excess mucus will be produced, and the birds try to expel them by coughing or sneezing. The worms may occlude the trachea in heavy infections, particularly in small birds, and asphyxiation may result. Exhaustion may occur from excessive coughing, while appetite will decrease followed by gradual weight loss and emaciation. Worms may often be seen through the glottis when the beak is opened widely. Prevention by good husbandry is the preferred method of control.

Adult birds with just a few worms may pose a serious threat to nestlings and should be separated from them. Further, earthworms and other potential paratenic hosts should be withheld from debilitated birds. Where birds are maintained in outdoor aviaries efforts should be made to shield them from the droppings of wild birds such as starlings. A roof (fiberglass or plastic) over the cage would achieve the desired result. In large birds it may be possible to remove the worms manually, using a cotton and wire pipe-cleaner. Oral administration of the drug, thiabendazole, may be quite effective.

Other parasites associated with the respiratory and circulatory systems include the filarial worms that are most likely transmitted by blackflies (*Simulium* spp.) and midges (*Culicoides* spp.). These worms may cause pneumonia, inflammation of the air sacs, clogging of capillaries (by microfilariae, or larvae, in the blood), and enlargment and thickening of arterial walls (resulting in fibrosis, necrosis and stenosis). No drug is available for their control, and once again prevention is the keyword.

Threadworms (*Capillaria* spp.) inhabit the digestive tract (crop, esophagus, intestine, ceca) of many birds species and many cause problems if present in large numbers. Light infections appear to be of little importance. Their life-cycles are

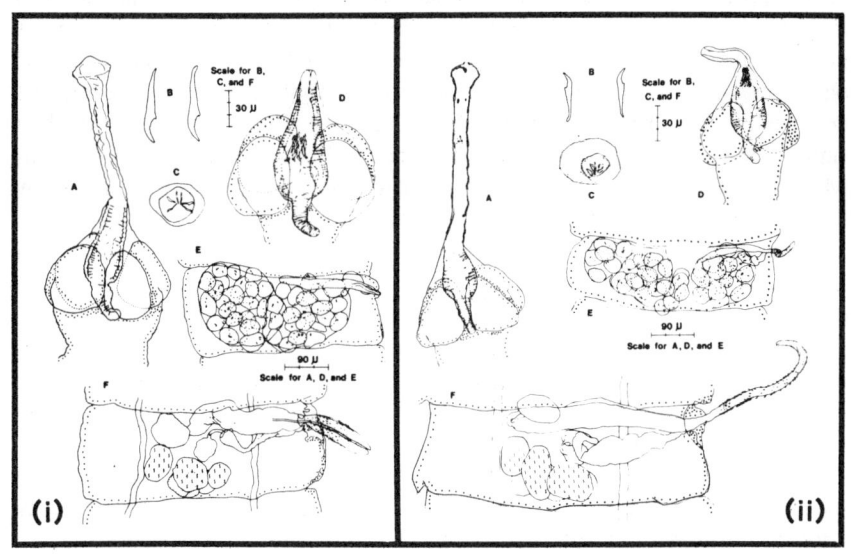

Figure 12. A single bird may contain thousands of tapeworms of several species and show no ill-effects. A number of characters are used to identify tapeworms, including among other things, the number, size and shape of the hooks; number and position of testes; and the size and shape of the cirrus. These tapeworms [and the one in Figure 4 (i)] were all recovered from a single common eider duck (*Somateria mollissima*). (i) *Hymenolepis (Microsomacanthus) somateriae*, (ii) *Hymenolepis (Microsomacanthus) microskrjabini*. A: scolex with everted rostellum; B: rostellar hooks; C: egg; D: scolex with rostellum inverted; E: gravid proglottid; F: mature proglottid (after Bishop and Threlfall, 1974).

poorly known, some appearing to be direct, others requiring an intermediate host. Clinical signs and their severity depend on the size of the infection, and range from poor appetite, emaciation, and anemia, to diarrhea. Yellow slimy or bloody diarrhea may result from heavy infections and is associated with the spearation of the mucous membrane lining the intestine. Diagnosis is by demonstrating the presence of eggs or adult worms in the feces. Absolute cleanliness is the key to controlling this worm and measures should be taken to ensure a minimal contact between free-living wild birds and those in the rehabilitation facility. Levamisole hydrochloride or tetramisole, administered orally, may be used to treat infected birds.

Proventricular and gizzard worms (e.g. *Acuaria* spp., *Amidostomum* spp., *Echinuria* spp., *Spiroptera* spp.) normally have direct life-cycles, and in the host burrow deeply into the mucosa of the infected organ. This may cause inflammation, ulceration and thickening of the organ wall resulting in impaired function. No satisfactory treatment is known.

Thus the best ways of preventing nematode-induced losses in a rehabilatation facility center around good husbandry and breaking the life-cycle of the parasite *before* it enters the host. A wide range of drugs is available to treat infected birds, with the most widely used medications being piperazine, tetramisole, thiabendazole, mebendazole, and levamisole hydrochloride.

Spiny-headed worms (Acanthocephala) are extremely common in birds. The adults appear to prefer the posterior small intestine where they become attached by embedding a hook-covered proboscis in the intestinal mucosa. Known life-cycles involve an intermediate host, usually an arthropod. Little work has been performed on the pathogenic effects of these parasites but heavy infections may cause enteritis and debility. Usually the worms remain undetected until necropsy, when the first sign of their presence is nodules on the outer wall of the intestine in the regions where probosces are, or were, embedded. Thiabendazole administered orally may be useful in controlling these worms (Arnall and Keymer 1975).

Individuals who handle large numbers of common birds, or small numbers of rare or exotic birds, can help advance the frontiers of science by collaborating with scientists interested in the taxonomy and ecology of parasites. When parasite-induced diseases are seen the rehabilitator should note the signs, symptoms and progress of the condition in the bird, and then collect the causative agents. The specimens collected would give information on what species of parasites are normally associated with a given bird species and in what numbers.

Ectoparasites may be collected while the birds are alive by removing them manually, or by the Kilner jar method (Fowler and Cohen 1983; Figure 13). Many arthropod parasites will leave a host soon after its death so that if ectoparasites are to be collected from a dead animal it should be as soon as possible after death. If a delay in examination is anticipated, birds may be placed individually in plastic bags and a wad of cottonwool soaked in chloroform inserted into each bag, or the bags may be completely covered in dry ice. The latter methods prevent movement of the parasites on the host and allow a worker to determine preferred sites for each parasite species, as well as allowing for an accurate count of the parasites present.

Eveleigh and Threlfall (1976) determined site preference of Mallophaga on auks (Alcidae) in Newfoundland and arbitrarily divided the bird's body into a series of regions for examination (Figure 14). Any parasites found may be fixed and preserved in 70 percent ethanol, or be placed directly into Rubin's fluid (Rubin 1951: Appendix); on removal from the bird, this latter method resulting in a permanent prepara-

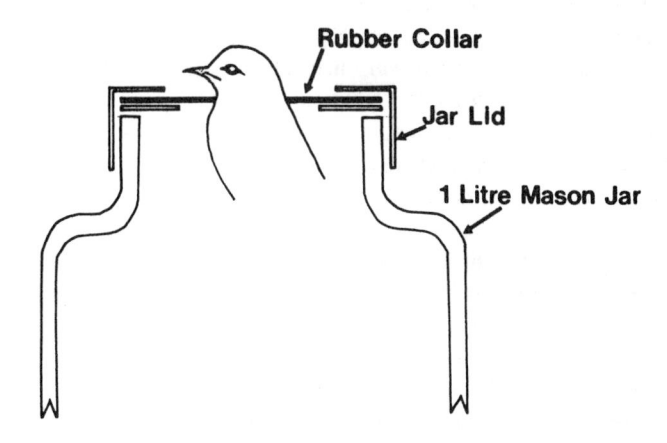

Figure 13. Kilner jar apparatus for collecting ectoparasites from live birds. The rubber collar was cut from a car tire inner tube and is thick enough to support the weight of small birds without the use of a clip (*see* Fowler and Cohen 1983). The diameter of the central hole in the rubber collar depends on the size of the bird being processed. The following list details the size of hole found to be most satisfactory for the birds named. Chloroform is placed in the jar and this will cause ectoparasites to drop off aproximately 15-20 minutes. The bird may then be released or returned to its cage. The parasites are then picked out of the jar with a paint brush and placed in 70 percent ethanol.

BIRD	DIAMETER (mm)
Kinglets (Muscicapidae)	10
Chickadees (Paridae)	12
Warblers, Small Sparrows (Emberizidae)	12
Finches (Fringillidae)	12
Small Flycatchers (Tyrannidae)	12
Starlings (Sturnidae)	15
Small Thrushes (Muscicapidae)	15
Large Sparrows (Emberizidae)	15
Robins (Muscicapidae)	20
Grosbeaks (Emberizidae)	20

tion. A series of voucher specimens for deposition in a recognized museum should be prepared [e.g. U.S. National Museum, British Museum, Biosystematics Research Institute (Canada)].

Blood and fecal samples may also be taken from the living bird. Blood is best taken and fixed using the method of Bennett (1970) and may be sent to the *International Reference Centre for Avian Haematozoa, (IRCAH) Department of Biology, Memorial University of Newfoundland, St. John's, Newfoundland, Canada, A1B 3X9*, to be examined for blood parasites (Figure 2). A series of pictorial guides to many of the haematozoa have been published (Greiner and Bennett 1975; Greiner et al. 1975; Herman et al. 1977).

Fresh feces may be examined for protozoans (trophozoites and cysts) and worm eggs using a variety of methods. Feces should be collected in a clean container and kept warm if trophozoites (motile, feeding stage in the life-cycle of protozoans) are to be detected. A smear of feces in 0.85 percent saline may be examined immediately for trophozoites. If the feces is to be examined for parasites at a later date it may be preserved in merthiolate-iodine-formalin (MIF), Burrow's polyvinyl alcohol (PVA) or 5 percent formalin (Appendix).

The methods used to concentrate protozoan cysts and worm eggs all rely on either flotation or sedimentation in a variety of media (Appendix), with the method of analysis used being a matter of personal preference. The basic procedures used in fecal analysis are detailed in a wide variety of works (Levine et al. 1960; Schell 1962; Cable 1965; Meyer and Olsen 1980; Pritchard and Kruse 1982; Faler and Faler 1984).

A number of disposable plastic kits are available commercially for the collection, preservation and analysis of feces. Bradley and Bradely (1982) evaluated three of these devices and found that the Ovatector® (BGS Medical) was the most efficient and cost effective. The problem with all such kits, including the Para-Pak Systems® (Meridian Diagnostics Inc.) is their cost. If fresh fecal samples are to be examined, and little or no delay is anticipated in processing, media may be made as needed in the laboratory and clean glassware used repeatedly at a much reduced cost. At the present time it is possible to identify to the generic level only a few of the many parasite eggs found in avian feces as no good key has yet been constructed for this purpose.

On the death of the host a necropsy may be performed to detect endoparasites (Meyer and Olsen 1980; Pritchard and Kruse 1982). With endoparasites it is essential that the worms are properly killed, fixed and preserved for later identification. Smears may be made with blood taken directly from the heart immediately after death of the host, air dried and fixed in absolute (100 percent) ethanol or methanol. Intestinal contents and feces may be examined for protozoa at necropsy, or if a delay is anticipated they may be preserved in PVA fixative. The latter preserves both trophozoites and cysts of protozoans.

Flukes and tapeworms should be washed thoroughly in 0.85 percent saline (Appendix) to remove mucus and debris and then relaxed in iced distilled water, or saline, in a refrigerator. The length of time for relaxation will depend to a large extent on the size of the worms, and many specimens must be flattened before fixation (see Pritchard and Kruse 1982). Flattening the worms facilitates subsequent straining, mounting and identification. The worms may be flattened between two glass slides or glass sheets which are then placed in a beaker or dish of fixative for several hours. The amount of pressure should be minimal as the worms may become distorted or enlarged if too much pressure is applied (Ulmer 1952). An excellent method for obtaining nicely relaxed intestinal worms is to remove the intestine from the bird, place it in an enamel dish and pour absolute ethanol chilled to 70°C with dry ice over the structure. This freezes the intestine within seconds and it may be kept frozen for subsequent examination (Bush 1980). Some workers prefer to kill the worms in hot, *not* boiling, water and transfer them a few seconds later to a fixative.

Entire organs may be heat-treated by pouring boiling water over them and then transferring them to fixative or the organs may be placed directly in 10 percent formalin (9 volumes of fixative for each volume of organs). In the case of the latter method parasites may be fixed *in situ* and any damage done to the host organ may be noted after appropriate processing. If whole animals are available but cannot be necropsied within an hour or so, 10 percent formalin injected directly in to the body cavity will preserve the organs and parasites. These birds should then be kept chilled or frozen. Freezing is a slow process and usually results in poor specimens as autolysis (self-digestion) of the intestine and parasites will occur. Placing birds in dry ice immediately after death results in rapid freezing and acceptable specimens.

Numerous fixatives (see Appendix for some of the more widely used types) are available for these helminths, with each person developing a preference for certain formulations. Two of the most popular fixatives are 10 percent formalin and

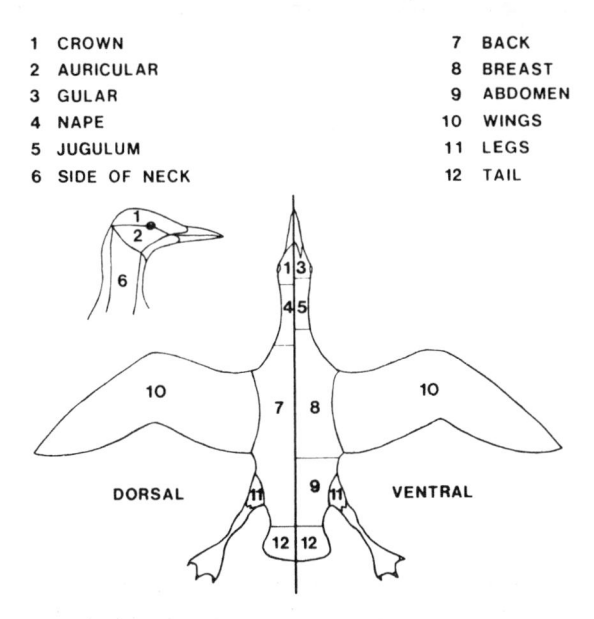

1	CROWN	7	BACK
2	AURICULAR	8	BREAST
3	GULAR	9	ABDOMEN
4	NAPE	10	WINGS
5	JUGULUM	11	LEGS
6	SIDE OF NECK	12	TAIL

Figure 14. Body regions to be examined for ectoparasites (after Eveleigh and Threlfall 1976).

alcohol-formalin-acetic acid (AFA). After fixation (small specimens a few minutes, large specimens several hours) the worms may be preserved in 70 percent ethanol or methanol.

Roundworms will tend to coil up if placed directly into a fixative making subsequent identification difficult. Live worms may be straightened, and killed, by placing them in cold glacial acetic acid, hot (almost boiling) 70 percent ethanol, or hot 70 percent glycerine alcohol (Looss's fluid: Appendix). After fixation, the roundworms are best preserved in glycerine alcohol. Lactophenol (Appendix) is used to clear the worms prior to identification.

Spiny-headed worms are usually attached to the intestine wall and care should be taken to ensure that the hook-covered probosces are not left embedded in the mucosa on removal. The number, size and shape of hooks, as well as the number of rows are important features in identification, thus the worms should be killed with their proboscis everted and not retracted. This is achieved by placing them in cold water in a refrigerator for as long as they live, during which time the proboscis will evert due to changes in internal pressure brought about by osmosis. Some researchers use hot 70 percent alcohol, or 10 percent formalin containing a few drops of glacial acetic acid to cause eversion much more rapidly. The worms may be fixed in AFA and then stored in 70 percent ethanol or methanol.

None of the specimens collected will be of any use if they are not correctly labelled. The label should include at least the data outlined on Figure 15. The best way of ensuring that the data will not be lost is to put a label in the vial of parasites. The label should be of white bond (rag) paper written in soft pencil or waterproof ink. If the vial is small an identification number may be placed in the vial and a cross-referenced detailed collection card completed. The present author prefers

```
HOST       COMMON NAME _____
           SCIENTIFIC NAME _____
           AGE _____ SEX _____
           LOCALITY _____ DATE COLLECTED ___
           COUNTRY OF ORIGIN _____
           NECROPSIED BY _____
           NECROPSY DATE _____

PARASITE   GROUP/SPECIES _____
           LOCATION (ON/IN HOST) _____
           FIXED IN _____ STORED IN _____

REMARKS    _____
           _____
```

Figure 15. Label to be included with parasites collected from birds. Alternatively an identification number may be placed in the vial of parasites. The number is then recorded on a label/form such as that illustrated.

to keep a "working copy" of the data sheets, and a "clean copy". This apparent duplication of effort is worthwhile as the original records may get lost or damaged. The host command *and* scientific names are asked for as common names are notorious for meaning different things in different places. [e.g. a pigeon to a Newfoundlander is a black guillemot (*Cepphus grylle*) whereas in Toronto it is a rock dove (*Columba livia*)]. The locality where the parasite was found and country of origin are included to preclude any incorrect geographical records being established [i.e. a number of parasites are now included in the faunal list of countries where the host does not live, except as a pet (Manter 1969)].

In closing, it is best to reiterate that with regard to parasites *"Prevention Is Better Than The Cure,"* and that good husbandry and good food should minimize any detrimental effects that parasites may have on a captive animal. It is best to break the life-cycle of the parasite outside the host animal thus preventing their acquisition, and animals should be checked regularly for both ectoparasites and endoparasites.

LITERATURE CITED

Anderson, R.C. 1976. Helminths. *In* Wildlife Diseases. (L.A. Page, ed.). Plenum Press, New York, NY. 35–44.

Arnall, L. and Keymer, I.F. 1975. Bird diseases. An introduction to the study of birds in health and disease. T.F.H. Publications Inc., Neptune City, NJ. 528 pp.

Bennett, G.F. 1970. Simple techniques for making avian blood smears. Can. J. Zool. 48: 585–586.

Bennett, G.F., Greiner, E.C. and Threlfall, W. 1976. Protozoans. *In* Wildlife Diseases (L.A. Page, ed.). Plenum Press, New York, NY. 25c33.

Bennett, G. and Laird, M. 1971. Reference Centre for avian malaria parasites. WHO Chronicle, 25 17-19.

Bennett, G.F., Whiteway, M. and Woodworth-Lynas, C. 1982. A host-parasite catalogue of avian haematozoa. Memorial Univ., Occ. Pap. Biol. #5. 243 pp.

Benson, C.W. 1973. Subfamily: Ox-peckers. *In* Grzimek's Animal Life Encyclopedia (B. Grzimek, ed.). Van Nostrand Reinhold Co, New York, NY. Vol. 9. Birds III, 475.

Benson, G.W. 1972. Family: coursers and pratincoles. *In* Grzimek's Animal Life Encyclopedia (B. Grzimek, ed.). Van Nostrand Reinhold Co., New York, NY. Vol. 8. Birds II, 199–202.

Bishop, C.A. and Threlfall, W. 1974. Helminth parasites of the common eider duck, *Somateria mollissima* (L.), in Newfoundland and Labrador. Proc. Helminthol. Soc. Wash. 41: 25–35.

Borror, D.J., DeLong, D.M. and Triplehorn, C.A. 1976. An introduction to the study of insects. 4th Ed. Holt, Rinehart and Winston, New York, NY. 852 pp.

Bradley, A.P. and Bradley, R.E. 1982. Evaluation of 3 disposable fecal flotation devices. Modern Vet. Practice. 63: 575–578.

Brandes, C.H. 1974. Snooks. *In* Grzimek's Animal Life Encyclopedia. (B. Grzimek, ed.). Van Nostrand Reinhold Co., New York, NY. Vol. 5. Fishes II and Amphibians. 74–117.

Bush, A.O. 1980. Faunal similarity and infracommunity structure in the helminths of lesser scaup. Ph.D. Thesis (Unpubl.), Univ. of Alberta, Edmonton, Alberta. 254 pp.

Cable, R.M. 1965. An illustrated laboratory manual of parasitology. Burgess Publ. Co., Minneapolis, MN. 165 pp.

Cheng, T.C. 1964. The biology of animal parasites. W.B. Saunders Co., Philadelphia, PA. 727 pp.
Clark, G.M., O'Meara, D. and Van Weelden, J.W. 1958. An epizootic among eider ducks involving an acanthocephalid worm. J. Wildl. Mgmt. 22: 204–205.
Cornwell, G. 1963. Observations on waterfowl mortality in southern Manitoba caused by *Echinuria uncinata* (Nematoda, Acuariidae). Can. J. Zool. 41: 699–703.
Cooper, J.E. and Eley, J.T. 1981. First aid and care of wild birds. David and Charles Inc., North Pomfret, VT. 288 pp.
Cowan, I. McT. 1946. Death of a Trumpeter Swan from multiple parasitism. Auk. 63: 248–249.
DeBary, A. 1879. Die Erscheinung der Symbiose. Karl J. Trubner, Strassburg.
Dogiel, V.A. 1962. General Parasitology. (translated Z. Kabata. 1964) Oliver and Boyd, Edinburgh, UK. 516 pp.
Ernst, E. 1975. Termites and earwigs. *In* Grzimek's Animal Life Encyclopedia. (B. Grzimek, ed.). Van Nostrand Reinhold Co., New York, NY. Vol. 2. Insects. 130–160.
Eveleigh, E.S. and Threlfall, W. 1974. The biology of *Ixodes* (*Ceratixodes*) *uriae* White, 1852 in Newfoundland. Acarologia. XVI(4): 621–635.
———. 1976. Population dynamics of live (Mallophaga) on auks (Alcidae) from Newfoundland. Can. J. Zool. 54: 1694–1711.
Faler, K. and Faler, K. 1984. Improved detection of intestinal parasites. Modern Vet. Practice. 65: 273–276.
Fowler, J.A. and Cohen, S. 1983. A method for the quantitative collection of ectoparasites from birds. Ringing and Migration. 4: 185–189.
Greiner, E.C. and Bennett, G.F. 1975. Avian Haematozoa. A color pictorial guide to some species of *Haemoproteus*, *Leucocytozoon*, and *Trypanosoma*. Wildl. Dis. 66, 59 pp., 52 color figs.
Greiner, E.C., Bennett, G.F., Laird, M. and Herman, C.M. 1975. Avian Haematozoa. Taxonomic keys and color pictorial guide to species of *Plasmodium*. Wildl. Dis. 68, 58 p., 44 color figs.
Herman, C.M. 1969. The impact of disease on wildlife populations. BioScience. 19: 321–325, 330.
Herman, C.M., Barrow, J.H. and Tarshis, I.B. 1975. Leucocytozoonosis in Canada geese at the Seney National Wildlife Refuge. J. Wildl. Dis. 11: 404–411.
Herman, C.M., Desser, S.S., Bennett, G.F. and Tarshis, I.B. 1977. Avian Haematozoa 3. Color atlas of *Leucocytozoon simondi* Mathis and Leger 1910. Wildl. Dis. 70, 58 pp., 48 color figs.
Herman, C.M., Steenis, J.H. and Wehr, E.E. 1955. Causes of winter losses among Canada geese. Trans. 20th N. Am. Wildlife Conf. 161–165.
Herman, C.M. and Wehr, E.E. 1954. The occurrence of gizzard worms in Canada geese. J. Wildl. 18: 509–513.
Hertig, M., Taliaferro, W.H., and Schwartz, B. 1937. The terms symbiosis, symbiont and symbiote. J. Parasitol. 23: 326–329.
Holland, G.P. 1949. The Siphonaptera of Canada. Tech. Bull. (70) Dominion Canada Dept. Agric., 306 pp.
Keymer, I.F. 1982. Parasitic diseases. *In* Diseases of cage and aviary birds (M.L. Petra, ed.). Lea and Febiger, Philadelphia, PA. 535–598, 657.
Kulachkova, V.G. 1953. [The parasites of the eider of the Kandalaksha Preserve, their pathogenic

importance and the prospects of combatting them.] Thesis, Leningrad State University. (In Russian.)
―――. 1954. [The life cycle and pathogenic importance of the eider trematode *Paramonostomum alveatum.*] Trudy Poblemnykh i tematicheskikh soveshchanii. Zool. Institi. U.S.S.R. #4. 118–122. (In Russian.)
―――. 1957. [The biology of the trematode *Paramonostomum alveatum* (Mehlis) and its role in the population dynamics of the common eider.] 9th Conf. on Parasit. Problems. Akad. Nauk SSR. Leningrad. (In Russian.)
―――. 1958. [An ecological and faunistic survey of the parasitic fauna of the common eider of Kandalaksha Gulf. Trudy Kandalakshkogo gosud. zapoved. #1: 103–159. (In Russian.)
Leslie, A.S. (ed.). 1912. The grouse in health and disease. Being the popular edition of the Report of the Committee of Inquiry on Grouse Disease. Smith, Elder and Co., London, UK. 472 pp.
Levine, N.D. 1973. Protozoan parasites of domestic animals and of man. 2nd Ed. Burgess Publ. Co., Minneapolis, MN. 406 pp.
Levine, N.D., Mehra, K.N., Clark, D.T. and Aves, J. 1960. A comparison of nematode egg counting techniques for cattle and sheep feces. Am. J. Vet. Res. 21: 511–515.
Limbaugh, C. 1961. Cleaning symbiosis. Sci. Am. 205(2): 42–49.
Manter, H.W. 1969. Problems in systematics of trematode parasites. *In* Problems in Systematics of Parasites. (G.D. Schmidt, ed.). University Park Press, Baltimore, MD. 93–105.
Meyer, M.C. and Olsen, O.W. 1980. Essentials of parasitology. Wm. C. Brown Co. Publ., Dubuque, IA. 266 pp.
Page, L.A. (ed.). 1976. Wildlife diseases. Plenum Press, New York, NY. 686 pp.
Pavlovski, E.N. 1934. [Organism as environment.] Priroda, Moskva. 1: 80–91. (In Russian.)
Pritchard, M.H. and Kruse, G.O.W. 1982. The collection and preservation of animal parasites. Univ. Press, Lincoln, NE. 141 pp.
Read, C.P. 1970. Parasitism and symbiology. An introductory text. Ronald Press Co., New York, NY. 316 pp.
Rietschel, P. and Rohde, K. 1974. The subkingdom of protozoa. *In* Grzimek's Animal Life Encyclopedia. (B. Grzimek, ed.). Van Nostrand Reinhold, New York, NY. Vol. 1. Lower animals. 89–137.
Rothschild, M. and Clay, T. 1952. Fleas, flukes and cuckoos. A study of bird parasites. Collins, London, UK. 304 pp.
Rubin, R. 1951. A rapid method for making permanent mounts of nematodes. Stain Technol. 26: 257–260.
Schell, S.C. 1962. Parasitology laboratory manual. John Wiley and Sons, Inc., New York, NY. 96 pp.
Schmidt, G.D. and Roberts, L.S. 1981. Foundations of parasitology. 2nd Ed. C.V. Mosby Co., St. Louis, MO. 795 pp.
Ulmer, M.J. 1952. Critique of methods for the measurement of parasitic worms. Pap. Mich. Acad. Sci. Arts Lett. 36 (1950): 149–151.
Warner, R.E. 1968. The role of introduced diseases in the extinction of the endemic Hawaiian avifauna. Confor. 70: 101–120.
Wobeser, G.A. 1981. Diseases of wild waterfowl. Plenum Press, New York, NY. 300 pp.

APPENDIX

Reagents, solutions and flotation media.

Alcohol-formalin-acetic acid (AFA).

Formalin (commercial)	6 ml
Ethyl alcohol (95%)	50 ml
Glacial acetic acid	4 ml
Distilled water	40 ml

An excellent solution for general work. Used for both killing and fixing. Specimens may remain in this solution for some time without harm. Many different formulations are used by different workers e.g. the proportions may be 10:50:2:40 respectively.

Alcohols

Methanol, ethanol and isopropyl alcohol may be diluted with water and used for fixation (hot or cold) and preservation. Fully denatured alcohols are usually unsuitable for biological work as they contain substances that cause them to become "milky" looking on the addition of water. Alcohols are usually purchased as absolute (100%) or 95%. They are then diluted with distilled water to the appropriate concentration, with 70% being the most widely used.

Bouin's fixative®

Picric acid (saturated aqueous solution)	75 ml
Formalin (commercial)	25 ml
Glacial acetic acid	5 ml

Used cold. Good for flukes, tapeworms and spiny-headed worms. Only disadvantage is that the picric acid colors the tissues yellow and must be removed before processing by passing through several changes of warm (35–40°C) 70% ethyl alcohol.

Flotation media

Several solutions are used to concentrate helminth eggs and protozoan cysts by flotation. Their efficacy is based on differences in specific gravity between the parasites and the solution used. The following are two of the more widely used solutions.

1. Zinc sulphate	336 g
Distilled water	1000 ml
(Specific gravity 1.18)	
2. Sucrose	910 g
Distilled water	1125 ml
Melted phenol	6.5 ml
(Specific gravity 1.20)	

Phenol is added as a preservative and to prevent growth of molds in the solution. Methanol crystals may also be used for the same purpose.

Other saturated salt solutions that may be used in flotation are sodium nitrate, calcium chloride, and magnesium sulphate.

Formalin (10%)

Formalin (commercial)	10 ml
Phosphate buffer solution (or water)	90 ml

Best fixative for general use. It is best used in the buffered form but normal (plain, made with water) formalin may be used.

Gilson's fluid® (fixative)

Corrosive sublimate (mercuric chloride)	5 g
Distilled water	220 ml
Nitric acid (80%)	4 ml
Glacial acetic acid	1 ml
Ethyl alcohol (70%)	25 ml

Best used cold. Good for some of the more delicate helminths.

Glacial acetic acid

This concentrated form of acetic acid will cause cells to swell and is used in many fixatives, as well as being used to "straighten" roundworms.

Glycerine-Alcohol solution

Ethyl alcohol (70%)	90 ml
Glycerine	10 ml

May be used as a fixative both hot and cold and for long-term storage of specimens. Also called Looss's fluid.

Hoyer's medium®

Gum arabic	30 g
Distilled water	50 ml
Glycerol	20 ml
Chloral hydrate	200 g

Mix in order given and filter. Used in preparation of mites for examination. Mites may be placed in a drop of this medium on a slide directly on removal from the bird or from 70% alcohol. Gentle heating expands the specimen, hastens clearing and sets the mounting fluid.

Lactophenol

Melted phenol	10 ml
Lactic acid	10 ml
Glycerine	20 ml
Distilled water	10 ml

Used to clear roundworms prior to identification.

Lugol's solution®

Distilled water	100 ml
Potassium iodide	4 g
Iodine	2 g

This solution may be used to detect protozoan cysts in fresh feces. It is also used in MIF fixtures. A slow deterioration of the solution necessitates the preparation of a new batch every 2-3 weeks.

Merthiolate–Iodine–Formalin (MIF) Stain-Preservation Technique

A. Direct Smear—used with fresh feces

Tincture of merthiolate 99	1:1000
Lugol's solution	5%
Formalin	(commercial)

Proportions used are related to the age of Lugol's solution e.g. (from Schell 1962).

Age of Lugol's solution (weeks)	Proportion of ingredients:		
	Merthiolate	Lugol's	Formalin
1	77.5	10.0	12.5
2	75.0	12.5	12.5
3	72.5	15.0	12.5

Feces is stirred into a drop of MIF diluted with an equal amount of distilled water, covered with a coverslip, and examined for protozoan trophozoites and cysts and worm eggs.

B. Indirect Method—when feces is to be examined at a later date. Two solutions are kept in separate bottles.

  i. Lugol's solution
 ii. MF stock solution

Distilled water	250 ml
Tincture of merthiolate	200 ml
Formalin (commercial)	25 ml
Glycerine	5 ml

When feces are obtained 0.5 gm is stirred into a solution of 0.3 ml 5% Lugol's solution to which has been added 4.7 ml of MF stock solution. The specimen may then be stored or shipped.

Phosphate buffer solution

Sodium phosphate, monobasic	3.31 g
Sodium phosphate, dibasic	33.77 g
Distilled water	1000 ml

May be used to dilute other solutions and to make them neutral (e.g. formalin).

Polyvinyl alcohol fixative (PVA or Burrow's® PVA fixative)

PVA fixative is made from two solutions that are prepared separately and then mixed.

  i. PVA mixture

PVA powder (e.g. Elvanol 71-30)	5.0 g
Glycerine	1.5 ml
Distilled water	62.5 ml

ii. Schuaddin's fixative® (modified)
   Mercuric chloride (crystals)   4.5 g
   Ethyl alcohol (95%)   31.0 ml
   Glacial acetic acid   5.0 ml

The PVA mixture is placed in a flask and heated to 70–75 °C in a waterbath. After approximately 10 minutes, or when all the PVA has dissolved, the Schuaddin's fixative is added. The solutions are mixed thoroughly and the resultant PVA fixative is allowed to cool before being placed in a screw-capped bottle.

This fixative is used to preserve protozoans (trophozoites and cysts) and worm eggs for subsequent examination. Fresh feces is mixed with the fixative and may be stored for months before permanent stained smears are prepared for analysis.

Rubin's fluid®

Polyvinyl alcohol (15 g) is dissolved in 100 ml distilled water at 80 °C to form a stock solution.

Polyvinyl alcohol (stock solution)	56 ml
Lactic acid	22 ml
Phenol crystals	22 ml

This substance may be used to make permanent preparations of nematodes and small arthropod ectoparasites. Specimens may be taken directly from a bird or any fixative (e.g. 70% ethyl alcohol) and placed in this medium.

Saline solutions

During necropsy of the host and processing of parasites recovered all biological materials should be kept moist with physiological saline. A basic 0.85% solution may be made, or more specialized salines may be used for cold or warm blooded vertebrates.

i. Basic salines   Fish   Amphibia/reptiles   Birds/mammals
   Sodium chloride   6.0 g   7.0 g   8.5 g
   Distilled water   1000 ml   1000 ml   1000 ml

ii. Ringer's solution-for cold-blooded vertebrates
    Ringer's chloride   8.0 g
    Sodium bicarbonate   0.2 g
    Potassium chloride   0.2 g
    Calcium chloride (anhydrous)   0.2 g
    Dextrose   1.0 g
    Distilled water   1000 ml

iii. Locke's solution-for warm-blooded vertebrates
     Sodium chloride   9.0 g
     Sodium bicarbonate   0.2 g
     Potassium chloride   0.4 g

Calcium chloride	0.3 g
Dextrose	2.0 g
Distilled water	1000 ml

Zenker's fixative®

Potassium dichromate	2.5 g
Mercuric chloride	4.0–5.0 g
Sodium sulfate	1.0 g
Glacial acetic acid	5.0 ml
Distilled water	100 ml

Excellent general fixative that shows fairly rapid penetration.

OILED BIRD REHABILITATION: FACT AND FALLACY

Lynne Frink

Tri-State Bird Rescue and Research, Inc.
2920 Duncan Road
Wilmington, DE 19899

and

Betsy Jones

WILD BIRDS Rehabilitation and Research
325 S. First Street
Surf City, NJ 08008

INTRODUCTION

Rehabilitating oiled birds is difficult; it is a time-consuming, urgent, laborious job requiring special materials and procedures. But oiled bird rehabilitation has been successfully carried out, time after time, with a number of species and dealing with a variety of oils. The secret to rehabilitating oiled birds is a simple one: Don't experiment, don't guess, don't play with an oiled bird: follow to the letter those procedures which have a *documented* positive result.

We have been rehabilitating oiled birds for a decade, yet we still know of only one successful way to deal with oiled birds. But we have read of hundreds of disastrous efforts.

There was the "dusty penguin" method, where Jackass penguins are rolled in Fullers earth, left to sit for a day or two, then rubbed with detergent (Edwards 1963). Rolling in cornmeal or sawdust, dipping in liquid paraffin (Westphal 1969) or hot butter (Martini 1953), rubbing with lard (Tottenham 1959), and continued testimonials for cooking oil, which we call the "Mazola duck" treatment (*New York Times* 1985), have all been tried with varying claims of success, but with *no* available documentation to back those claims. We have known of people reporting a 100% release rate in oiled birds; further investigation usually discloses that the oiled birds have been washed and tossed out the window the same day: no records were kept on individual birds, no weights, temperatures or pre-release evaluations were taken. These should not be considered successful rehabilitation efforts.

An article published in 1948, suggesting plucking an oiled bird, will be read by some earnest citizen, and become a dogma etched forever in stone. During a major oil spill, someone will *always* show up at the facility with a new wonder method, a miracle soap, letters of testimonial for his or her pet theory. And, in desperation and under the pressure of the moment, these people are often, tragically, allowed to determine treatment protocol.

At Tri-State Bird Rescue and Research, we have, over the last 10 years, spent thousands of dollars and hours studying the effects of oil on birds. We have studied the published papers and less formal accounts of others, and we have conducted carefully planned research on oiled birds to learn how to improve our techniques.

Tri-State and WILD BIRDS have, between them, rehabilitated over 27 species of oiled birds, ranging from Gannets and Loons through Peregrine Falcons and Barred Owls, to Bluebirds and Flickers. We don't have all the answers, but we sure have been working on them. Our release rates vary with species. We have been able to return 93% of our Anseriformes to the wild; 76% of our rehabilitated diving ducks have been set free, while our release rates with Gaviiformes remains just under 50%, despite our utmost effort.

We have travelled throughout the U.S. and to other countries and spoken to thousands of people in an effort to share our very hard-earned knowledge. Our plea to them, and to you, is: understand the rationale for the current oiled bird protocol; plan, now, how you will respond to an oil spill; follow time-tested procedures; and keep accurate records.

Some of the difficulties in rehabilitating oiled birds concern the numerous ways that oil affects birds. These effects can be broadly categorized as behavioral, environmental, internal and external. A current review article is available which discusses these types of effects in more detail (Leighton 1983).

In this paper, we will only discuss external and internal physiological effects of oil on birds.

The external effects of oil are the most noticeable and most immediately debilitating. Oil destroys the waterproofing and insulating properties of plumage.

The bird may suffer from chilling; it is often unable to fly or remain afloat in the water. The bird has difficulty obtaining food or escaping predators. Irritation and ulceration of the eyes, and clogging of the nares and mouth often accompany oil contamination. The weakened bird becomes susceptible to secondary infections, such as aspergillosis.

Internal effects of oil, while not as obvious, are equally life-threatening. Direct toxic consequences to the gastrointestinal tract, pancreas and liver have all been documented (Langenberg et al. 1983). These effects frequently result in loss of digestive and absorptive efficiency. Oil aspiration pneumonia is not uncommon in oiled birds. Visceral gout due to kidney damage as a direct toxic effect of oil or due to dehydration has been documented (Langenberg et al. 1983).

Extensive laboratory studies have been done on the effects of different types of oil on a specific biochemical or physiological response in a certain species of birds. While these studies can be very valuable, it would be inaccurate to apply them too broadly to actual field responses involving species or oil other than those studied.

We find that different species respond quite differently to the same types of oil and oiling conditions. For example, we have found that one type of light crude oil posed few problems to Canada and Snow Geese, Black Duck, and Laughing Gulls, while Double-crested Cormorants involved in the same spill experienced significant physiological abnormalities and high mortality. Although costs are great in running diagnostic tests (such as blood gasses and chem screens), it should be a priority that those of us who deal with a significant number of oiled birds secure funding to investigate the physiological responses of different species in actual oil spill conditions.

TREATMENT OF OILED BIRDS

Oiled bird rehabilitation can be thought of as 5 basic procedures:

1. Stabilizing the bird
2. Removing the oil from the feathers
3. Removing the cleaning agent from the feathers
4. Restoring the waterproofing
5. Acclimating the bird for release.

Table 1 presents these steps in a chart that can be posted on the wall during a major oiled bird rehabilitation effort.

STABILIZING THE BIRD

A complete physical should be given to every oiled bird. In addition to standard procedures, the examiner should band the bird with a temporary, numbered plastic leg band, note the amount and distribution of oil on the body, and record weight

TABLE 1. OILED BIRD REHABILITATION—WATERFOWL

1. STABILIZE THE BIRD:
- Flush eyes with saline or water.
- Clean mouth and nares.
- Check body temperature, weight musculature.
- Give fluids (Lactated Ringers and 2.5% Dextrose, Normosol M) by gavage or subcutaneously. Give Pepto-Bismol® by gavage. Repeat fluids until intake of food and water by bird is adequate.
- Keep from chilling; avoid external stressors.

2. REMOVE OIL FROM FEATHERS:
- Large tubs of water at 103° to 105° F.
- Lux Liquid Amber® industrial detergent or Dawn® dishwashing liquid, at 5% to 12% concentration. (Test wash one feather cut from bird, or dead bird.)
- Ladle solution over feathers; stroke gently in direction of growth; do not scrub.
- Avoid eye area; flush areas when necessary (frequently).

3. REMOVE CLEANING AGENT FROM FEATHERS:
- Large amounts of water, 103° to 105° F.
- Spray hoses and tubs of clean water.
- *Water MUST roll off back in diamond droplets.*
- Belly, underwings, tail, need special attention.

4. RESTORE FEATHER STRUCTURE:
- Dry under free access to heat lamps in draft-free area.
- Keep people away.
- Allow access to swimming after 24 hours. Tepid water first time, cool to cold thereafter.
- Waterproof birds can remain in water 20 to 90 minutes depending on species, with dry feathers. (In some diving birds, the outermost contour feathers are allowed to get wet, but the down is *absolutely dry*.
- Acclimate to external temperatures before release.

and cloacal temperature. Oil should be removed from the mouth and the nares. The vent should be checked to make sure oil and matted feathers are not causing impaction. The eyes should be flushed with sterile saline or opthalmic irrigation. If possible, blood should be taken at this time to check packed cell volume and total solids. A number of oiled birds are dehydrated because of enteritis.

The bird should be tubed with a warm electrolyte solution (Lactated Ringers and 5% Dextrose, Normosol, etc.), and an enteric coating agent (we suggest Pepto-Bismol® at 2–5 mg/kg; Milk of Magnesia® and mineral oil are not recommended). Nutrients can later be added to the tubing solution, and tube-feeding should be repeated every 4–6 hours until the bird is permitted free access to food and water after cleaning.

The bird should be kept in a warm, quiet environment, away from people and other external stressors. Mortality of oiled birds is affected by the stressors they experience during rehabilitation (Rowan 1983).

Excessive preening of oil-covered feathers must be discouraged (especially after contamination with highly-refined oils). Do not tape the bird's bill shut. A poncho can be made for the bird with a disposable diaper or a pillow case, loosely wrapped around the bird. Holes should be cut in the pillow case for the head and legs, and an opening left for the cloaca.

Some birds benefit by being placed with a conspecific, but over-crowding can be stressful. Sheets can be hung to prevent visual contact with humans. People must not speak in loud voices when in the bird-holding area.

Although prophylactic medications (corticosteroids and tranquilizers) have been recommended in the past, there is no evidence that they are efficacious (Lauer et al. 1982).

The bird should not be washed until it is alert, responsive, and restored to normal fluid balance. Efforts should be made to stabilize the bird and wash it within 8 to 24 hours; the longer the oil is allowed to remain on the feathers, the more difficult it will be to remove, and the more damage can be done to the skin. Highly refined oils can be absorbed through the skin, intensifying internal problems.

One Tri-State study conducted on 56 Ruddy ducks (*Oxyura jamaicensis*) found a strong correlation between body weight and body temperature for survival in washed birds (Lauer et al. 1982). The average weight and temperature of the affected birds was determined. Those birds that tested at or above normal in weight and temperature for their sex in the oiled group had a 100% release rate. Those birds under the norm in one or both areas evidenced reduced release rates (temperature—66%, weight—75%, both 38%). Body temperature in waterbirds varies considerably, but certainly a bird with a temperature under 101°F should not be washed.

REMOVING THE OIL FROM THE FEATHERS

Oil must be removed from the feathers without damaging the delicate feather structure. We find the safest, most effective cleaning method to be a detergent bath. Oiled birds should not be washed unless large amounts of hot water are available. Eighty to one hundred gallons of 103–105°F water are needed over a 20 minute period to wash one bird. This quantity of water can only be assured through a series of hot water heaters or a rented steam generator. The water must be above 102°F in order to lift the oil. Anyone who has tried to wash a greasy frying pan in cold water will understand this necessity.

Numerous cleaning agents have been tested for their ability to remove oil from feathers (Berkner et al. 1977). Only a few of them meet the following requirements:

1. The detergent must suspend the oil and hold it in suspension.
2. The detergent must be minimally irritating to the body and must not destroy the structure of the feather.
3. The detergent must rinse off the bird; detergent has a wetting effect and detergent residue can prevent waterproofing.
4. The detergent should not hinder restoration of feather alignment or prevent reoiling from the uropygeal gland.

TABLE 2. DETERGENT CONCENTRATION (CUPS/GALLON AND OUNCES/GALLON)

%	Cups/1 Gal.	Oz./1 Gal.	Cups/5 Gal.	Oz./5 Gal.	Cups/10 Gal.	Oz./10 Gal.
15%	2.4	19.2	12.0	96.0	24.0	192.0
12%	1.92	15.36	9.6	76.8	19.2	153.6
10%	1.6	12.8	8.0	64.0	16.0	128.0
9%	1.44	11.52	7.2	57.6	14.4	115.2
8%	1.28	10.4	6.4	51.2	12.8	104.0
7%	1.12	8.96	5.6	44.8	11.2	89.6
6%	0.96	7.68	4.8	38.4	9.6	76.8
5%	0.8	6.4	4.0	32.0	8.0	64.0
4%	0.64	5.12	3.2	25.6	6.4	51.2
3%	0.48	3.84	2.4	19.2	4.8	38.4
2%	0.32	2.56	1.6	12.8	3.2	25.6
1%	0.16	1.28	0.8	6.4	1.6	12.8

Equivalents

8 oz.	=	1 cup
4 cup	=	1 qt.
32 oz.	=	1 qt.
4 qt.	=	1 gal.
16 cup	=	1 gal.

We currently use Lux Liquid Amber® industrial detergent (Lever Bros.) or Dawn® dish-washing detergent (Procter & Gamble). The cleaning procedure should be done in a warm, quiet area, free from drafts.

For the actual cleaning process, a single bird is placed in a 10 gallon tub containing 4%-15% detergent in 103-105°F water (see Table 2). A ten-gallon tub is adequate for birds ranging in size from small ducks to a small Canada goose. Swans and large geese must have larger containers. We suggest kiddie pools or human bath tubs holding at least 15-20 gallons of water. Do not wash any bird larger than a songbird in little (3-5 gallon) plastic dishpans; they are too small to hold enough detergent solution to clean the bird effectively.

One person should ladle the detergent solution over the bird's body and wings, while a second person gently strokes the bird in the direction of feather growth. A third person may be needed to hold a large bird. It is important that the feathers never be rubbed, scrubbed, or picked since this could damage the delicate feather structure so vital to waterproofing. A container of clear water or normal saline and eye-droppers should be kept handy and the bird's eyes should be flushed frequently to prevent detergent irritation. The bird's head must be gently restrained during washing; many birds attempt to duck their heads under the water.

The bird should be removed from the tub when the water is dirty. The entire washing process is then repeated using a clean tub of water-detergent solution at the same temperature.

The bird may require three (sometimes more) tub washings. Weathered and heavy crude oils are particularly difficult to hold in suspension. If the oil is not lifting easily, at Tri-State we will try the following: Remove the bird, dripping wet with detergent solution, from the tub. Wrap the bird's body in a large dry towel, and place it in a quiet, dark box for 4–6 minutes. This allows the bird to calm down slightly and also provides time for the detergent solution to soak into the oiled feathers. Continue with the procedure. Very stubborn oils may require softening with a warm mineral oil. This should only be used as a *last* measure, since mineral oil itself is a contaminant which will then have to be washed out of the plumage.

REMOVING THE CLEANING AGENT FROM THE FEATHERS

The feathers must be *completely* rinsed if the bird is to be rehabilitated. Any detergent residue can impede waterproofing (Russell et al. 1981).

Rinsing is carried out with a combination of spray rinses and tubs of clean water. The water temperature should be still 103–105 °F. Special attention should be given to the undertail coverts, underwings and neck of bird. The bird is not acceptably rinsed until *diamond-like beads of water roll freely* from the feathers. This is the one sign of a successfully cleaned oiled bird, and once you see it, you will recognize it as the end point in every oiled bird cleaning effort.

The failure to rinse the bird adequately is probably the most common cause of unsuccessful rehabilitation efforts. Do not succumb to the impulse to give up the rinsing process prematurely.

The bird's feathers are blotted dry with a clean towel, and the eyes are flushed one last time.

If the materials have all been assembled in advance, and the tubs of water are pre-drawn, the entire cleaning time should take from 15–30 minutes. If a bird becomes extremely stressed during washing, it should be rinsed and put in a pen separate from clean birds, to dry. After stabilization (24 or more hours) the bird will have to be rewashed.

RESTORING FEATHER STRUCTURE

The newly-washed bird should now be placed in a clean holding pen to dry. The pen should be lined with sheets or towels, curtained to minimize human intrusion, and provided with heat lamps to allow the bird to find a comfortable ambient temperature. The heat lamps should be of two heights from the bottom of the pen (approx. 24″ and 36″ for a mallard-sized bird) and an unheated area should also be available. We eliminated use of our specially designed pet driers when we found that birds behaved more normally under ambient warm air, and frequently began preening their feathers back into alignment immediately.

Diving ducks require as much as 3 inches of foam padding under the sheeting to prevent breast abrasions and open sores. For birds which are totally unable to walk on dry land (e.g. Common Loons), we provide small plastic bags which have been stuffed with shredded foam to make a slightly flat pillow; these bags are placed under the sheeting. The birds soon learn to position these pillows under their keels in a comfortable position. Scrupulous care must be given to the pens of those birds which are not mobile on land. The birds can incur serious feather damage if they become contaminated with feces and old food.

Free access to water and food should now be provided. Make every effort to provide a variety of food. Observe the birds to see which ones are self-feeding. Check the droppings for blood and oil, and treat these birds for enteritis with more Pepto-Bismol® and tubings of easily absorbed nutrients. (See Table 3 for Nutrient Solution recipe.)

Wait 24 hours before allowing the birds access to swimming water. The birds should be provided with enough water to actually swim and preen. For birds that are smaller than Canada geese, we use 4' × 8' pens with a sloped ramp which allows the birds to enter the water and leave it at will (see illustration, Figure 1). Our pens are curtained and the elevated platform has a heat lamp on one side to prevent chilling. Kiddie pools with access ramps can be used, but should be changed 3–4 times a day, or more, if many birds are using the same pool. Use tepid water for the first swim, then use cool to cold water.

Birds usually take to the water readily; when they begin to get wet, they leave the water to preen. As the bird continues its efforts to swim, then preen, it realigns its feathers and restores original feather structure.

TABLE 3. COMPOSITION OF A DIET FOR FEEDING OILED BIRDS[1]

Ingredient[2]	Approximate Amount
Soy Protein formula (Isomil, Neo Mul Soy or an equivalent product)	60.0
Rice pablum (or similar baby food product)[3]	35.0
Electrolyte powder (containing calcium, copper, cobalt, manganese, potassium, sodium, zinc)	0.1
Water soluble vitamin mix	0.05
Vitamin A (International units)	1500 IU
Vitamin K (milligrams)	2.0

Note: At Tri-State, we have good results using High Protein Baby Cereal (and, in fish-eating birds, Strained Baby Beef) in our tubing mixes, although caution must be used to minimize the length of time a bird receives a reduced calcium diet.

[1] Reprinted from: Nutrition and disease relationships that may serve as models for feeding oiled birds. John Serafin. In Rosie, D.G. and S.N. Barnes (eds.). 1983. *The Effects of Oil on Birds: Physiological Research, Clinic Applications, and Rehabilitation.*

[2] Diets of similar composition (with customary amounts of vitamins K and A) have been used for keeping young birds alive at Patuxent Research Center.

[3] Follow manufacturer's direction. Many products contain a combination electrolytes and vitamins.

This alignment of the feathers is what ensures the bird's water-proofing. The feather structure does not require, but is further enhanced by, the application of uropygial gland oil to the feathers. The uropygial gland oil is no longer thought to be vital to water-proofing, but it does seem to assist in maintaining the structure, much as hair spray might hold a hairstyle (Rijke 1970).

Birds which are waterproof will demonstrate the diamond beading of water on their feathers. They will also be able to remain in the water, depending on species, anywhere from 10 to 50 minutes without getting wet. Certain diving birds (loons, ruddy ducks, grebe sp.) may have slightly wet outer contour feathers, but the down should remain *absolutely* dry.

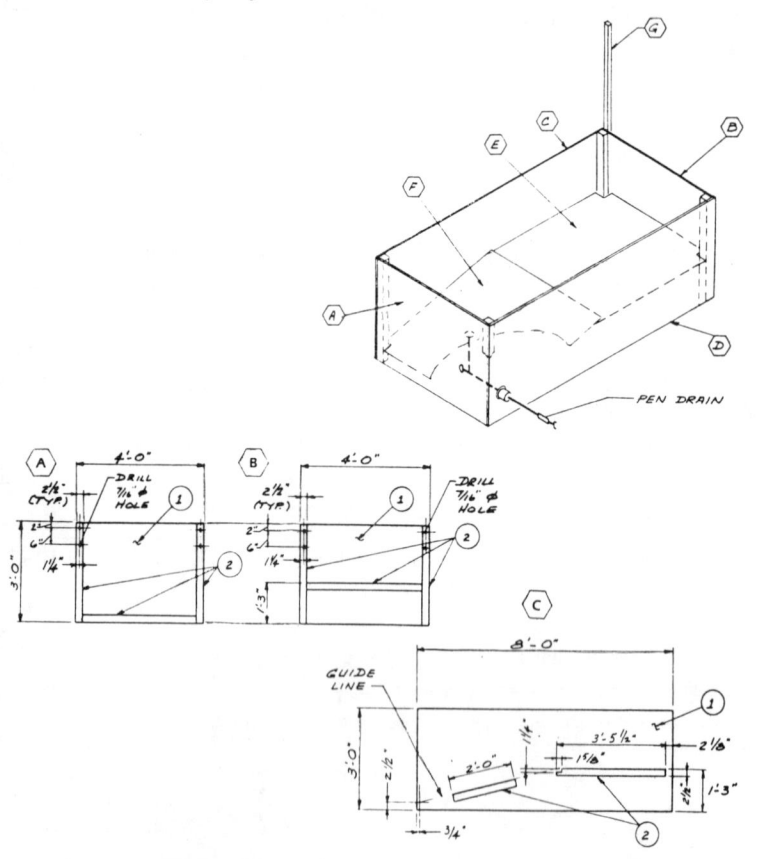

Figure 1. THE PUDDLE PEN: Oiled birds undergoing rehabilitation need free access to a pool. The "Puddle Pen" can be easily constructed with plywood, double-headed 6 d. nails and bulkhead fittings if continual drainage is desired. (The bulkhead fittings and gasket should be installed first, and then the PVC piping fitted by force.)

Install 2 sheets of 6 mil polyethylene (8' × 12') with staples. Lay clean indoor-outdoor carpet or sheets over section "E" (elevated, dry area of pen) with excess trailing onto ramp of "F" and secured there to provide footing for birds. Fill pool to edge of "E." Hang sheeting/drapes from posts, "G," to screen area and prevent dabbling ducks and geese from jumping out of pen. Diving ducks can not take flight from these pens.

ACCLIMATE FOR RELEASE

A bird which is waterproof should slowly be exposed to temperatures comparable with outside weather. This, of course, is critical in cold winter months.

A rehabilitated oiled bird should be of average weight for its species and sex. It should be adequately muscled so that it can forage normally in the wild. The bird should not show any signs of disease. Birds should be banded with Fish and Wildlife Service bands and released early in the day in suitable habitat. Do not return birds to any sites which still have oil contamination.

Seabirds must be prepared for return to the ocean by being given a tubing solution of normal saline (0.9%) for 3 days before release. This allows the nasal salt gland to resume functioning.

MAJOR OIL SPILL CRISES

For those rehabilitators who are not set up for oil spill response, even five or six oiled birds can present a serious challenge. The necessity for human-intensive labor, the immediacy of the effort, and the need for special equipment (water, detergent, pools, etc.) can make the job seem an Herculean task. A spill involving fifty or more birds taxes the resources of even those of us who like to think we are always prepared for oil spills.

There are certain steps that can be taken to ensure a more smoothly running oil spill response (Zimmerman et al. 1976). The most important task is to determine what the protocol will be before beginning the rehabilitation effort. While the birds are being brought to the facility and/or stabilized, training of volunteers and acquisition of supplies must occur.

1. Control Access: do not open the facility to every interested visitor who knocks on your door. Oiled bird rehabilitation is not a spectator sport. Set up a desk near the door, and give all of the volunteers trained to work with you a name tag. Hand all other visitors a notice explaining:
   (a) why they can't come in;
   (b) what items you need (cash, towels, fresh fish, etc.);
   (c) the date, time and place of the workshop you will be holding for people who want to be trained to help (they must be able to guarantee you a certain number of hours over the next 2 weeks).
2. Set up a training workshop for your staff and any volunteers. Go over the entire process of cleaning an oiled bird from start to finish. Make it clear that the protocol you have just covered will be carried out without change unless a special meeting of all chairpersons decides otherwise. Then set up the following committees, allowing volunteers to serve on no more than two committees. Choose committee chairs and give them all the support you can.

3. Operations Control:
   (a) controls access to the Center;
   (b) accepts in-coming birds and begins the record sheet on them;
   (c) schedules shifts to make sure enough volunteers come in at specified times;
   (d) provides a rest area away from the birds for the volunteers, and stocks that area with food. Answers the phones. Does periodic safety checks. Sends distressed people home to rest.
4. Medical—Rehabilitation:
   (a) performs the initial physicals on all birds and treats any secondary problems and/or injuries;
   (b) cares for the birds while they are stabilized for cleaning;
   (c) oversees care of the newly-washed birds during the rehabilitative period and examines and bands each bird before release.
5. Cleaning: Is responsible for setting up the cleaning area and cleaning, rinsing, and drying all birds.
6. Supplies—Set-Up:
   (a) acquires the needed supplies;
   (b) constructs the necessary pens and pools.
   (During major oil spills, an entire facility can be set up with separate treatment areas using typar plastic, 1 × 2's and nails.)

If a major spill occurs, it is imperative that the rehabilitator keep in close contact with the Fish and Wildlife Field Response Coordinator who is responsible for the welfare of all migratory wild birds, including oiled birds. These professionals, in our experience, have been dedicated and committed to oiled bird rehabilitation. If they are convinced that the rehabilitator is experienced and prepared for the crisis, they will do all they can to assist in the rehabilitation effort. Birds *must* be retrieved as quickly as possible for rehabilitation; a day's delay can increase mortality. Fish and Wildlife Service resources, including aerial surveys, Coast Guard assistance, and hazing equipment, all contribute significantly to reducing mortality after oil spills.

Only one person should be appointed to talk with the news media, and he or she should be conservative in all remarks, discussing only the birds at the facility, *not* offering judgment on the oil spill response events outside the facility. Media coverage, in our opinion, should always be a lower priority than the quality of non-stressful care given to the birds.

Teams should be set up for 6 to 8 hour shifts and not allowed to work beyond those hours. Oiled bird rehabilitation is intensive work and the pressure can be great. One tired or emotionally distraught person can undo the good work of many.

CONCLUSION

We find that most oiled birds can be rehabilitated successfully using the above techniques, although special modifications must be made for passerines and raptors. As with many procedures, experience is the greatest tool for carrying out the job quickly and efficiently.

Anseriformes can usually be rehabilitated in 3 to 4 days. Problems occur most frequently when shortcuts or "small substitutions" are made in the rehabilitative process (e.g. using a different detergent, tubs which are too small, a lower water temperature).

Keep accurate records of all that you do and share your experiences with others; in this way your efforts will help us to improve oiled bird rehabilitation techniques and continue to provide other rehabilitators with the most current methods.

ACKNOWLEDGEMENTS

We extend our appreciation to Bob Lobou (SUNY) for a literature search on past oiled bird rehabilitation methods, and to the Delaware Bay and River Cooperative and Texaco, Inc., for funding to develop rehabilitation protocol.

REFERENCES

Edwards, R.A. 1963. Treatment of "washed up" penguins. *Bokmakerie*, 15:8.

Westphal, A. 1969. Jackass penguins: their treatment, care and release after contamination by crude oil and other oil products. *Marine Pollution Bull.*, 14:2–7.

Martini, E. 1953. Oil plague—Observation on the North Sea island Spiekeroog. Ornithologische Mitteilungen 5(3):44–48.

Tottenham, Katherine. 1959. The oil menace. *Audubon*, 61:28–30.

New York Times, April 4, 1985.

Leighton, F.P. 1983. The pathophysiology of petroleum oil toxicity in birds: A review. In Rosie, D.G. and Barnes, S.A. (eds.). *The Effects of Oil on Birds: Physiological Research, Clinical Applications, and Rehabilitation*. Tri-State Bird Rescue & Research, Wilmington, DE.

Langenberg, J.A., Dein, F.J. 1983. Pathology of ruddy ducks contaminated with #6 fuel oil. In Rosie, D.G. and Barnes, S.A. (eds.). *The Effects of Oil on Birds: Physiological Research, Clinical Applications and Rehabilitation*. Tri-State Bird Rescue & Research, Wilmington, DE.

Rowan, Eileen. 1983. Stress: its effect on the pituitary/adreno-cortical axis and its importance in latent infections. In Rosie, D.G. and Barnes, S.N. (eds.). *The Effects of Oil on Birds: Physiological Research, Clinical Applications, and Rehabilitation*. Tri-State Bird Rescue & Research, Inc. Wilmington, DE.

Lauer, D.M., Frink, J.A. and Dein, F.J. 1982. Rehabilitation of ruddy ducks (*Oxyura jamaicensis*) contaminated with oil. JAVMA 181:1398–99.

Berkner, A.B., Smith, D.C. and Williams, A.S. 1977. Cleaning agents for oiled wildlife. In Proc. 1977 Conference on Prevention & Control of Oil Pollution. Washington, D.C. American Petroleum Institute.

Russell, W.C., Choules G.L., and Gauthier, D.A. 1981. Detergents and Waterfowl. *J. Zoo. Anim. Med.* 12:10–13.

Rijke, A.M. 1970. Wettability and phylogenetic development of feather structure in water birds. *J. Expl. Biol.*, 52:469–479.

Zimmerman, J. and Frink, J.A. 1976. *Oiled Bird Rescue: Government and Volunteer Action.* Tri-State Bird Rescue & Research, Inc. DAS. Wilmington, DE.

COMMON PROBLEMS AMONG REPTILES PRESENTED TO REHABILITATION CENTERS

Stephen L. Barten, D.V.M.

Vernon Hills Animal Hospital
1260 Butterfield Road
Mundelein, IL 60060

I. NON-NATIVE WILDLIFE
   A. Source:
      - Released as unwanted pets.
      - Abandoned in apartments when people move.
      - Confiscated in cities that outlaw ownership of snakes or in humane law violation cases.
      - Escapees.
      - Accidental importations.
   B. Why Non-Native Reptiles or Wildlife Should Not be Released Outside Their Range:
      - Inability of that specimen to adapt to a new environment (finding food, shelter, surviving new climate) could doom it to a premature death.
      - Potential for that specimen to survive and establish breeding colonies, displacing native wildlife (i.e. walking catfish, starlings displacing bluebirds, pheasants, marine toads, fire ants).
      - Potential for specimen to introduce new pathogenic parasites, viruses, or bacteria to the native population.
      - Potential for the specimen to introduce undesirable genes to the established population by breeding, thus changing the population in untold ways with untold consequences.
      - Potential for the specimen to accidentally be included in a study of native wildlife, (i.e. garter snake from Manitoba being collected in Ohio) introducing false data and rendering the results invalid (i.e. establishing current range of a species: or size, color, scale counts).
   C. Identification and Disposition:
      - Field guides.
      - Regional herpetological societies (see Appendix).
      - Local zoos and museums.
   D. Venomous Reptiles:
      If you are not experienced at handling them, *leave them alone, contact an expert.*

TABLE 1. ANTIBIOTIC DOSAGES FOR REPTILES

Anesthetic	Dosage
Amikasin	2.5 mg/kg every 72 hrs.*
Carbenicillin	100 mg/kg/day
Cefoperazone	125 mg/kg/day
Chloramphenicol	50–75 mg/kg/day
Gentamicin	2.5 mg/kg every 72 hrs.*
Ketamine	20–60 mg/kg
Netilmycin	2.5 mg/kg every 72 hrs.*
Tetracycline	50–75 mg/kg/day
Tobramycin	2.5 mg/kg every 72 hrs.*
Trimethoprim-sulfa	15 mg (combined) orally/day or injectable 30 mg (combined)/kg/day for 2 days then every 48 hrs. for 7 injections
Tylosin	50–75 mg/kg/day

*For amikasin, gentamicin, netilmycin, and tobramycin, the dosage given is for most snakes. The dosage for turtles and tortoises is 10 mg/kg every 48 hours. Mader (1985) recommends an initial loading dose of 5 mg/kg for snakes. The dosage should be lowered by 1/3 if one of these 4 antibiotics is used for longer than 2 weeks.

For mouth infections Ross (1984) recommends dividing the dose in half, diluting half with saline and injecting it intralesionally and giving the rest IM or SQ as usual.

II. SICK AND INJURED WILDLIFE

A. General (provide proper husbandry).
- Clean dry cage. Newspaper, substrate, hiding box, water bowl.
- Proper temperatures:
  Tropical species; 85–90°F day—80°F night.
  Temperate species; 80–85°F day—75°F night.
  If sick; 90°F.
- Heat lamps, heating pads, hot rocks (measure temperature with a thermometer).
- Proper nutrition: consult field guides and herpetological societies. Feed natural diets if available. Pre-kill all rodents.

B. Sick, Wild Reptiles—rarely seen (usually die of bacterial infections before being caught):
- Most are sick due to gram negative bacteria, so use appropriate antibiotics.
- Use dosages established for reptiles (Table 1).
- Pay attention to nursing care: temperature, hydration (15–25 ml/kg/day parenteral fluids. Jacobson and Frye believe Ross' dosage of 2.0–2.5 ml/kg/day to be too low), Nutrition.
- Clean and debride necrotic tissue from infected areas (mouth, skin). Establish drainage.

C. Injured Wildlife
  1. Use same principles you would for mammals...
     a. Treat for shock, stablize patient.
     b. Relieve pain with anesthetics.
        - There is little place for hypothermia.

- Ketamine 20–60 mg/kg.
- Metofane, halothane, isoflurane.
- Facemask or intubate.
- Positive pressure ventilation 2/minute.
  c. Aseptic technique.
    - Close wounds with slight eversion of skin edges; (horizontal mattress), incise between scales, establish drainage.
    - Remove stitches at 3–4 weeks.
  d. Faster anesthetic recovery, better healing at warmer temperatures 90°F.
    - Treat secondary problems, (i.e. infections).
    - Watch for dysecdysis during healing.

2. Wounds:
Debride nectotic tissue, suture or leave as open wound. If open wound, don't use ground-up bedding. Cover with antibiotics.

3. Amputations:
Should be done at the level of the shoulder or hip to avoid trauma to the remaining stump.

4. Fractures:
Same principles of fracture fixation as those used in mammals (i.e. rigid fixation, usually internal, until radiographic evidence of healing).
    - Cage rest.
    - Splint.
    - Pins, plates, K.E. apparatus.
    - Surgical glue for small patients.

5. Fractured Shells:
    - Examine for and treat concurrent injuries.
    - Appropriate anesthesia.
    - Thorough flushing of exposed tissues.
    - I prefer to wire fragments in place prior to sealing with 5-minute epoxy or dental acrylics. Can use fiberglass mesh (preferably sterilized). 5-minute epoxy is readily available, but if you see a lot of cases, consult a local dentist for acrylics.
    - Penrose drains for drainage.
    - Antibiotics.
    - Unless turtle is full grown, the artificial splint should be removed with a Dremmel tool after healing to allow for shell growth. Wear a facemask to avoid inhalation of epoxy particles.
    - See Mr. Heinrich's following paper on Chelonian Shell Repair for more details.

REFERENCES

Frye, F. *Biomedical and Surgical Aspects of Captive Reptile Husbandry.* V.M. Publications, Inc., Bonner Springs, Kansas. 1981.

Jacobson, E., et al. Dosages for Antibiotics and Parasiticides Used in Exotic Animals. Compendium Contin. Educ. Pract. Vet. 5: 315–325. 1983.

Ross, R. *The Bacterial Diseases of Reptiles*. The Institute for Herpetological Research, P.O. Box 2227, Stanford, California. 1984.

Mader, D. et al. Effects of Ambient Temperature on the Half-Life and Dosage Regimen of Amikasin in the Gopher Snake. J. Am. Vet. Med. Assoc. 187: 1134–1136. 1985.

APPENDIX
Regional Herpetological Society Directory

Arizona Herpetological Association
2459 W. Claire
Phoenix, AZ 85032

Bay Area Turtle & Tortoise Society
P.O. Box 17
Berkeley, CA 91701

Desert Tortoise Council
350 Golden Shore
Long Beach, CA 90802

California Turtle & Tortoise Society
Box 90252
Los Angeles, CA 90009

Sacramento Valley Herpetological Society
Bob Pedder
6007 Watt Ave.
North Highlands, CA 92111

Bay Area Amphibian & Reptile Society
3037 Huntington St.
Oakland, CA 98108

San Diego Turtle & Tortoise Society
c/o 6957 Tanglewood Rd.
San Diego, CA 92111

Southwestern Herpetological Society
P.O. Box 7469
Van Nuys, CA 91404

Colorado Herpetological Society
P.O. Box 15381
Denver, CO 80215

Connecticut Herpetological Society
George Whitney, DVM
Whitney Clinic, Oakwood Rd.
Ornage, CT 06477

Florida West Coast Herpetological Society
John Lewis
1312 South Evergreen Ave.
Clearwater, FL 33515

Gopher Tortoise Council
c/o Florida State Museum
University of Florida
Gainsville, FL 32611

Florida Herpetological Society
Dennis R. Magee
5488 North River Rd.
Jacksonville, FL 32211

Palm Beach Herpetological Society
Greg Longhurst
P.O. Box 125
Loxahatchee, FL 33470

South Florida Herpetological Society
Saul Friess
9972 N. Kendall Dr., #45
Miami, FL 33176

Georgia Herpetological Society
c/o Reptile House
Atlanta Zoological Park
800 Cherokee Ave., S.E.
Atlanta, GA 30315

Chicago Herpetological Society
2001 North Clark St.
Chicago, IL 60614

Mid-Mississippi Valley Herpetological Society
Mike Lodato
925 Park Plaza Dr.
Evansville, IN 47715

Iowa Herpetological Society
P.O. Box 191
Norwalk, IA 50211

Kaw Valley Herpetological Society
Rt. 1, Box 29B
Eudora, KS 66025

Kansas Herpetological Society
Museum of Natural History
University of Kansas
Lawrence, KS 66045

APPENDIX
Regional Herpetological Society Directory *(continued)*

Kentucky Herpetological Society
John MacGregor
102 Fourth St.
Nickolasville, KY 40358

Maryland Herpetological Society
Natural History Society of Maryland
2643 North Charles St.
Baltimore, MD 21218

Massachusetts Herpetological Society
P.O. Box 1082
Boston, MA 02103

Toledo Herpetological Society
c/o Marlene Sterling, Secretary
8151 Summerfield Rd.
Lambertville, MI 48144

Michigan Society of Herpetologists
c/o Theresa Moran
1603 Massachusetts
Lansing, MI 48906

Great Lakes Herpetological Society
c/o Jeff Gee
4308 N. Woodward
Royal Oaks, MI 48072

Minnesota Herpetological Society
Bell Museum of Natural History
10 Church St.
Minneapolis, MN 55455

South Mississippi Herpetological Society
c/o Ted Crawford
404 Ridge Dr.
Biloxi, MS 39532

St. Louis Herpetological Society
P.O. Box 9216
St. Louis, MO 63117

Nebraska Herpetological Society
Johnny Martinez
2326 S. 12th St.
Omaha, NB 68108

North New Jersey Herpetological Society
P.O. Box 94
Augusta, NJ 07822

East Seaboard Herpetological Society
David Hulmes, Coordinator
122 Second Ave.
Hawthorne, NJ 07507

Association for the Conservation
of Turtles and Tortoises
c/o Mrs. Sandra Jordan, Secretary
RD #4, Box 291
Sussex, NJ 07461

New Mexico Herpetological Society
Department of Biology
University of New Mexico
Albuquerque, NM 87131

New York Herpetological Society
P.O. Box 1245
Grand Central Station
New York, NY 10017

North Carolina Herpetological Society
North Carolina State Museum
of Natural History
P.O. Box 27647
Raleigh, NC 27611

Greater Cincinnati Herpetological Society
Cincinnati Museum of Natural History
172 Gilbert Ave.
Cincinnati, OH 45202

Northern Ohio Association of Herpetologists
Department of Biology
Case Western Reserve University
Cleveland, OH 44106

Central Ohio Herpetological Society
2621 Muskingum Ct.
Columbus, OH 43210

Oklahoma Herpetological Society
Jeffrey Black
Oklahoma Baptist University
Shawnee, OK 74801

Oregon Herpetological Society
Mr. David Olson, Treasurer
981 W. 8th Ave., #10
Eugene, OR 97402

Philadelphia Herpetological Society
Harry Hance, President
739 Rosyln Ave.
Glenside, PA 19038

South Texas Amphibian & Reptile Society
c/o Greg Luther
P.O. Box 233
Angleton, TX 77515

APPENDIX
Regional Herpetological Society Directory *(continued)*

Dallas Herpetological Society
Dallas Museum of Natural History
P.O. Box 26193
Dallas, TX 75226

North Texas Herpetological Society
c/o Fort Worth Museum
of Science & History
1501 Montgomery St.
Fort Worth, TX 76107

Gulf Coast Herpetological Society
John Zapata
P.O. Box 1562
Houston Zoo
Houston, TX 77001

Lubbock Turtle & Tortoise Society
c/o Dr. Carl Anderson
3311 24th St.
Lubbock, TX 79410

Texas Herpetological Society
309 South 4th St.
Wylie, TX 75098

Utah Herpetological Society
Hogel Zoological Gardens
P.O. Box 8475
Salt Lake City, UT 84108

Virginia Herpetological Society
c/o Don Merkle
Longwood College
Farmville, VA 23901

Washington Herpetological Society
Scott Rae
317 Adahi Rd.
Vienne, VA 21180

Wisconsin Herpetological Society
Milwaukee Public Museum
800 West Wells
Milwaukee, WI 53233

Canadian Amphibian & Reptile
Conservation Society
9 Mississauga Rd., N.
Mississauga, Ont. L
Canada L5H 2H5

A TECHNIQUE FOR THE REPAIR OF CHELONIAN SHELL FRACTURES, WITH A HISTORICAL REVIEW OF SHELL FRACTURE REPAIR

George Heinrich

Dept. of Herpetology
Memphis Zoo and Aquarium
2000 Galloway Avenue
Memphis, TN 38112

and

Donna Heinrich

Wildlife Rehabilitation
Lichterman Nature Center
5992 Quince Road
Memphis, TN 38119

ABSTRACT

A brief history of the repair of turtle and tortoise shell fractures is reviewed. The use of fiberglass cloth and epoxy resin enables injured specimens to be repaired and released after a variable period of recuperation. Step-by-step instruction on the application of this technique is presented. Post-repair captive maintenance (e.g. medical care in addition to physical, social and climatic requirements) is covered. This technique can be a valuable conservation tool when applied to rare and vanishing species.

INTRODUCTION

One of the greatest threats to turtles and tortoises (excluding loss of habitat or human encroachment) is the automobile. The numbers of individuals that are injured or killed on our roads annually is staggering.

Wilson and Porras (1983) report, "Vehicular traffic has long been known as an important agent in reducing populations of amphibians and reptiles." Barbour (1944) notes, "...in Florida the slaughter of reptilian life on the roads has been devastating.... There they have been killed literally by the millions."

Most encounters with automobiles result in death. However, some chelonians manage to survive the initial trauma. These individuals generally walk away with varying degrees of shell fracture. The majority of automobile induced shell fractures occur during migratory periods. Though not as great a threat as the automobile, attacks by predators, as well as encounters with agricultural machinery are additional causes of shell fracture.

Based on the extent of the fracture and degree of trauma to the underlying internal organs, some individuals are capable of surviving the lengthy process of shell regeneration. Cagle (1945) reports collecting (on May 17, 1940) a painted turtle (*Chrysemys picta*) that had recently received a serious injury from a rifle shot. In his words:

> "The bullet had entered the 2nd right costal and considerable bleeding had occurred in the vicinity of the wound. Although the injury had appeared serious the turtle was marked and released.
>
> This turtle was subsequently recovered four times during the next two years. At the time of the first two recoveries (June 6, 1940; July 19, 1940) the wound was open and there was little evidence of repair. Recovered again on May 22, 1941, there was some evidence of scar tissue developing about the bullet hole and the fractured plate was healed. The turtle appeared to be normally active. The turtle was recovered again on June 18, 1942. The injury was completely closed and the turtle gave no evidence of being handicapped."

HISTORICAL REVIEW

Over the past two decades, several researchers have experimented with various techniques for the repair of chelonian shell fractures (Table 1). A review of the literature indicates nearly all papers dealing with this subject were written by members of the veterinary profession.

One of the earliest reported cases of shell fracture repair was by LyVere (1966). The Denver Zoological Gardens presented LyVere with an adult Galapagos tortoise (*Geochelone elephantopus*) whose carapace had been damaged by vandals. The wound was allowed to heal while antibiotics were administered. After ten months, the soft-tissue wounds had filled in with scar tissue. However, two holes had remained in the shell. At that time Hoff Repair Material (H.D. Justi Division, William Gold Refining Co., Philadelphia, PA) was utilized to repair the damage. Since the tortoise was used for public display, shoe polish was used to camouflage the clear plastic. LyVere feels that even though the material used generated high heat, it had a lasting quality because the shell repair remained intact until the tortoise's death from an unrelated accident ten years later (pers. comm.).

Zeman et al. (1967) report the use of a rapid gelling and curing styrene modified-polyester resin "...to surgically fill a traumatic defect in the carapace" of an eastern box turtle (*Terrapene carolina carolina*). The animal was accidently injured by a power mower, resulting in a hole approximately 35 mm in diameter, exposing the underlying respiratory organs. When the peritoneum has been penetrated and the underlying internal organs are exposed, the opening must be closed before any further repair work can be undertaken.

After standard veterinary treatment of the wound, two elliptical wafers of cured polylite were made for placement under the shell. This covered and protected the exposed internal organs and surrounding tissue. The authors note that, "This served as a bed for the further application of successive layers of plastic resin." The authors report a total surgical time of approximately one hour. This procedure is recommended when treating chelonians with injuries of this nature. The turtle was

TABLE 1. LIST OF CHELONIAN SPECIES REPARIED, NAMES OF RESEARCHERS AND DATES OF PUBLICATION (PRESENTED IN CHRONOLOGICAL ORDER PER SPECIES)

Species	Researchers	Dates of publication
Galapagos tortoise (*Geochelone elephantopus* ssp.)	LyVere, D.B.	1966
Eastern box turtle (*Terrapene c. carolina*)	Zeman, W.V., F.G. Falco, and J.J. Falco	1967
Eastern box turtle (*Terrapene c. carolina*)	Miller, M.F.	(pers. comm., 1986)
Eastern box turtle (*Terrapene c. carolina*)	This publication	
(*Gopherus* sp.)	Northway, R.B.	1970
(*Gopherus* sp.)[1]	Rosskopf, W.J., Jr., and R.W. Woerpel	1981
Desert tortoise (*G. agassizii*)	Bissett, D.	1971
Desert tortoise (*G. agassizii*)	Frye, F.L.	1973
Texas tortoise (*G. berlandeiri*)	Frye, F.L.	1973
Blanding's turtle (*Emydoidea blandingii*)	Barten, S.L.	(pers. comm., 1985)
Painted turtle (*Chrysemys picta* ssp.)	Barten, S.L.	(pers. comm., 1985)
Red-eared slider (*Pseudemys scripta elegans*)	This publication	
Eastern box turtle x Three-toed box turtle (*T. c. carolina* x *T. c. triunguis*)	This publication	
Florida box turtle (*T. c. bauri*)	This publication	

[1]Identification is based on photographs in paper.

observed for five months post-surgery during which time it revealed no toxic signs of symptoms.

Frye (1973) reports the use of a rapid curing epoxy resin (Devcon 5-Minute Epoxy, Devcon Corporation, Danvers, MA) for the repair of carapacial and plastral fractures in a desert tortoise (*Gopherus agassizii*) and two Texas tortoises (*Gopherus berlandieri*).

Originally, Frye experimented with epoxy resin-impregnated cloth for repairing the shells of tortoises. The material employed was commonly available sport vehicle repair material.

Frye states, "The main disadvantage of this method has been the relatively long period of polymerization when equal parts of a catalyst-containing hardener and epoxy resin are used. Adding more catalyst shortens polymerization time but causes a marked increase in the temperature resulting from exothermic reaction."

With the Devcon 5-Minute Epoxy, polymerization time is greatly reduced with less heat generated. The animals in this case were also accorded standard veterinary treatment in preparation for surgery. Frye also reports, "Although epoxy compounds are recognized as irritants to living tissues, no untoward reactions or generalized toxicity were noted...."

Another technique utilizing a standard bone-pinning chuck or drill and heavy-duty surgical wire is described by Rosskopf and Woerpel (1981). Although not stated in their article, the tortoise in the photographs is a *Gopherus* species. Small holes were drilled alongside the fracture and then sutured with surgical wire. The authors state that their preference for the use of wire sutures over acrylic resin is based on fewer potential complications although no further explanation is offered.

Barten (pers. comm.) also employs wire sutures. Originally, epoxy resin-impregnated fiberglass mesh was employed. However, this was abandoned due to prolonged surgical time. Suturing with 22-gauge orthopedic wire and then covering the sutures with fiberglass cloth and epoxy proved more successful.

This technique has been applied to both painted turtles (*Chrysemys picta*) and Blanding's turtles (*Emydoidea blandingii*). In addition, Barten places Penrose drains between the shell and the underlying tissue with the drain exiting through the skin next to the shell. This allows fluids and discharge to exit through the hole in the skin around the drain. Also, antibiotics can be flushed into the wound via the drain.

In addition to the previously described methods, some researchers are working with dental acrylics (Wallach 1969). This material can be molded to the shape of the shell and does not generate a great deal of heat. One of its most desirable qualities is that it can be used in contact with mucous membrane with neither toxic nor caustic effects (Williams, pers. comm.).

SHELL FRACTURE REPAIR AT LICHTERMAN NATURE CENTER

At Lichterman Nature Center (L.N.C.) we employ epoxy resin-impregnated fiberglass cloth (based after Frye 1973). Since 1984, ten turtles (including both aquatic and terrestrial species) have been successfully repaired using this technique (Table 2).

Some adult specimens have been released with the patch still intact. This is acceptable for adults due to their limited potential growth. However, with young turtles the patch was always removed. Subsequent shell growth can cause deformities in young chelonians that have not had the patch removed prior to release (Rosskopf et al. 1983). The relief and removal of patches is discussed within this paper under the section titled, "Post-Repair Captive Maintenance."

The authors would like to note that although the technique of shell fracture repair used at L.N.C. is a fairly basic method, veterinary consultation and some supervision is recommended. The diagnosis and treatment of injured wildlife without veterinary consultation is unacceptable (Evans and Evans 1986). It is not the intention of either author to use this paper for instructing rehabilitators as to the treatment of critically injured chelonians. Only after a veterinarian has stabilized the individual can the rehabilitator play his part in repairing the shell fracture.

EXAMINATION

The first step upon receiving an injured turtle or tortoise is to examine and stabilize the individual. Quite often the animal arrives bleeding and/or in shock. Critically injured chelonians should be accorded treatment by a well trained and equipped staff. Therefore, it is imperative that individuals in this condition be treated by a veterinarian. While in transport, injured animals should be immobilized and kept warm. Chelonians arriving in a stabilized condition can obviously forego the above treatment.

TABLE 2. BREAKDOWN OF CHELONIAN SPECIES REPAIRED AND THEIR DISPOSITION AT LICHTERMAN NATURE CENTER (PRESENTED IN ORDER REPAIRED PER SPECIES)

Species	Released	Rehabilitating	Other	Total #
Eastern box turtle (*Terrapene c. carolina*)	4	2		6
Red-eared slider (*Pseudemys scripta elegans*)	1		1[a]	2
Eastern box turtle x Three-toed box turtle (*T. c. carolina* x *T. c. triunguis*)		1		1
Florida box turtle (*T. c. bauri*)		1		1
Totals	5	4	1	10

[a] One (1) specimen of *P. s. elegans* died from an unrelated accident while rehabilitating.

1. Is the peritoneum punctured or torn?
2. Is infection present?
3. Are there larvae present?
4. How old is the damage?
5. Has healing already begun?

Only after considering these questions can the rehabilitator begin to judge each individual's chances for survival and determine where to draw a line on suitable candidates for repair.

In order to gain experience without endangering the health of a live animal, it is advisable to practice this technique on "D.O.R." (dead-on-road) turtles and tortoises. "Road-kills" are a valuable resource and an excellent way to practice and refine one's technique. Until the rehabilitator has become more proficient, shell fracture repairs on rare and vanishing species are best left to those more experienced.

During the examination, an arrival weight and temperature should be recorded and compared to normal baseline. Cloacal temperatures vary with each species. An excellent reference for weights and temperatures of North American species is Ernst and Barbour (1972). Another source of information on preferred body temperatures is Marcus (1981). Radiographs should be taken at this time to aid in determining the extent of the damage. In addition, they can be compared to later radiographs to assess healing. Although radiographs are an additional expense, they are well worth the cost.

Based on their conditions upon arrival, some cases warrant the use of antibiotics to achieve stabilization. At L.N.C., lincomycin hydrochloride (Lincocin®—made by The Upjohn Company, Kalamazoo, MI) is administered IM b.i.d./s.i.d. at a dosage of 6 mg/kg (Frye 1981). Individuals are maintained on this antibiotic therapy for approximately seven days. Lincocin® should not be used in presence of impaired renal or hepatic function or dehydration (Frye 1981). For other injectable antibiotics that are suitable for use in chelonians. See Frye (1981).

Prior to the commencement of shell repair, care should be taken to assure that the proper equipment and materials are available (Table 3). As noted in Table 3, some equipment and materials must be sterilized before use.

PREPARATION OF SHELL FOR REPAIR

The following steps should be completed in preparing the shell for repair:

1. Insert tele-thermometer probe (use lubricant) into cloaca at this time and begin to monitor temperature.
2. Some cases warrant the use of injectable anaesthetics. At L.N.C., ketamine hydrochloride (Ketaset®—made by Veterinary Products, Bristol Laboratories, Division of Bristol-Myers Co., Syracuse, NY) is administered IM at a dosage of 20–60 mg/kg (Frye 1981). This dosage may be inadequate for some surgical procedures (Frye 1981). Burke (1978) recommends a dosage of 88 mg/kg.

Beginning with a low dose, subsequent injections are given at 30 minute intervals, if needed. Burke also reports doses greater than 132 mg/kg have necessitated respiratory assistance to prevent death. This anaesthetic has a rapid induction time and reasonable recovery period (Frye 1981). Ketamine hydrochloride should not be used in reptiles with suspected renal disease or dehydration (Frye 1981). In addition, the manufacturer warns against using it on animals with hepatic insufficiencies.

3. Clean entire shell with a soft brush using a surgical scrub. Caution should be exercised so as not to damage scutes.
4. Clear fracture of all debris using forceps and hemostats.
5. Clean fracture with a toothbrush using a surgical scrub.
6. Flush fracture liberally with lactated Ringer's solution.
7. If fracture is immediately fresh, attempt to realign shell as is. If not, use a Dremel Moto-Tool® (Dremel, Division of Emerson Electric Co., Racine, WI) to debride bone (see following section titled "Debridement of Bone" for instructions on the proper use of this tool). Then realign shell.
8. Repeat steps 4 through 6.
9. Dry entire shell with gauze pads. Special attention should be given to the fracture site. Allow time for complete drying.

DEBRIDEMENT OF BONE

In some cases the use of a Dremel Moto-Tool® is required to debride bone. Generally, this is in cases where the fracture site has already begun regenerating and is not aligning properly. It is recommended that one wear goggles when using this tool. The Dremel Moto-Tool® has a range of 5,000–28,000 r.p.m. At a high speed a slight slip can result in severe damage to the animal and/or worker. It cannot be stressed enough to practice extreme caution when using this tool.

Some practice is required before using this tool on a live animal. Therefore, it is advisable that one practice on deceased chelonians.

Marking the shell with a surgical skin scribe will aid in debriding only as much bone as is necessary. Using a steel saw (Dremel attachment #406), carefully cut away dead bone. Extreme caution should be practiced to avoid cutting through the peritoneum, located immediately below the shell. Minor bleeding is necessary to assure that debridement has reached living bone. Care should be taken so as not to confuse blood from the peritoneum with that from the latter. Friction from the use of this tool generates heat. Periodically, the facture site should be allowed to cool. When cutting the opposing side of the fracture, be sure it follows the same outline as the first side. This is important so that there will be good apposition which will facilitate regeneration.

APPLICATION OF FIBERGLASS CLOTH AND EPOXY RESIN

The next step involves the application of fiberglass cloth and epoxy resin. Using the initial radiograph or the live animal itself, measure and draw the fracture on paper. This will be used when cutting the fiberglass pieces. Each piece can then be checked against the fracture before application.

Using surgical scissors, fiberglass pieces should be cut either round or oval shaped to prevent wrinkling and puckering (Frye 1981). Each piece should be cut to extend approximately 1.5 to 3.0 cm beyond the edge of the fracture (Frye 1981). In addition, each successive layer should overlap the previous layer to increase structural strength. As noted in Table 3, the fiberglass cloth should be sterilized.

TABLE 3. LIST OF EQUIPMENT AND MATERIALS USED FOR SHELL REPAIR AT LICHTERMAN NATURE CENTER (PRESENTED IN ORDER USED)

lubricant: to ease insertion of tele-thermometer probe.
tele-thermometer: to monitor cloacal temperature.
adhesive tape: for taping temperature probe wire to shell; also used when suspending animal during of epoxy resin.
Ketaset®: or other comparable injectable anaesthetic; must be obtained from and used under direct supervision of a veterinarian.
*****insulin syringes:** must be obtained from a veterinarian.
soft brush: suitable for scrubbing fracture site.
surgical scrub: preferably a povidone-iodine scrub.
*****forceps:** for cleaning fracture.
*****hemostats:** for cleaning fracture.
toothbrush: for scrubbing fracture.
lactated Ringer's solution: for flushing fracture.
*****60 cc irrigation syringe:** for flushing fracture.
skin scribe: for marking area to be debrided.
goggles: to protect eyes while using Dremel Moto-Tool®.
Dremel Moto-Tool®: used when debriding bone, butting and sanding excess patch.
*****steel saw (Dremel attachment #406):** used for debriding bone.
*****gauze pads:** for drying fracture site.
*****surgical scissors:** capable of precisely cutting fiberglass cloth.
*****fiberglass cloth:** tightly woven; a good source is an automotive paint dealer.
Devcon® 5-Minute Epoxy: available at most department or hardware stores.
*****flat applicator sticks:** for mixing and application of epoxy resin.
steel ring: used when suspending the animal.
chain or cord: to suspend animal during curing of epoxy resin.
disposable respiratory mask: used to prevent inhalation of epoxy resin-impregnated fiberglass dust.
cutting wheel (Dremel attachment #409): used for cutting away excess patch.
mandrel (Dremel attachment #402): used with cutting wheel.
drum sander (Dremel attachment #407): for sanding rough areas of patch.
drum sander bands (Dremel attachment #408): used with drum sander.

*Items marked with asterisk must be sterilized before use.

Immediately prior to use, thoroughly mix a small amount of epoxy resin. Experiment with epoxy resin in order to become familiar with its qualities (e.g. composition, curing time, etc.). Due to rapid curing time, fresh epoxy resin will need to be mixed several times during the course of each shell fracture repair.

When applying epoxy resin to shell, do not get on tissue or in fracture as this will prevent regeneration. Apply epoxy resin for approximately 2 cm around the margin of the fracture (Frye 1981). After aligning the edges of the fracture, place the first layer of fiberglass cloth so that the margin adheres to the epoxy resin. Do not put any epoxy resin on the center area of the first layer. This will prevent excess epoxy resin from leaking through into the fracture. Work the epoxy resin into the interstices of the patch margin. After the first layer has polymerized place a second layer on in the same manner. However, with the second layer work epoxy resin into the entire piece of fiberglass. This should adhere to the first layer. After the second layer has polymerized, place the third layer on in the same manner. Generally, three layers are sufficient. However, some cases warrant the use of additional layers.

An area that requires special attention is the bridge. Bridge fractures usually involve additional damage to either the plastron or the carapace. When working on a bridge, care should be taken to avoid contact of epoxy resin with tissue or limbs. Care should also be taken so that hinges are not accidently immobilized. However, in some cases this is desirable. When a fracture involves the hinge area and/or bridge, it is sometimes necessary to immobilize the hinge. This will limit stress on the bridge. However, due to the turtle's inability to close its shell, high stress is placed on the animal psychologically. Animals in this condition should be monitored closely during rehabilitation. Obviously, turtles repaired in such a fashion should never be released.

CURING OF EPOXY RESIN

During the curing period, it is necessary to suspend chelonians with plastral fractures in a sling. This allows the epoxy resin to cure without adhering to any substrate matter. In addition, this allows the animal to breath easier during recovery (Rosskopf et al. 1983). At L.N.C. we securely affix a steel ring to the carapace with adhesive tape. A chain or cord is attached to this ring with the opposite end attached to an aquarium top. The individual is suspended in an aquarium approximately 15–20 cm above the base. A soft substrate is placed below the turtle in case of accidental falling. Rosskopf et al. (1983) report the use of a coat hanger apparatus to allow drying.

Large species (e.g. *Geochelone*) will require the researcher to employ some creativity. Whatever the method of suspension, care should be taken that the animal does not sustain further injuries. In addition, one should avoid placing additional stress to the fracture site while in suspension. Generally, "slinging" is required for only a few hours.

After curing, it is usually necessary to cut away excess patch. All rough spots should be sanded down to limit any possible abrasion. It is advisable that one wear goggles and a disposable respiratory mask when conducting this work. The dust caused by this procedure is extremely irritating to the ophthalmic, respiratory and gastrointestinal epithelium in man (Frye 1981). Frye also reports it may be a carcinogenic agent.

The cutting can be done using a cutting wheel (Dremel attachment #409) attached to a mandrel (Dremel attachment #402). Sanding can be done with a drum sander (Dremel attachment #407) and drum sander bands (Dremel attachment #408). Areas of patch bordering the neck or legs should be carefully examined to assure no sharp edges are present. In applicable cases, be sure hinges are clear and working.

POST-REPAIR CAPTIVE MAINTENANCE

As is the case with all rehabilitating animals, the individual should be maintained in as close to a stress-free environment as possible. Chelonians should be kept warm immediately after surgery (Rosskopf et al. 1983). During this period antibiotic therapy similar to that described earlier is recommended. Antibiotics should be administered for ten days postoperatively (Rosskopf and Woerpel 1981). Marcus (1981) reports a seemingly better response to antibiotic therapy when the ambient temperature is maintained at 29.4–33.2°C. Rosskopf et al. (1983) use intracoelomic lactated Ringer's solution administered at a dosage of 10–20 cc/0.45 kg daily for the first five days or longer when indicated. Chelonians should not be allowed to get wet for approximately seven days postoperatively, to allow a perfect seal to develop between the resin and shell (Rosskopf et al. 1983). Hibernation, which retards healing, should be avoided for at least six months (Rosskopf et al. 1983).

It is advisable to hold off on all food and water for approximately 24 hours post-repair. If the animal does not begin eating or drinking voluntarily, assistance may be necessary. Food supplements can be force fed until normal alimentation returns (Rosskopf et al. 1983). Water should be available *ad libitum*. Diets in captivity should be as natural as possible. An excellent reference for diets of North American species is Ernst and Barbour (1972). Weight should be monitored the entire time the animal is in captivity. Again, this can be compared to the arrival weight and normals for each particular species.

Periodic radiographs should be taken and compared to earlier ones in order to determine rate of regeneration. This will help eliminate maintaining animals that are ready for release or vice versa.

When weather permits, rehabilitating turtles and tortoises can be taken outside. Provide shade and shelter from inclement weather and predators. Be alert to drastic changes in temperature. Some species appear to do better when maintained in groups. This can be advantageous when limited cage space is available. Be sure species maintained together are compatible.

It is necessary to maintain some individuals for up to two years in captivity. During this period the patch must occasionally be relieved to allow for new growth. This growth occurs at the interface of the bony plates and scutes (Frye 1981). The patch can be relieved from the areas immediately overlying the expanding growth rings by carefully routing away with a hand held motorized file or burr (Frye 1981). With young turtles and tortoises this should be done approximately six months to one year post-repair. The patch can be removed entirely by manually peeling it off. Care should be taken so as not to further injure the regenerating fracture.

Time in captivity should be reduced to as short as possible. The sooner the animal is released (within reason) the better. Full-grown adults that are difficult to maintain in captivity can be released as soon as they are stable and show no signs of complications. The patch can permanently remain on the shell. Additional sources of information on the captive husbandry of chelonians are Ernst and Barbour (1972), Frye (1981), Marcus (1981), Murphy and Collins (1983) and Pawley (1984).

REINTRODUCTION

Reintroduction is synonymous with rehabilitation. Returning the animal to the wild is the main objective of wildlife rehabilitation. When releasing a repaired chelonian, select an area as close as possible to where it was originally collected. This is necessary to preserve population characteristics and is of the utmost importance when undertaking wildlife rehabilitation projects involving reintroduction of native wildlife.

Individuals may feel their contributions are too small to make a difference. However, as a group, rehabilitators in conjunction with veterinarians can and do make a difference. Numerous turtles and tortoises throughout North America, as well as world-wide, are threatened with extinction. In the United States alone, two species of the genus *Clemmys*, three *Gopherus* species, and several *Graptemys* species, among others, are all in need of assistance. This technique can be a valuable conservation tool when applied to rare and vanishing species.

FUTURE WORK

In the future we hope to work with the gopher tortoise (*Gopherus polyphemus*) and begin to apply what we have learned with the turtles of the mid-south to this rapidly disappearing species. In addition, we are currently coordinating a radio telemetry study of post-release "shell fracture repaired" chelonians to help answer questions regarding the effects of this technique on the individual's life in the wild (e.g. acceptance by a mate, reproduction, defense from predators, etc.).

In closing, we would like to note that the possibilities for the development of new techniques are exciting. Shell fracture repair has come a long way in the last 20 years: from simple taping to the use of dental acrylics. We look forward to future papers reporting more effective methods of accomplishing the same goal.

ACKNOWLEDGEMENTS

We would like to thank the Memphis Zoo and Aquarium and the Lichterman Nature Center for making it possible to conduct this project. Special thanks is offered to Larry Pickens for much needed support; Lois Jones for assistance during repair work and rehabilitation; Michael S. Lifsey, M.D. and Thereasa Bond for consultation and support; and to Pete Money for planting the seed that grew into L.N.C.

Additional thanks goes to Bob Barni, Stephen L. Barten, D.V.M., Charles R. Beck, Jr., Bill Cupo, Joan Diemer, Kaki Dowling, Fredric L. Frye, D.V.M., Kathy Goble, Dave Hill, Earl Jones, Donald B. LyVere, D.V.M., Eugene H. Mcgehee, D.V.M., Gerald A. Olson, D.V.M., Kelee Overgaard, Steve Reichling and Lisa Sisk.

We would also like to thank Sarah, our daughter, for understanding frequent trips to the Center, pulling all-nighters; and turtles everywhere. To all of the above we are most heartily thankful, for without their combined assistance this project would not have been possible.

LITERATURE CITED

Barbour, T. 1944. That vanishing Eden. Little, Brown and Co., Boston. 250 pp.

Barten, S.L. 1985. Personal communication.

Bissett, D. 1971. A tortoise by accident. Intern. Turtle & Tortoise Soc. J. 5(3):6–9, 34.

Burke, T.J. 1978. Chemical restraint and anaesthesia. In Burke, T. (ed.), Reptiles. In Fowler, M.E. (ed.-in-chief), Zoo and wild animal medicine. Pp. 132–134. W.B. Saunders Company, Philadelphia. 951 pp.

Cagle, F.R. 1945. Recovery from serious injury in the painted turtle. Copeia 1945:45.

Ernst, C.H., and Barbour, R.W. 1972. Turtles of the United States. Univ. Press Kentucky, Lexington. 347 pp.

Evans, A.T., and Evans, R.H. 1986. Raising raccoons for release. Part IV. Medical management and readiness for the wild. Vet. Tech. 7(1):37–48.

Frye, F.L. 1973. Clinical evaluation of a rapid polymerizing epoxy resin for repair of shell defects in tortoises. Vet. Med./Small Anim. Clin. 68:51–53.

———. 1981. Biomedical and surgical aspects of captive reptile husbandry. Veterinary Medicine Publishing Company, Edwardsville, Kansas. 456 pp.

LyVere, D.B. 1966. Repair of the shell of a Galapagos tortoise. Mod. Vet. Pract. 47:76.

———. 1986. Personal communication.

Marcus, L.C. 1981. Veterinary biology and medicine of captive amphibians and reptiles. Lea & Febiger, Philadelphia. 239 pp.

Miller, M.F. 1986. Personal communication.

Murphy, J.B., and Collins, J.T. 1983. A review of the diseases and treatments of captive turtles. AMS Publishing, Lawrence, Kansas. 56 pp.

Northway, R.B. 1970. Repair of a fractured shell and lacerated cornea in a tortoise. Vet. Med./Small Anim. Clin. 65:944.

Pawley, R. 1984. Reptiles and amphibians: their needs are different. In Wildlife Rehabilitation, Vol. 2. Pp. 77–80. Beaver, P. (ed.), Exposition Press, Inc., Smithtown, New York. 188 pp.

Rosskopf, W.J., Jr., and Woerpel, R.W. 1981. Repair of shell damage in tortoises. Mod. Vet. Pract. 62:938–939.

———, et al. 1983. Abdominal surgery in turtles and tortoises. Anim. Health Tech. 4(6)326–329.

Wallach, J.D. 1969. Medical care of reptiles. J. Am. Vet. Med. Assoc. 155(7): 1017–1034.

Williams, C.A. 1986. Personal communication.

Wilson, L.D., and Porras, L. 1983. The ecological impact of man on the south Florida herpetofauna. Univ. Kansas Publ. Mus. Nat. Hist., Lawrence. 89 pp.

Zeman, W.V., Falco, F.G., and Falco, J.J. 1967. Repair of the carapace of a box turtle using a polyester resin. Lab. Anim. Care 17(4):424–425.

Rearing Orphans

THE USE OF BIRD SKIN PUPPETS IN REARING ORPHANED BIRDS

Paul Beaver, Ph.D., Denise Steenblock, Ruth Iannazzi and Mike Ayers

Quabaug Bird Sanctuary
315 Palmer Road
Ware, MA 01082

Hand-rearing orphaned birds is a problem frequently discussed in these wildlife rehabilitation proceedings. It's an incredibly time-consuming affair; and unless you're willing to devote the proper time and resources, the mortality rate will be very discouraging.

Some rehabilitators have suggested alternatives to captive rearing, such as replacing orphaned birds in existing nests. While this approach works well in some situations, it should be avoided as a general practice, for the following reasons: first, you can attract predators to the nest site; second, you may be spreading disease; third, you can overload a nest, leading to decreased fitness for the young or the parent; fourth, if ages are not correctly matched, mortality may result; fifth, some species can recognize their young and will kill strange young; and sixth, if you are mixing species (i.e. cross-fostering), you will have inappropriately imprinted birds. Tinkering with nature in this fashion typically gives rise to more problems than solutions.

If you do choose to rear your orphaned birds in captivity, you have to provide an adequate diet, feeding schedule, proper heat and humidity, and generally healthful conditions. Quite a bit has already been published in the rehabilitation literature on the proper management of young birds.

But beyond simply keeping your charges alive, you have to make sure that they are being adequately prepared, behaviorally, for successful reintroduction into a wild population. Rehabilitators have not given enough attention to the importance of behavioral aspects in rearing orphaned birds. In the past few years I have published papers in this proceedings series on developmental aspects of: foraging; migratory orientation; and predator recognition and avoidance.

Perhaps the most crucial aspect of a young bird's environment is the social aspect. A bird cannot be successfully reintroduced unless it has been properly imprinted.

Imprinting is the process by which a young bird acquires its sense of species identification. Birds which have not been imprinted on their species type, which have become imprinted on humans or another inappropriate species or object, must be considered as behaviorally crippled and unfit for release. It is a serious problem, because once imprinting has been completed, it is often not fully reversible. Taming is another social pathology, different from imprinting, though often confused with it, which must also be avoided in the preparation of animals for release.

So, our problem is: how do we go about properly imprinting our infant birds? Perhaps the easiest solution, if permanent cripples are on hand, is to rear the young in the presence of adults. This procedure has worked very well for Katherine McKeever in owls. Siblings as social partners also seems to work in at least some species. Robins reared in broods of more than a single individual will become robin imprinted, even though they are not exposed to adult robins until fledglinghood.

Still another approach is to use puppet fascimiles of the natural parent to interact with your young birds. This approach has been used for several years by the California Condor Recovery Project in the captive rearing of Condors.

At the Quabaug Bird Sanctuary, we have experimented with the use of puppets as surrogate parents in rearing orphaned passerines. The puppets are fabricated from the skins of bird carcasses. This work was supported, in part, by a grant received from the National Wildlife Rehabilitators' Association.

The puppets are used when feeding the birds. The food is scooped up by a stainless steel brain spoon, which is fixed in place, inside the puppet's mouth. When not feeding, the puppet is sometimes fixed in position near the baby birds.

The only mechanical problem we have encountered in using the puppets is their lack of durability. When used frequently, they tend to fall apart in 2-3 weeks. So if you have a lot of baby birds to care for, you'll need a steady supply of carcasses for skins.

We have used the puppets in rearing several species, including: jays, robins, cardinals, waxwings, mockingbirds, grosbeaks, bobolinks and orioles. We have had great success with this technique. Even birds reared in isolation from adult or sibling conspecifics will properly imprint if hand-reared by a bird skin puppet.

According to imprinting theory, you shouldn't have to use puppets during the entire infancy of your birds, rather just during those ages which form the critical period for imprinting. Unfortunately, the critical periods for imprinting have not yet been delineated for most species of native passerines. Our research in the robin has shown that the critical period for imprinting in this species lies between the 7th to 9th day post-hatch.

Besides being a valuable tool for the inducement of biologically appropriate imprinting in orphaned birds, we have found that the use of bird skin puppets has another benefit. In certain sensitive species which are hard to rear in captivity, the use of puppets may settle the bird down so it will eat and survive. Some birds which did not readily gape for food held by human hands or tweezers, gaped instantly in response to food held by a puppet.

Puppets were also effective in rearing such hard-to-rear birds as Wood Ducks. Typically, when received at an age of about 3-7 days post-hatch, these little guys are so hyperactive that they continuously jump around, up and down, until they drop dead. Wood Ducks have precocial young which imprint before 2 days of age; indeed, they are fully imprinted before leaving the nest. If they are subsequently separated from the parent, they become very unhappy little ducklings and will not do well in captivity.

We put a stuffed Wood Duck in with a single Wood duckling and had great results. This was surprising since the stuffed duck lacked natural articulated motion. In fact, the stuffed duck lacked motion of any sort and also lacked vocalization; but the little duckling accepted it as its parent. It would run and hide under the stuffed duck whenever we approached. The duckling settled down, ate well and matured without complications until it was released.

So it may be that the use of puppets is also effective to help those hard-to-rear orphaned birds.

HAND-REARING CHIMNEY SWIFTS©

Paul and Georgean Kyle

Wildlife Rescue, Inc.
401 Deep Eddy
Austin, TX 78703

INTRODUCTION

The Chimney swift (*Chaetura pelagica*) is one of four regularly occurring species of swifts found in North America, and the most common one found east of the Rocky Mountains. As their name implies, they are accustomed to building their nests in chimneys as well as old buildings and occasionally stone wells. Because of their close association with man, the adults and their young are frequent candidates for rehabilitation.

Adult chimney swifts are most commonly seen in flight. When soaring, their long scythe-shaped wings span about 31.75 cm (12.5″) to support a proportionally short body with a squared-off tail. The flickering, bat-like flight when flapping is due to short, massive wing bones. Usually seen in groups, chimney swifts' flight is accompanied by a sharp "chippering" or "ticking" call.

At rest, an average 122 cm (5″), 22.8 gram (.8 ounce) adult is sooty-grey to black with the throat slightly lighter or even silvery-grey in color. Both sexes are identical in appearance. The long wings cross by an inch or more over the tail feathers, which are tipped by pointed bristles. Both the claws and tail bristles are useful in clinging to rough vertical surfaces. Swifts are unable to perch.

Chimney swifts winter in the Amazon Basin of Peru. They appear in Texas in March and are gone by early November. Nesting begins in May, and has been known to continue into August. The female normally lays four to five (rarely two to seven) white eggs in a nest of twigs glued together with saliva and attached to a vertical surface. Because the nest is unlined, the eggs must be constantly incubated by alternating adults. After 18 to 19 days, the eggs begin to hatch.

DESCRIPTION OF HATCHLINGS

They are pink and naked at birth, have sharp claws which enable them to cling to textured surfaces, and they chatter loudly when stimulated.

DEVELOPMENT

The average growth rate for hand-raised chimney swifts should be one to two grams of body weight per day for the first three weeks. A weight gain of less than .5 gram may indicate a metabolic problem often related to a systemic infection. However, a fluctuation in weight after a bird reaches 20 grams is normal. Within a few days, black pinfeathers begin to appear. They are able to climb, and they exhibit preening behavior, even with no feathers.

8 to 10 days — Feathers begin to unfurl.
15 to 17 days — Eyes open. They are subtle blue in color at first, but turn brown by 21 days. (Birds which are stressed by excessive heat or emaciation may have their eyes open at a much earlier age.)
21 days — Fully feathered and "practice flapping."
30 days — Flying.

TABLE 1. DISPOSITION OF CHIMNEY SWIFTS HAND-RAISED WITH AND WITHOUT SALIVA "INOCULATION"

Age in Days	1	2	3	4	5	6	7	8	Totals
Without saliva (N = 8)									
Expired	—	2	2	2	1	—	—	1	8
Released	—	0	0	0	0	—	—	0	0
With saliva (N = 40)									
Expired	2	2	0	1	0	0	0	1	6
Released	0	1	3	6	4	16	3	1	34

NESTLING HOUSING

Line the sides of a tall box or basket with a snag-free cloth such as muslin, and place unscented facial tissue in the bottom to facilitate cleaning. Until feathered, the birds will need external heat (85°F) and high humidity (60% to 70%). Until the birds are feathered, it is preferable to use a "hospital box" or incubator/brooder with automatic thermostat and indirect or filtered sunlight.

NATURAL DIET AND FEEDING HABITS

Chimney swifts catch flying insects on the wing and will dive at trees and shrubs in passing, to pick insects, bugs, spiders, etc. from the tips of leaves and branches. During the first week of life, baby chimney swifts are fed by regurgitation from the gullet of the adult. After six or seven days, the parents no longer regurgitate, but will form a ball of insects or "pellet" which is stored in a throat pouch until it is fed to the young.

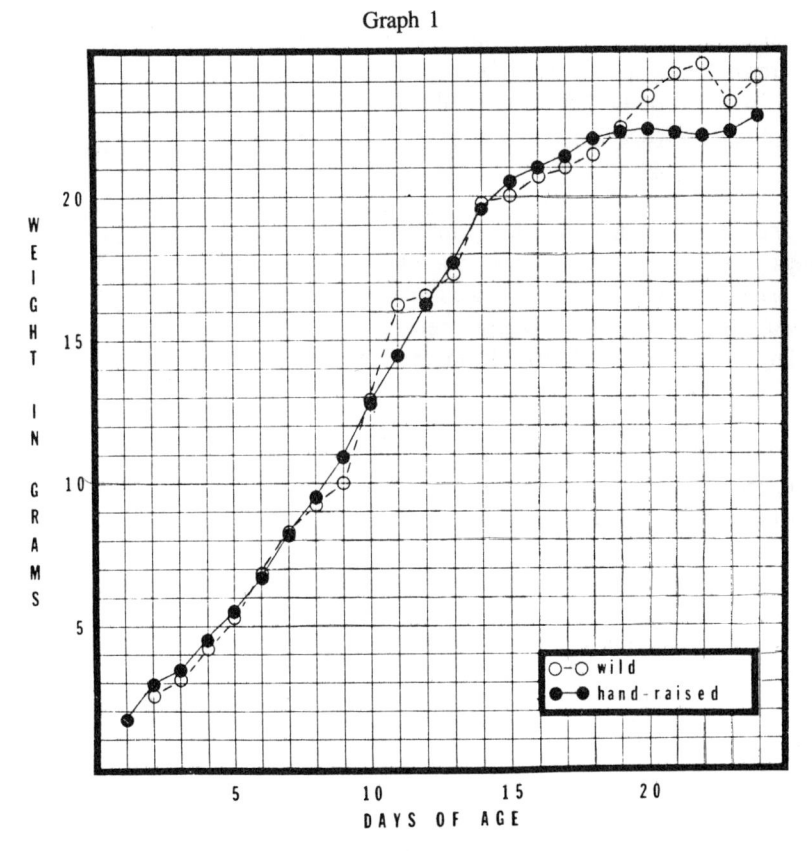

Graph 1

Growth Rate Comparison of Chimney Swifts:
Hand-raised (Kyle 1985) vs. Wild (Fischer 1958)

REHYDRATION

Because chimney swifts nest during the hottest time of the year, the vast majority of babies presented for rehabilitation will be dehydrated—at least to some degree. Birds fed under these conditions will not be able to digest food properly, and may die if not rehydrated first. As soon as a swift is acquired for rehabilitation, it should be given three to four drops of 10:1 Gatorade®: Nutri-cal® mix. This should be repeated every 30 minutes, regardless of the bird's age, until a moist stool is observed. Once a normal stool is observed, small amounts of the "Substitute Diet" should be introduced. Fluid therapy may take as long as 12 hours.

SUBSTITUTE DIET

Small mealworms (not the jumbo kind from bait stores which contain steroids) are drowned in a small amount of:

- 1 Tbsp.   Avimin® liquid mineral supplement;
- 1/4 tsp.   Plex-sol® C or 1/2 tsp. Avi-Con® powdered vitamin supplement (high in folic acid);
- 8 oz.   distilled water;

The mealworms must then be sprinkled with Plus Yeast® protein powder (for essential amino-acids) and dipped in a 50/50 mixture of full-strength Nutri-cal® and plain, active-culture yogurt. Once feathers begin to unfurl, part of a small piece of soaked-until-soft Purina High-Protein Dog Meal® should be added to each feeding. Both the yogurt/Nutri-cal® mix and the soaked dog food must be prepared fresh every two hours to prevent spoilage.

When feeding unfeathered birds, the mealworms should at first be "tenderized" by pinching the head and all along the body with tweezers. If this is not done, the birds may have difficulty swallowing or digesting the food and will sometimes pass a mealworm whole.

TABLE 2. CHIMNEY SWIFT DIET: PROPORTIONS OF CONSTITUENTS (weight in grams)

Constituent	Weight
Mealworms (50)	5.00
Hi-Pro® (dry weight—three small pieces)	0.60
Yogurt	0.45
Nutri-cal®	0.40
Plus Yeast®	0.10
Plex-Sol® C/Avimin® drowning mix (1.1 cc)	1.30
Distilled water (for soaking Hi-Pro)	1.80
Total average daily consumption	9.65

FEEDING

Chimney swifts' feeding responses can be triggered by tapping the basket, tapping their beaks, gently brushing their faces with a facial tissue, or gently blowing on the birds (simulates parents' wings). They respond by bobbing their heads down, chattering loudly and gulping at anything close by. With a little practice, they can be taught to feed from above with a pair of tweezers.

Each bird should be given as many mealworms (prepared as described in "Substitute Diet") every 30 minutes, 12 to 13 hours per day until its eyes are open, then every hour until fully feathered, and then every two hours until released. Older fledglings may have to be force-fed four to six mealworms every hour until they learn to accept food from the tweezers. Juveniles and adults may never learn to take food and may have to be force-fed up until the time of release. Remember: *Never feed solid food* until the bird has been properly rehydrated. Because swifts feed on the wing and are unable to perch, they will never learn to self-feed in captivity.

One or two drops of distilled water from a curved-tip irrigating syringe should follow each feeding. Place the drops on the bird's beak—NOT IN ITS THROAT.

TABLE 3. CHIMNEY SWIFT DISPOSITION IN TEXAS

	Released	*Expired*	*Totals*
1980–1984[1]			
Miscellaneous Diets			
Adults	19	15	34
Immature	76	223	299
Totals	95	238	333
Percent	29%	71%	
1983–1984[2]			
Substitute Diet[3]			
Adults	7	10	17 (15)[4]
Immature	71	31	102 (21)[4]
Totals	78	41	119 (36)[4]
Percent	66%	34%	
1985[2]			
Substitute Diet[3]			
Adults	2	2	4 (4)[4]
Immature	116	31	147 (24)[4]
Totals	118	33	151 (28)[4]
Percent	78%	22%	

[1] Statistics taken from the active Scientific Permits file, Texas Parks and Wildlife Department, September, 1985.

[2] Statistics taken from Animal Care and Research Committee Archives, Wildlife Rescue, Inc. of Austin, Texas.

[3] Mealworms, Purina High-Protein Dog Meal®, yogurt, Nutri-cal®, Plus Yeast Protein Powder®, Avimin®, Plex-Sol® C (or Avi-Con®), prepared as described.

[4] Number of birds which were ill or injured when acquired.

Chimney swifts become fond of these droplets and may begin biting them from the tip of the syringe.

Caution: Because of the frantic nature of their feeding response, special care must be taken to keep the birds' faces clean. A swift's nares are very far forward. Be careful not to get food in them. It will harden and be difficult to remove. Always clean the bird's face with a damp tissue after each feeding.

FLEDGLING HOUSING

Fledgling swifts require a large area for practice flying—at least 10' × 15' × 8' tall...the larger, the better. Any windows should be covered to prevent the birds from flying into them and becoming injured. Some textured surface (such as burlap) should be provided on at least two opposite walls for the swifts to cling to. Once swifts begin to fly, they must have access to this area during all daylight hours until release. Any less than complete access will lead to improper development and may render a swift unreleasable.

TABLE 4. GROWTH RATE OF HAND-RAISED CHIMNEY SWIFTS
(average of twelve individuals/five broods)

Days of age	Average weight in grams			Development
	High	Low	Average	
1	1.9	1.7	1.8	Pink, blind and naked.
2	3.0	3.0	3.0	Pin feathers begin to appear.
3	3.6	3.6	3.6	Exhibiting preening behavior.
4	4.5	4.5	4.5	
5	6.0	5.3	5.5	
6	7.2	5.9	6.7	
7	8.4	7.5	8.1	
8	10.3	9.3	9.5	Feathers begin to unfurl.
9	12.2	8.3	10.9	Feathers begin to unfurl.
10	14.7	11.4	12.7	Feathers begin to unfurl.
11	15.5	13.1	14.5	
12	18.7	13.2	16.3	
13	20.4	16.0	17.7	
14	21.0	16.6	19.5	
15	22.1	17.5	20.5	Eyes begin to open (15 to 17 days)—
16	22.9	19.0	21.0	pale, milky blue at first.
17	23.5	19.9	21.5	
18	23.8	20.0	22.0	
19	23.6	19.0	22.1	
20	24.4	19.1	22.3	Eyes have turned brown.
21	24.3	21.0	22.3	Fully feathered.
22	24.7	20.8	22.2	"Practice flapping."
23	25.1	20.3	22.3	
24	24.0	21.8	22.9	

After 24 days, the weight of each bird fluctuated greatly, and no clear pattern of growth was evident.

RELEASE

After a week of practice flying, and when the birds' wings cross by an inch or more when at rest, release should be considered. In order to survive in the wild, chimney swifts must be perfect flyers. They should be able to maneuver and turn sharply, hover, and act "restless" prior to release. A swift which is reluctant to fly probably has some physical problem or is too young to release. Release weight for hand-raised chimney swifts should be approximately 20 grams, and the wing cord (measured from the epaulet to the tip of the longest primary) should be approximately 127 mm.

Chimney swifts are migratory and very communal. Always release them into a known population at least two weeks prior to normal migration time. Early on a calm morning, locate a group of chimney swifts and toss the bird skyward as they fly overhead. Usually, if the new bird strays, some of the others will swoop down to show it the way.

Another method for release is to place the bird above the damper inside a chimney where other swifts are living. If all goes well, the bird will climb up to

TABLE 5. WEIGHT AND WING CORD OF HAND-RAISED CHIMNEY SWIFTS[1] (N = 116)

Wing Cord		Weight	
Millimeters	Number	Grams	Number
115[2]	1	16.5	3
116[2]	1	17.0	1
120	1	17.5	7
123	1	18.0	14
124	5	18.5	18
125	7	19.0	23
126	1	20.0	10
127	9	20.5	9
128	9	21.0	2
129	10	21.5	3
130	14	22.0	2
131	8		
132	11		
133	8		
134	4		
135	12		
136	4		
137	5		
138	1		
139	2		
140	1		
141	1		

[1] At the time of release, 1985.
[2] Tips of the primaries were broken off, but flight ability was adequate for release.

the others and join their colony. Check the chimney periodically to make certain the bird has not fallen back down or gotten into a bind. Back-up feeding is usually not possible. However, if released where they are raised, some swifts will return for a few days after release.

SPECIAL CONSIDERATIONS

If aspiration does occur when giving a bird water from a syringe, using distilled water will minimize the chances of causing pneumonia. Distilled water has no suspended particles to irritate the lungs.

Unlined baskets have caused problems of injured feet and broken primary feathers. These accidents can be avoided by lining the basket with a snag-free material such as muslin. An empty mealworm bag works quite well.

Young swifts which are not given yogurt will not be able to properly digest their food and may develop visible problems such as excess mucus in the mouth, off-color droppings, poor feathering, and may actually die. Similarly, swifts raised on a diet lacking the protein powder have suffered from poor feather development. Yogurt and protein powder are essentials—not extras.

Baby swifts are subject to several injuries simply because of the location of their nests. The sounds they make when begging for food are often mistaken for those of bats or even snakes. Fires intended to drive them off cause poisoning from toxic fumes and burns. Inhalation problems should be treated with oxygen therapy immediately by a veterinarian. Burns should be flooded with sterile water or isotonic saline once or twice daily until new tissue begins to grow. Eyes should be checked for corneal damage and kept moist with an "artificial tears" solution.

Because they cling so well, claws are sometimes damaged or ripped out when the youngsters are pulled from their chimney or handled too roughly. An ointment such as Panalog® will reduce swelling and the chance of infection. Be sure to consult your veterinarian before using any medication.

INJURED ADULTS

Injured adults must be force-fed about six to ten drowned mealworms (prepared as described in "Substitute Diet") and a part of a piece of Purina High Protein Dog Meal® every two hours during daylight. They also need the water supplement. Until able to fly, the bird should be confined in a small cage with a rough

TABLE 6. WEEKLY ACQUISITION OF IMMATURE CHIMNEY SWIFTS: 1985 (N = 141)

Week ending:	June 8 15 22 29	July 6 13 20 27	August 3 10 17
Number:	13 6 26 24	15 2 19 22	6 7 1

log or brick for it to cling to as well as muslin lining on at least one side. Because injured swifts will often lie flat on the bottom of their cage, care must be taken to keep the vent clean and open. Several days of practice flying in a large room is necessary prior to release.

RELATED SPECIES

In Texas, the only other species of swift likely to be encountered is the white-throated swift (*Aeronautes saxatalis*). It is a larger bird: six to seven inches, 26 to 36 grams, and is usually not found east of the Trans-Pecos region. Characteristics are a white throat and flanks, a slightly notched tail and feathered feet with thicker, shorter claws than those of the chimney swift. Because roosting and nesting sites are caves and crevices rather than shafts, caging should include hollow logs and rocks.

These birds do cling to vertical surfaces, but they will walk around and investigate the cage. They will usually burrow into a tight spot to sleep. Limited experience has shown that the "Substitute Diet" described for chimney swifts is satisfactory for adult white-throated swifts.

ONGOING RESEARCH

Prior to July of 1985, all chimney swifts which were acquired under six days of age died following three to four days of apparently normal development. Because necropsies revealed a bacterial infection by a different Gram-negative organism as the cause of death in each case, immune incompetence was suspected rather than equipment contamination. Whether this condition was due to the young age of the birds, stress, or the absence of some substance provided by the parents during the feeding process was unknown, but the latter was assumed.

After this time, all swifts under seven days of age (feathers sheathed) were fed a mealworm coated with the saliva from the throat of an injured but otherwise healthy adult three or four times each day in addition to the standard "Substitute Diet," until they were approximately sixteen days of age (eyes open). Once this procedure was initiated, 94 percent of all uninjured birds acquired at three days of age or older (and one individual no more than 48 hours old) survived, developed normally and were subsequently released.

Because the constituents of the saliva and the mechanisms involved are unknown at this time, and because concurrent controls were not used, the results are not conclusive. However, the improved success rate presents a strong case in favor of recommending saliva transfer or "inoculation" as a standard practice in hand-rearing very young chimney swifts.

TABLE 7. REASON FOR ACQUISITION OF
IMMATURE CHIMNEY SWIFTS: 1985 (N = 141)

Fell from nest	41
Entire nest fell	46
Forcibly removed*	33
Other	21

*By homeowner or professional chimney sweep at homeowner's request.

EVALUATION OF THE SUBSTITUTE DIET

Prior to July, 1983 and the introduction of the diet described in this paper, the known percent of releases for hand-raised chimney swifts in Texas was no more than 29 percent. Since that time, the overall success rate for young, uninjured birds raised on the diet has been approximately 78 percent.

Additional evidence in favor of the diet includes two individuals that were kept for extended periods of time. A white-throated swift recovering from a slow-healing head injury was released after eighteen months of care, and a chimney swift which was acquired as a nestling in July, 1984 is still in captivity (September, 1985) due to a shoulder injury. Both birds maintained a normal body weight and went through a complete moult with perfect feather replacement.

The average daily consumption of the "Substitute Diet" by a hand-raised chimney swift weighing 18 to 24 grams (13 days old to adult) was as listed in Table 2.

SOURCES

Avi-Con®: Vet-A-Mix, Inc., Shenandoah, Iowa 51601 and available from veterinarians.
Avimin®: Lambert-Kay, Cranbury, New Jersey 08512 and pet stores.
Berry baskets: Grocery stores (used to package strawberries, cherries, mushrooms, etc.).
Brooders: Sears, Roebuck and Company and local feed stores.
Gatorade®: Stokely-Van Camp, Inc., Chicago, Illinois 60654 and grocery stores.
Hospital box: A "hospital box" is a ventilated enclosure which provides an environment with a constant air temperature and relative humidity. A satisfactory set-up can be made by laying an aquarium on its side on a heating pad and taping a flap of clear plastic to the open side to act as a door. A damp sponge placed in the corner will act as a good humidity source. The temperature in an improvised system must be constantly monitored with a thermometer placed on the same level as the nest of baby birds. With the door on the side rather than on top, less heat escapes during the frequent feedings, and the environment remains more stable. If condensation begins to appear, the humidity is too high and must be adjusted. The ideal hospital box will have an automatic thermostat which can be set for the desired temperature. The heating element and thermostat for such a system may be available at feed stores specializing in poultry equipment.
Hygrometers: Sears, Roebuck and Company and local feed stores.
Incubators: Sears, Roebuck and Company and local feed stores.
Mealworms: Rainbow Mealworms, 126 E. Spruce Street, Compton, California 90224, 213/635-1494. Do not use jumbo or mealworms from bait shops because they contain steroids.
Nutri-cal®: Evesco Pharmaceuticals, Buena, New Jersey 08310 or your veterinarian.
Plex-Sol C®: Vet-A-Mix, Inc., Shenandoah, Iowa 51601 and available from veterinarians.
Plus Yeast Protein Powder®: Plus Products, Irvine, California 92714 and health food stores.
Purina High Protein Dog Meal®: grocery or feed stores.
Syringes (curved irrigating), Monoject #12: available at pharmacies.
Thermometers: Sears, Roebuck and Company and local feed stores.

REFERENCES

Bull, J. and Farrand, J., Jr. 1977. *The Audubon Society Field Guide to North American Birds—Eastern Region*. Alfred A. Knopf, Inc., New York.

Fischer, Richard B. 1958. *The Breeding Biology of the Chimney Swift*. New York State Museum and Science Service, Bulletin #368.

———. Secrets of the Swift. *The Living Bird Quarterly*. (Vol. 2, No. 4): pp. 5-8.

Hickman, M. and Guy, M. 1973. *Care of the Wild Feathered and Furred*. Unity Press, Santa Cruz.

Kyle, Georgean. 1984. An Introduction to the Role of Vitamin, Mineral and Amino-Acid Supplements in the Avian Diet. Animal Care and Research Committee Archives, Wildlife Rescue, Inc., Austin, Texas.

Lyons, Jane. 1979. Supplement to Care of Orphaned or Injured Birds. *Wildlife Rehabilitation Course Manual*. Wildlife Rescue, Inc., Austin, Texas.

National Geographic Society. 1983. *Field Guide to the Birds of North America*. Washington, D.C.

Peterson, Roger Tory. 1963. *A Field Guide to the Birds of Texas*. Houghton Mifflin Co., Boston, Massachusetts.

Terres, John K. 1982. *The Audubon Society Encyclopedia of North American Birds*. Alfred A. Knopf, New York.

Welty, Joel C. 1982. *The Life of Birds*. Saunders College Publishing, Philadelphia.

Whittemore, Margaret. 1981. *Chimney Swifts and Their Relatives*. Nature Book Publishers, Jackson, Mississippi.

Financial and technical assistance with chimney swift care and research were provided in part by Wildlife Rescue, Inc., Austin, Texas, and its members, Katherine A. Van Winkle, DVM, of Barton Creek Animal Clinic, Austin, Texas, and the Avian Diagnostic Lab, Texas A&M University, College Station, Texas.

Some chimney cleaning companies openly advertise bird removal, and will illegally remove nests and baby swifts from chimneys for a fee. This activity should be reported to state and federal game wardens.

This paper is copyrighted 1985 and is a revised edition of *Care of Chimney Swifts*, copyright by Paul Kyle (1984).

HAND-REARING CAROLINA AND BEWICK'S WRENS©

Paul and Georgean Kyle

Wildlife Rescue, Inc.
401 Deep Eddy
Austin, TX 78703

INTRODUCTION

Wrens are "plump, stumpy, energetic" little birds with upcocked tails and long, slightly down-curved beaks. The most common nesting species in the central Texas area are Bewick's (*Thyromanes bewickii*) and Carolina (*Thyrothorus ludovicianus*).

The 13 mm to 14 mm (5" to 5½") adult Bewick's is grey to grey-brown with a white breast, a conspicuous white eye stripe and white corners on the outer tail feathers. The adult weighs about 12 grams (.4 ounces) and has an average wingspan of 18.4 cm (7").

The 14 mm to 15 mm (5½" to 6") adult Carolina is a slightly larger, stockier bird and reddish brown in color with a buff-colored breast. It also has a white eye stripe, but lacks the white tail corners of the Bewick's. The adult weighs about 16 grams (.56 ounces) and has an average wingspan of 18.5 cm (7.25"). Both sexes of each species are outwardly identical in appearance.

These species of wrens nest in rural and urban areas, often in close proximity to or actually in man-made structures. Favorite nest sites include nest boxes, hanging plants, pockets of clothing, grills of automobiles, motor boats and sometimes even hollow trees. Pair bonding and nest building begin in March and continue throughout the summer. The male Carolina will build several nests, and the female will line the one of her choice before settling in to lay her eggs. Both species will lay three to nine white eggs with brown speckles (Bewick's 16 × 13 mm, Carolina 19 × 15 mm). Incubation is by the female and takes 12 to 14 days. The young are fed by both parents.

EGGS

Because of their ubiquitous nesting habits, an entire clutch of eggs—nest and all—is often "rescued" by the public. If replacement is not possible, the eggs should be placed in a small, tissue-lined basket in a commercial incubator with a constant temperature of 95 to 100°F with a constant humidity source. They should be carefully turned 1/4 turn every hour until hatched.

Note: Birds which are less than three days of age may not have received necessary antibodies or a normal balance of beneficial flora from the parents and lack sufficient immunity to common bacterial infections. At the time of this writing, no positive solution to this problem exists, except proper hygiene.

DESCRIPTION OF NESTLINGS

- Altricial with sparse, grey down on head, back and thighs.
- Pale yellow gape flanges with brighter yellow mouth.
- Dark, narrow, pointed beak.
- The tip and spurs of a Carolina wren's tongue are dark. Bewick's wrens lack these markings.

DEVELOPMENT

The average growth rate for hand-raised wrens should be about .5 to 1 gram of body weight per day for the first two weeks. A weight gain of less than .3 gram during this period may indicate a metabolic problem, usually related to a systemic infection. However, a sharp weight loss directly after a bird fledges is normal.

2 days — Pin feathers begin to develop on the wings.
5-6 days — Pin feathers on the wings and tail are prominent, and the eyes are open.
10 days — Wing and tail feathers are breaking out of the sheaths, and the body pin feathers are prominent.
14 days — All feathers are out of the sheaths, and the birds are hopping out of the nest.
21 days — Birds are able to fly well and are pecking at everything. A Bewick's tail will be noticeably longer than a Carolina's at this age. Both species will begin to experiment with a variety of vocalizations by three weeks.
30 days — Wrens should be well on the way to self-feeding.

NESTLING HOUSING

The babies should be placed in a berry basket or margarine tub lined with unscented, white facial tissue. The tissue should be changed whenever soiled. Wrens are very susceptible to problems related to drafts, temperature fluctuations and dehydration. A heating pad alone *is not adequate.* They must be housed in an incubator/brooder or "hospital box" with constant temperature (88°F), humidity (60% to 70%) and indirect sunlight until fully feathered.

NATURAL DIET

Wrens eat spiders, flying insects, ants, beetles, scale insects, grasshoppers, caterpillars, etc. Less than three percent of the diet may include some fruits and berries.

NATURAL HABITAT

Woodlands with thick underbrush, rotting wood and a good water source will usually have a strong wren population.

SUBSTITUTE DIET

Small mealworms (not the jumbo kind from bait stores which contain steroids) are drowned in a small amount of:

- 1 Tbsp. Avimin® liquid mineral supplement.
- 1/4 tsp. Plex-sol C® (or 1/2 tsp. Avi-Con®) powdered vitamin supplement (high in folic acid).
- 8 oz. Distilled water.

The mealworms must then be sprinkled with Plus Yeast® protein powder (for essential amino-acids) and dipped in a 50/50 mixture of full-strength Nutri-cal® and plain, active-culture yogurt. Once feathers begin to unfurl, part of a small piece of soaked-until-soft Purina High-Protein Dog Meal® should be added to each feeding. Both the yogurt/Nutri-cal® mix and the soaked dog food must be prepared fresh every two hours to prevent spoilage. When feeding unfeathered birds, the mealworms must first be "tenderized" by pinching the head and all along the body with tweezers. If this is not done, the birds may have difficulty swallowing or digesting the foods, and will sometimes pass a mealworm whole.

TABLE 1. WREN DISPOSITION IN TEXAS (Bewick's and Carolina)

	Released	Expired	Totals
1978–1984[1]			
Miscellaneous diets	38	51	89
Percent	43%	57%	
1983–1984[2]			
Substitute diet[3]	23	11	34 (8)[4]
Percent	68%	32%	
1985[2]			
Substitute diet[3]	31	11 (7)[4]	42 (4)[5]
Percent	74%	26%	

[1]Statistics from Texas Parks and Wildlife Department, active Scientific Permit files, September, 1985.
[2]Statistics taken from Animal Care and Research Committee archives, Wildlife Rescue, Inc. of Austin, Texas.
[3]Mealworms, Purina High-Protein Dog Meal®, yogurt, Nutri-cal®, Plus Yeast Protein Powder®, Avimin®, Plex-Sol C® (or Avi-Con®), prepared as described.
[4]Less than 2 days of age when acquired.
[5]Ill or injured when acquired.

FEEDING

Because a wren's mouth is so tiny, the use of tweezers (with rounded tips) is strongly recommended. Their mouths will open readily when they are stimulated, but close quickly. Each gaping bird should be fed as many mealworms (prepared as described in "Substitute Diet") as it wants every 30 minutes from sunrise until 9:00 p.m. to 10:00 p.m. (25 to 30 feedings per day) until feathered and picking up food on its own, then every hour until completely self-feeding. One or two drops of *distilled* water from a curved irrigating syringe should follow each feeding. Place the drops of water on the bird's beak; never put water or any liquid directly into a bird's throat. (See more under heading, "Special Problems").

FLEDGLING HOUSING

Once wrens are feathered and out of the nest, a 2' × 2' × 4' long wire cage is minimum. Fiberglass window screening is preferable because it will "give" when the birds become excited and frantically bounce off the walls—as they quite often do. Also, moths and other small flying insects can be contained to encourage self-feeding. The only drawback to window screening is that it provides no protection for the birds from predators, and such a cage cannot be safely left outdoors.

Because wrens are such nervous, inquisitive little birds, careful attention must be paid to their environment to ensure them a safe, secure habitat until the time of release. The habitat should have a paper-lined floor, smooth and rough perches, a potted plant and a "brush pile" of small branches with the leaves still attached. Young wrens like to sleep high in the cage and in a pile, so a sleeping shelf in a darkened upper corner will be well-used.

While Carolina wrens are fond of splashing around in a shallow dish of water, Bewick's wrens are partial to dust baths in loose, fine soil. Both water and soil should be provided as well as live food and some full sun for basking.

Once completely self-feeding, wrens should be allowed at least one week of exercise prior to release in a flight cage measuring at least 4' × 4' × 6' tall.

> *Note:* No more than six or seven wrens should ever be housed together, and then only birds of the same age. Young and mature alike are quarrelsome, even in a large flight cage, and have been know to kill a cagemate in overcrowded conditions.

RELEASE, BACK-UP FEEDING AND SUPPORT

It is very common for young wrens to return to the aviary for a few nights until they find another suitable roost, so ideally their final housing situation should be at the release sight. Wrens can be released at seven to eight weeks of age when they no longer wish to be hand-fed. Carolina and Bewick's wrens should weigh about 15 gm and 11 gm (respectively) at the time of release. The approximate wing cord (length of the wing measured from the epaulet to the tip of the longest primary) should be about 55 mm for Carolina and 50 mm for Bewick's. They are very territorial and should be released where some of the same species reside but density is low. Wrens will revert somewhat when released and must have back-up feeding for as long as two weeks or more in the form of mealworms and small pieces of soaked Purina High Protein Dog Meal®.

SPECIAL PROBLEMS

A healthy nestling wren's fecal sac is very large and dark brown in color. If yogurt is not added to the diet, the color will become progressively lighter (possibly indicating poor digestion) and the bird may die within 24 hours. Additionally, wrens raised on a diet lacking the protein powder have suffered from poor feather development. Yogurt and protein powder are essentials in the diet—not extras.

TABLE 2. GROWTH RATE OF HAND-RAISED WRENS
(Bewick's and Carolina)

Days of age	Bewick's[1]	Carolina[2]	Development
1	1.1	1.5	Sparse down on head, back, and thighs.
2	1.5	2.0	Pin feathers show on wings.
3	1.9	2.3	
4	2.2	3.5	
5	2.4	4.5	Eyes open.
6	2.5	5.5	Pin feathers on wing and tail prominent.
7	2.9	6.5	
8	3.7	7.5	
9	3.8	8.5	
10	4.7	9.5	Wing and tail feathers opening.
11	5.8	10.5	Body pin feathers prominent.
12	6.7	11.4	
13	7.2	12.4	
14	7.3	13.8	Completely feathered.
15	8.0	14.4	Out of the nest.
16	8.7	15.2	
17	9.2	15.8	
18	9.4	16.6	
19	10.0	17.0	
20	9.5	17.5	
21	9.9	18.2	Flying well, pecking at food.
22		19.3	
23		19.0	

[1]Average of 13 individuals/9 broods.
[2]Average of 7 individuals/4 broods.

Wrens have an extremely high metabolism and must be fed more frequently for a longer term than larger species of the same age. If a wren has gone a long time without food, it must be rehydrated before feeding. Failure to do so will usually result in the death of the bird. To be safe, any incoming baby wren should be given several drops of a 10:1 Gatorade®:Nutrical® mix (warmed) every 15 minutes until a wet stool is observed. Feeding can then be gradually started and fluid continued until a normal, well-contained stool is observed.

Wrens which have not been fed a proper diet may exhibit poor equilibrium or seizures due to low blood sugar or calcium deficiencies. If caught in time, this can sometimes be turned around. Treatment consists of one drop of dexamethasone (2 mg/ml) orally and the Nutrical®/Gatorade® fluid therapy as mentioned above. Check with your veterinarian before using any medication.

Because wrens are so prone to dehydration, they must have a constant water supplement. Even if a nestling skips a feeding (not uncommon), it should still be given a drop or two of water. Distilled water contains no suspended particles and will minimize problems of aspiration. Early signs of dehydration may be a lack of mucus around the fecal sac and incomplete expulsion of fecal material.

Wrens are nervous and high-strung. They should be transported as little as possible and not subjected to loud noises, music or too much disturbance around their cage. Wrens are also curiously disturbed by boldly striped or patterned clothing.

IMPLICATIONS FOR OTHER SPECIES

While the care techniques detailed in this paper are specifically for Carolina's and Bewick's wrens, the basic substitute diet has been used successfully with other avian insectivores including titmice, chickadees, nightjars, woodpeckers, chimney swifts, swallows and yellow-billed cuckoos. Even omnivores and seed-eaters such as jays, blackbirds and finches have done well on the diet as nestlings, but must have a greater variety as they begin to self-feed. Mockingbirds and flycatchers required additional calcium.

SOURCES

Avi-Con®: Vet-A-Mix, Inc., Shenandoah, Iowa 51601 and available from veterinarians.
Avimin®: Lambert-Kay, Cranbury, New Jersey 08512 and pet stores.
Berry baskets: Grocery stores (used to package strawberries, cherries, mushrooms, etc.).
Brooders: Sears, Roebuck and Company and local feed stores.
Gatorade®: Stokely-Van Camp, Inc., Chicago, Illinois 60654 and grocery stores.
Hospital box: A "hospital box" is a ventilated enclosure which provides an environment with a constant air temperature and relative humidity. A satisfactory set-up can be made by laying an aquarium on its side on a heating pad and taping a flap of clear plastic to the open side to act as a door. A damp sponge placed in the corner will act as a good humidity source. The temperature in an improvised system must be constantly moditored with a thermometer placed on the same level as the nest of baby

birds. With the door on the side rather than on top, less heat escapes during the frequent feedings, and the environment remains more stable. If condensation begins to appear, the humidity is too high and must be adjusted. The ideal hospital box will have an automatic thermostat which can be set for the desired temperature. The heating element and thermostat for such a system may be available at feed stores specializing in poultry equipment.

Hygrometers: Sears, Roebuck and Company and local feed stores.
Incubators: Sears, Roebuck and Company and local feed stores.
Mealworms: Rainbow Mealworms, 126 E. Spruce Street, Compton, California 90224, 213/635-1494. Do not use jumbo or mealworms from bait shops because they contain steroids.
Nutri-cal®: Evesco Pharmaceuticals, Buena, New Jersey 08310 or your veterinarian.
Plex-Sol C®: Vet-A-Mix, Inc., Shenandoah, Iowa 51601 and available from veterinarians.
Plus yeast Protein Powder®: Plus Products, Irvine, California 92714 and health food stores.
Purina High Protein Dog Meal®: Grocery or feed stores.
Syringes (curved irrigating), Monoject #12: Available at pharmacies.
Thermometers: Sears, Roebuck and Company and local feed stores.

REFERENCES

Hickman, M. and Guy, M., 1973. *Care of the Wild Feathered and Furred.* Unity Press, Santa Cruz.

Kyle, Georgean, 1984. An Introduction to the Role of Vitamin, Mineral and Amino-Acid Supplements in the Avian Diet. Animal Care and Research Committee Archives, Wildlife Rescue, Inc., Austin, Texas.

Lyons, Jane, 1979. Supplement to Care of Orphaned or Injured Birds. *Wildlife Rehabilitation Course Manual.* Wildlife Rescue, Inc., Austin, Texas.

Peterson, R.T., 1963. *A Field Guide to the Birds of Texas.* Houghton Mifflin Co., Boston, Massachusetts.

Terres, John K., 1982. *The Audubon Society Encyclopedia of North American Birds.* Alfred A. Knopf, New York.

Welty, Joel C., 1982. *The Life of Birds.* Saunders College Publications, Philadelphia.

Financial and technical assistance with wren care and research were provided in part by Wildlife Rescue, Inc. of Austin, Texas, and its members, Katherine A. Van Winkle, DVM, of Barton Creek Animal Clinic, Austin, Texas, and the Avian Diagnostic Lab, Texas A&M University, College Station, Texas.

This paper is copyrighted 1985 and is a revised edition of *Care of Orphaned Carolina and Bewick's Wrens,* copyright by Paul and Georgean Kyle (1983).

Programs for Particular Species

CONSERVATION PROGRAM FOR THE GOLDEN LION TAMARIN: CAPTIVE RESEARCH AND MANAGEMENT, ECOLOGICAL STUDIES, EDUCATIONAL STRATEGIES, AND REINTRODUCTION

Devra G. Kleiman, Benjamin B. Beck, James M. Dietz, Lou Ann Dietz and Jonathan D. Ballou

National Zoological Park
Smithsonian Institution
Washington, D.C. 20008

and

Adelmar F. Coimbra-Filho

Centro do Primatologia de Rio de Janeiro (FEEMA)
Rio de Janeiro, Brazil

ABSTRACT

This paper summarizes the conceptual framework and methodology of an integrated conservation program for the endangered Golden Lion Tamarin (*Leontopithecus rosalia*), including the preparation and reintroduction of captive-born Tamarins into the southeastern coastal rain forests of Brazil.

To ensure the long-term conservation of the Golden Lion Tamarins and their primary habitat, we have pursued research on behavior, genetics, medical problems, and management of the species in captivity; protection of remaining forest and restoration of degraded habitat within the species' original range; professional and public education in the areas of wildlife managment and conservation biology; and field studies of the behavioral ecology of the species, with regular censuses of the remaining wild population.

This program exemplifies the potential for fruitful interactions between zoo and field conservation efforts and is a unique case where collaborative efforts on an international scale have saved an endangered species from certain extinction.

INTRODUCTION

The future conservation of most threatened species will require not only the preservation and management of critical habitats but also scientifically managed propagation programs for captive animals by zoos. Zoos will undoubtedly have primary responsibility for the preservation and protection of genetic diversity through the maintenance of viable captive populations (or their deep-frozen equivalents). However, they should also have a role to play in supporting and contributing to the preservation of natural habitats through research and public education on environmental issues.

Conservation programs by zoos, by international and national conservation organizations, and by governments should converge, as the size of critical habitats and refuges becomes smaller and the amount of land available to zoos and their involvement with endangered species become greater.

A successful conservation program involves a management plan, and an educational strategy. Basic research is essential for the development of scientifically-based recommendations on preservation and management, whether the management plan is within a zoo or field context, and for educational programs.

Traditionally, the fields of psychology, physiology, behavior, reproduction, and genetics have been emphasized in zoo research. The results of such research can lead to improved management of a captive population. Field research in similar disciplines, as well as in ecology, not only improves the preservation of a single species, but also often results in the protection of a portion of the natural habitat within a refuge or national park.

Basic research also provides the foundation upon which the educational elements of a conservation program must be built. Creating a public constituency sensitive to and supportive of conservation programs cannot be accomplished without the attractive presentation of research information which is appropriate for the target audience. There is an enormous need to improve the public image of conservation in developing and developed countries. Systematically-developed educational programs—based on the presentation of results from scientific research—are thus ultimately indispensable to successful long-term conservation.

Additionally, conservationists in developed countries must recognize that the support and conduct of future conservation programs must ultimately be in the hands of trained professionals from the less-developed countries. Thus, scientists from developed countries should include in their overseas budgets support for training in conservation biology to ensure that a cadre of professional wildlife managers and biologists can continue programs initiated from outside.

One major area where zoo conservation interacts with programs of maintaining and preserving natural habitats involves the use of reintroductions, translocations, and introductions of endangered species (see Konstant and Mittermeier 1982 for definition of terms). These techniques are being developed and may be used to increase the chances of survival of a natural population, mainly when the wild population and its critical habitat are exceedingly vulnerable.

Konstant and Mittermeier (1982) have summarized the limited attempts to translocate, reintroduce, and introduce various primate species within South America. Many appear to have been unsuccessful, although the results have often been difficult to evaluate. One major flaw has been the paucity of long-term monitoring of individuals to determine the impact of the release on the local fauna and flora or the effectiveness of the preparation of the animals prior to the release (most are not prepared). Konstant and Mittermeier (1982) recommend the use of these techniques in only limited cases, especially because of the potential damage that the introduction of animals may have on an already established fauna and flora.

This paper summarizes a conservation program which includes reintroduction of captive-born animals into the wild, in the context of a broad strategy to save a species from extinction. In this case, the reintroduction created local interest in and support for habitat and species protection, fostering the development of techniques to prepare (rehabilitate) animals for a return to the wild, and repopulated areas devoid of the species, while paving the way for an increase in genetic diversity of the captive and wild population.

HISTORY OF GOLDEN LION TAMARIN CONSERVATION EFFORTS

The Golden Lion Tamarin was historically found in the coastal forests of the states of Rio de Janeiro and Espírito Santo, south of the Rio Doce. The original range is now reduced to remnant and scattered forests within the state of Rio de Janeiro. Available habitat is probably less than two percent of the original forest inhabited by Golden Lion Tamarins (Hershkovitz 1977; Coimbra-Filho and Mittermeier 1977; Kleiman 1981).

The Golden Lion Tamarin's precarious condition has resulted primarily from the near total destruction of the Atlantic coastal rain forests of Southeastern Brazil. Intensive logging, initially for the commercially valuable tree species and then for other human activities such as farming and cattle ranching, has contributed to the nearly complete deforestation of this region. More recently, forest destruction has intensified, with charcoal being used as an alternative fuel to petroleum both for home consumption and to fuel ceramics factories.

Finally, a relatively new threat to the remaining forest has arisen from the construction of condominiums and weekend cottages near beaches with some of the only remaining Golden Lion Tamarin habitat. These condominiums are being developed for the wealthier inhabitants of Rio de Janeiro, a city within a two hour drive of the major remaining Golden Lion Tamarin population.

In addition to habitat destruction, Golden Lion Tamarins have traditionally been captured for pets and for exhibition in zoos both within and outside of Brazil. It has been illegal to capture and/or export wild Golden Lion Tamarins since the late 1960's, thus international trade in this species has declined significantly within the past 15 years. However, individuals still occasionally appear for sale in the markets of major cities like Rio de Janeiro.

Adelmar Coimbra-Filho and his colleagues have been working within Brazil for nearly 20 years to ensure the survival of wild Golden Lion Tamarins. These efforts have resulted in (1) the creation of the Poço das Antas Biological Reserve for *Leontopithecus rosalia* in 1974 and (2) the development of a breeding facility for endangered primates endemic to Brazil (Rio de Janeiro Primate Center CPRJ-FEEMA)(Coimbra-Filho and Mittermeier 1977).

International zoo involvement with the preservation of Golden Lion Tamarins was initiated in the United States in the late 1960's when the Wild Animal Propagation Trust (WAPT—now disbanded) convened a conference entitled "Saving the Lion Marmoset" (Bridgwater 1972).

This conference reviewed the status of the species in captivity and in the wild, and recommended research areas that needed immediate attention for the future reproduction and management of the species in captivity. Shortly thereafter, Marvin Jones (1973) published the first International Studbook for the Golden Lion Tamarin which contained information on natality, mortality and animal pairings for this species in captivity. The existence of the Studbook permitted the development of an aggressive program of management for the captive population.

Following the 1972 WAPT Conference, the National Zoological Park, Smithsonian Institution initiated long-term studies on the reproduction, social behavior, and husbandry of this species in captivity. The initiation of this captive research and management program occurred simultaneously with Coimbra-Filho's efforts to protect remaining habitats in Brazil and develop a captive breeding program for endangered Brazilian primates. These two efforts were the basis for the Golden Lion Tamarin Conservation Program as it exists today, with its five major elements.

GOLDEN LION TAMARIN CONSERVATION PROGRAM

The Captive Population: Cooperative Research and Management

When the National Zoological Park (NZP) initiated a research program with Golden Lion Tamarins in the early 1970s, it was estimated that there were fewer than 80 individuals of this species remaining in captivity. At that time all projections suggested that the captive population was destined for extinction since the mortality rate of the captive animals was exceeding natality (see Kleiman 1977a; Kleiman and Jones 1977; Kleiman, Ballou and Evans 1982).

The major goal of the NZP research program was to find methods to improve the poor reproductive performance and survivorship of animals in captivity. Thus studies of reproduction, social behavior, and nutrition were initiated with the aim of applying the results of the studies to the captive management of the species.

Simultaneously, the major biomedical problems were being defined and physiological norms established. The results of these studies have been summarized and published in a variety of periodicals (see Bush et al. 1980; Bush et al. 1982; Hoage 1977, 1982; Kleiman 1977, 1981, 1983; Kleiman, Hoage and Green, in press; Kleiman, Ballou and Evans 1982; Montali et al. 1982), and have enabled us to manage better this captive population, resulting recently in a phenomenal growth in numbers.

Some of the major behavioral findings include confirmation that (1) Golden Lion Tamarins breed best in captivity when maintained in monogamous pairs and nuclear family groups and (2) monogamy appears to be maintained by both physiological and behavioral suppression of maturing offspring (Kleiman 1978, 1979).

Both parents and older juveniles participate in the raising of infants within the family group, and juvenile experience with younger siblings appears to be important for their later sexual and parental competence (Hoage 1977, 1982). Among the behaviors exhibited by family groups which are critical to the successful development of young are the carrying of infants, and the active sharing of food with the young during and after weaning, a behavioral attribute found in few mammals (Brown and Mack 1978; Hoage 1977, 1982).

Additionally, a major finding with a powerful impact on captive management has been that females, including related females, exhibit incredibly high levels of aggression towards each other (Kleiman 1979). Deaths of several daughters (and one pregnant mother) have occurred while they were still living with their families, prior to and during the time of puberty. Aggression towards daughters by mothers occurs even before sexual maturity, when the daughters are likely to be reproductively inactive.

Coimbra-Filho and colleagues have also contributed to our understanding of Golden Lion Tamarin biology, with studies of taxonomy, reproduction, distribution, and ecology (Coimbra-Filho 1969, 1977; Coimbra-Filho and Mittermeier 1973, 1977, 1978; Coimbra-Filho and Maia 1979ab; Rosenberger and Coimbra-Filho 1984). These studies have provided considerable groundwork for the ecological research and the reintroduction.

In 1974, D.G. Kleiman assumed responsibility for the International Golden Lion Tamarin Studbook and began to manage the captive Golden Lion Tamarin population at an international level. In the late 1970s as the captive population of Golden Lion Tamarins began to grow, it first became possible to send pairs to institutions which had not previously been involved in the Golden Lion Tamarin breeding program. Concurrently, an international Cooperative Research and Management Agreement (CRMA) was drawn up and signed by the owners and new holders of Golden Lion Tamarins. The standards for Golden Lion Tamarin management and maintenance were defined, and both owners and holders agreed to adhere to decisions on population management made by an elected Management Committee. The agreement also included a prohibition on permitting Golden Lion Tamarins to enter commercial trade.

Major decisions by the Management Committee in recent years have involved providing animals for exhibit and breeding to institutions wishing to join the Golden Lion Tamarin consortium, and developing a management plan to ensure the long-term viability of the captive population through demographic and genetic management. The latter has involved (1) the removal of a certain number of individuals from the breeding pool via vasectomy, hormone implants, and single-sexed groupings; (2) altering the genetic composition of the captive population by pairing animals to maximize the contribution from individual founders which are under-represented in the captive gene pool; and (3) developing mechanisms for putting a ceiling on the total size of the captive population (see Kleiman, Ballou, and Evans 1982; Ballou 1985).

Recent studies in genetics and physiology have also affected the captive breeding program. In the late 1970s a diaphragmatic hernia was discovered in an animal born at the National Zoo (Bush et al. 1980). Careful screening of living and dead animals suggested that the diaphragmatic hernia was present in between five and ten percent of the captive population. Although it initially appeared that the defect could have been the result of a single recessive gene, recent analyses of the pedigrees of affected individuals suggest that this problem is either polygenic or not genetic at all. Moreover, attempts to breed for this trait have generally had negative results (Kleiman, Ballou and Evans, unpublished). The diaphragmatic hernia has now been found in the majority of lineages of captive Golden Lion Tamarins and thus is not a characteristic which selective breeding could easily remove from the population.

Since the average inbreeding coefficient for the captive population is not particularly high (Ballou 1985) the diaphragmatic condition is unlikely to be the result of inbreeding. However, when inbreeding has occurred in Golden Lion Tamarins, it has resulted in reduced viability of offspring, as is the case with numerous other primate species (Ralls and Ballou 1982).

From a captive population of fewer than 80 outside of Brazil in 1971, there were approximately 370 animals by the end of 1983. Recently, the population has been increasing at a rate of 20 to 25 percent per year (Ballou 1985). The major management efforts are currently being devoted to slowing population growth and balancing the contribution of the various founders to the population.

The Wild Population: Field Research on Population Size and Behavioral Ecology

By 1981 it was clear that the captive population was secure and that there were animals surplus to the needs of the breeding program. However, the wild population's status was still precarious. In 1974, the Poço das Antas Federal Biological Reserve in the state of Rio de Janeiro had been established, and a director (D. Pessamilio) was appointed in 1977. A survey in 1980 by K.M. Green (unpublished) suggested that although Golden Lion Tamarins existed in the Reserve, there were major problems to be solved before protection and long-term conservation of the Golden Lion Tamarin could be guaranteed.

Shortly thereafter, Kleiman initiated discussions with officials from IBDF (Instituto Brasileiro de Desenvolvimento Florestal), World Wildlife Fund—U.S. and with Adelmar Coimbra-Filho, Director of the Rio de Janeiro Primate Center (CPRJ-FEEMA), to determine the feasibility of developing a formal collaborative program for Golden Lion Tamarin conservation involving species preservation in the wild and captivity, and possibly the release of captive-born Golden Lion Tamarins into suitable natural habitat in Brazil.

It was clear from initial discussions that deforestation continued to erode the remaining natural habitat and that only tiny, isolated and unprotected populations of tamarins existed outside the Poço das Antas Reserve. Green (unpublished) had estimated that fewer than 100 individuals were likely to exist in the Reserve, and had emphasized the degraded nature of the habitat, its extreme vulnerability due to human development, and the need for rapid implementation of and support for a management plan to increase the carrying capacity of the Reserve and protect it from further degradation.

The small size and uneven habitat quality of Poço das Antas suggested that a viable natural population of Golden Lion Tamarin could *not* be sustained in the long-term without remedial action. Thus, it became evident that we needed to develop methodologies for: (1) genetic exchange between wild and captive populations through reintroduction, translocation, and pinpoint genetic intervention; (2) increasing carrying capacity of the Reserve through rehabilitating degraded tropical forest habitats; and (3) developing a conservation education strategy which would ensure public support for the protection and expansion of remaining forest blocks outside the Reserve.

Although reintroduction of captive-born animals to the wild was considered an aim of our collaborative conservation program, the necessity for, and feasibility of a release needed to be evaluated prior to any reintroduction plans. Release of captive-born animals required prior knowledge of (1) the behavioral ecology of the species including home-range sizes, group size and composition, feeding and foraging patterns, habitat preferences, and group movements; (2) the status of the wild population within the Poço das Antas Reserve; and (3) availability of suitable habitat. Additionally, (4) assurance was needed that the release of captives would in no way jeopardize the safety of the remaining natural population.

Studies of the behavioral ecology and status of Golden Lion Tamarin were initiated in the Poço das Antas Reserve in 1983 by James Dietz. The relevant data have been collected by Dietz and Brazilian students through a trap, mark, and release program, with selected tamarins being outfitted with radio collars in order to follow the movements of individuals and family groups. Table 1 presents a summary of

TABLE 1. CAPTURES AND HANDLING OF WILD AND REINTRODUCED GOLDEN LION TAMARINS
(Nov. 1983 to June 1985)

	Wild Tamarins	Released Tamarins	Total
Captures (trapped)	169	53	222
Individuals captured	101	28	129
Chemical immobilizations	153	47	200
Number of individuals outfitted with radio transmitters	21	12	33

the trapping and handling which has occurred in the field through June 1985.

Table 2 provides some information on the size and composition of free-living Golden Lion Tamarin groups in the wild. For purposes of this table, adults were considered to be individuals weighing more than 500 grams, juveniles and subadults weighed between 200 and 500 grams, and infants weighed less than 200 grams. There tends to be a sex ratio of 1:1, with no more than two adults of each sex per group. The trapping program has provided insufficient data to confirm whether or not wild Golden Lion Tamarins are strictly monogamous (Kleiman 1977b), but it does appear that only one litter is raised at a time, thus suggesting that only a single female breeds within a group.

Home-range size for individual groups is approximately 40 hectares within the Reserve, with home-range overlap of adjacent groups averaging about 10 percent. Golden Lion Tamarins are dependent on the use of holes in trees for shelter at night and thus good tamarin habitat includes sufficient holes for denning (see Coimbra-Filho 1977), especially since each tamarin group depends on several tree holes within their home-range (Dietz, unpublished). Tamarins also depend on bromeliads as a source of food with high protein content (e.g. small vertebrates and insects). Good tamarin habitat thus additionally includes forest with a profusion of bromeliads.

Systematic censuses of the wild population have resulted in estimates of the overall numbers and distribution of remaining free-living Golden Lion Tamarin. Table 3 summarizes the most recent estimates of Golden Lion Tamarin numbers in currently protected sites. There may be an additional 100 animals existing precariously in tiny isolated forest patches. These data clearly indicate that Golden Lion Tamarins continue to be severely threatened in the wild. The 5000 hectare Poço das Antas Reserve, with its slightly more than 100 individuals, is the only long-term protected plot of land in Brazil for this species. All additional animals existing

TABLE 2. SEX AND AGE COMPOSITION OF CAPTURED GROUPS OF GOLDEN LION TAMARIN (October 1983–October 1984)

Group	Adults ♂	Adults ♀	?	Subadults and Juveniles ♂	Subadults and Juveniles ♀	?	Infants ♂	Infants ♀	?	Total ♂	Total ♀	?	Σ
PW	1	1	3						2	1	1	5	7
P20	2	1			1					2	2		4
RS	1	2		1	1					2	3		5
NW	2	2		2	1					4	3		7
AR	2	3		3						5	3		8
RN	2	3		1	2					3	5		8
OS	2	1	1	2						4	1	1	6
P10	2	3		1			2			4	4		8
VA	2	2		2			1	1		3	5		8
CO	2	2		3	2				2	5	4	2	11
TOTALS	18	20	4	12	10		3	1	4	33	31	8	72
Mean (n = 10)	1.8	2.0	0.4	1.2	1.0		0.3	0.1	0.4	3.3	3.1	0.8	7.2

in the remaining southeastern coastal rain forests of Brazil are inhabiting vulnerable habitat which is being deforested at unprecedented rates.

Preliminary studies on the genetics of the captive and wild population, through the biochemical analysis of blood proteins, suggest that free-living Golden Lion Tamarins may be less genetically diverse than the captive population (Forman et al. submitted). These tentative findings suggest that inbreeding may be a major problem with remaining wild Golden Lion Tamarins, and that an exchange of genetic material is likely to be required in the future to maintain a vigorous and viable wild population.

The Habitat: Protection, Management, Preservation, and Restoration

The mechanisms whereby one can rapidly increase the carrying capacity of currently degraded habitat for Golden Lion Tamarins while paving the way for a natural regrowth of the forest is of basic research interest as well as being of major conservation importance. The Poço das Antas Reserve is a patchwork of primary and secondary forest and pasture land (Ferreira et al. 1981). Estimates by Green (unpublished) of the amount of forest cover suggest that less than 40% of the entire 5,000 hectare reserve is forested, with perhaps 10% in undisturbed climax forest.

At the beginning of the field studies project we initiated a major protection and restoration effort for the Poco das Antas Reserve. Much of the support for the Reserve's rehabilitation has come from contributions by zoos which hold and own Golden Lion Tamarins outside of Brazil, and from the World Wildlife Fund—U.S.

Major problems which were addressed and remedied between 1981 and 1983 included: (1) making and placing signs indicating the existence of the Reserve and its protected status; (2) hiring and training guards to patrol and enforce anti-hunting regulations within the Reserve; (3) providing additional vehicle fuel to enable the Reserve's guards to get to and from work and to monitor the Reserve's boundaries; and (4) eliminating most squatters involved in slash-and-burn agriculture and periodic hunting.

More recently, we constructed fire breaks to improve fire control, since the Poco das Antas Reserve has been exposed to continued degradation through fires which annually burn nearly 20% of its area.

TABLE 3. THE APPROXIMATE NUMBERS OF GOLDEN LION TAMARINS REMAINING IN THE WILD IN PROTECTED HABITAT

Available forest	Approximate size of area (ha)	Estimated number of groups	Estimated number of individuals*
Poco das Antas Reserve	5,000	16	115
Campos Novos Naval Reserve (Sao Pedro de Aldeia)	500	15	108

*Based on mean group size of 7.2 individuals.

Long-term management and restoration of this Reserve must involve the development of innovative techniques for the rehabilitation of tropical forests. One of our first efforts was to distribute lime over a 500 hectare area to elevate the pH of the soil in degraded areas and to encourage natural regeneration of woody species where grasses have been dominant for many years. Also, several experimental plots have been established to determine which species will regenerate most rapidly given different soil types. From these efforts we hope to improve our understanding of how rapidly a tropical forest with structural complexity and species diversity can regenerate through selective plantings (Dietz and Pessamilio, unpublished).

Despite these major gains, there are several remaining problems within the Poço das Antas Reserve which may retard the creation of additional habitat for Golden Lion Tamarins.

For example, a railroad track still bisects the Reserve and trains pass through several times a day. Moreover, a dam has recently been completed which, when operational, may flood 15–20% of the Reserve. Additionally, there is a 2,000 hectare plot of land adjacent to the Reserve which is owned by the Government of Brazil and may be turned over to the Department of Agriculture for development. Any intensive farming operation bordering the Poço das Antas Reserve would further jeopardize the remaining habitat through the additional human impact and application of insecticides. We have encouraged annexation of this block of land to the Reserve by IBDF, with limited success to date.

Finally, the Poco das Antas Reserve may be too small to maintain a genetically viable population of Golden Lion Tamarins in perpetuity. Thus, we need to identify and protect additional blocks of forest which are already inhabited by Golden Lion Tamarins or which can support the species. We are currently encouraging the protection of any significant blocks of forested land by public and private owners.

Conservation Education

The long-term preservation of species or habitats cannot be accomplished without public and professional education at every level which results in community support for conservation. One of our major educational goals has involved the training of students and young professionals in up-to-date techniques of wildlife management and conservation biology.

As biologists and educators from a developed country, we must encourage future environmental protection and conservation of uniquely Brazilian ecosystems through the identification, involvement, and support of as many interested Brazilian students as are available and logistically possible. Essential to our whole program is the training of a cadre of Brazilian wildlife ecologists, behaviorists and conservation educators to maintain the long-term continuity of this, and future conservation programs.

Secondly, L.A. Dietz is coordinating our public education programs and educational research efforts. We are attempting to obtain local, national and international attention to foster increased public interest in and support generally for environmental protection and conservation. Finally, we hope to serve as a catalyst for other, much-needed conservation education programs in Brazil by contributing to the development of education as a conservation tool. Each step of the program is being documented and its effectiveness evaluated.

The Golden Lion Tamarin ecological studies in the Poço das Antas Reserve have provided the information necessary to define the major threats to the species' survival and thus establish specific objectives for the education program:

1. To reduce deforestation in the lowland areas around the Reserve;
2. To assure the permanent conservation of at least a part of the privately owned forests in the area;
3. To reduce fires in forests and cleared areas in the region;
4. To reduce commerce of Golden Lion Tamarin; and
5. To reduce hunting within the limits of the Reserve.

Changing human opinions and behaviors is a slow process, and therefore, this education program must be on-going. Thus, we have encouraged major community involvement in the planning and implementation of the program. We have found that the local community is more interested in implementation if it has invested in the development of a project.

Our efforts have been concentrated in the three municipalities surrounding the Poço das Antas Reserve. The area (2292 km^2) has a total population of 89,000 inhabitants (1980 census) with a relatively low density of 39 inhabitants per square kilometer. The principal economic activities are agriculture and fishing. We have worked with the entire population, more specifically the Reserve staff, local authorities, teachers, students, landowners and other adult residents.

The education level of this target population is relatively low for the state of Rio de Janeiro. Forty-one percent of the population have had no formal instruction (1980 census), and only a fourth of the population over ten years old have completed fourth grade. The large landowners (over 50 hectares) have a higher level of education and generally live in metropolitan areas outside the three target municipalities.

In January and February 1984, with the help of 30 local volunteers, we conducted 519 interviews with a sample of the population of the rural and urban communities of the municipality of Silva Jardim (in which the Reserve is located). We collected information concerning knowledge, attitudes and behaviors regarding the Golden Lion Tamarin, the Reserve, and the conservation of local flora and fauna which helped us to plan appropriate educational strategies and materials. The initial results will be compared with similar interviews to be conducted in September 1985, from which we can evaluate the effectiveness of our educational activities and the conservation education program in general.

The following are responses to some questions from the first round of interviews:

1. 92% listen to radio and 76% watch television although much of this rural area has no electricity. The use of radio and T.V. to transmit our conservation program, therefore, became a priority.
2. 58% recognized the Golden Lion Tamarin from a photo, but they knew very little regarding the animal's habits, or that it is endangered and close to extinction.

3. In answer to the question: "What is the major problem in your municipality?" the majority of those interviewed responded "deforestation" (28%) while other common responses were "roads" (12%), a local dam (10%), and "unemployment" (7%).
4. 94% of respondees indicated that they had never been harmed or had property damaged by wild animals.
5. Of the landowners interviewed, 74% responded that they wanted to "leave alone" or protect the wildlife on their properties.
6. 76% did not know if Golden Lion Tamarins were beneficial to man. The benefits which were mentioned included "cure of diseases," "beauty" or "happiness."
7. To the question: "Does the forest provide you any benefits?" 88% responded "yes." The benefits most often mentioned were "pure air," "firewood," "wood" and "watershed protection."

In general, we found that we did not have to confront negative attitudes about the Golden Lion Tamarin or the forest. Instead, we needed to increase the level of knowledge and global thinking, principally concerning the long-term consequences of human actions on the local environment and the interrelations of humans, fauna, habitat, and the well-being of all.

In the communities, we first talked with local authorities and invited them to visit the Reserve, where we explained our goals, the problems we were facing, and the help we needed. They have been fully supportive. These first contacts have also led to the formation of a group of young people interested in conservation whose ideas and interests largely contributed to the educational materials we have produced. We tested prototypes of all materials with members of the target population before final production and use.

Materials we have produced include:

1. *Press releases.* An informed press can help tremendously in communicating to the public the necessity for conservation and environmental protection.
2. *30-second public service messages for television and radio.* The Brazilian Roberto Marinho Foundation helpfully donated air time on national and local stations.
3. *Video copies of the television news reports and public service messages.* These and other films of Brazilian flora and fauna were provided for local showings.
4. *A pamphlet which serves as the cover for a school notebook.* It contains a story about the Golden Lion Tamarin and the forest, the problem of deforestation and some suggestions for solutions. It is distributed in the schools.
5. *A factual pamphlet.* Current scientific information about the Golden Lion Tamarin, the Poço das Antas Biological Reserve, and the conservation of the Atlantic Coastal Forest has been prepared and is distributed to students, teachers, the press, and others interested in the subject.

6. *An educational poster.* The Reserve guards and local students distribute the poster to public places in the region.
7. *Short slide-tape programs.* These can be presented in various locations to different target audiences.
8. *A package of materials, "Profit While Conserving Nature."* This explains to landowners the benefits (financial and otherwise) of establishing "Private Wildlife Refuges" on their properties.
9. *A Golden Lion Tamarin logo.* This logo (prepared by the National Zoo's Office of Graphics and Exhibits) is used on all project materials and is now a symbol for the Poço das Antas Reserve.
10. *T-shirts, buttons, and stickers.* These are presented as recognition for those who contribute to the conservation of the lion tamarin and the forests, as prizes for school activities related to conservation, and for sale by local conservation groups to finance their activities.
11. *Other existing materials.* Posters, pamphlets and books produced by the Brazilian Foundation for Nature Conservation (FBCN) and by the World Wildlife Fund are also used, as well as the children's book "Artes e Manhas do Mico Leão" by Yves Hublet.

The activities we have employed in the education program have included:

1. *Lectures* for local authorities, conservation groups, farmers, high school and university students, and other interested people;
2. *Training courses* for Reserve guards and local teachers;
3. *Promotion of the formation of conservation groups*;
4. *Press events.* We have capitalized on the tremendous interest in this project shown by the Brazilian press;
5. *A travelling exhibit* which has now been presented in six communities to approximately 4,500 people;
6. *A children's play* based on the book "Artes e Manhas do Mico-Leão" presented in three municipalities to a total estimated audience of 1,500. All the actors are young, local residents;
7. *Special classes on conservation of local wildlife in local schools.* With the help of a team of local young people we have given over 150 presentations reaching all the students of our target population (approximately 7,000);
8. *Educational field trips to the Reserve.* The guides are Reserve guides and members of local conservation groups. Participants have an opportunity to see the reintroduced tamarins free in the forest and to learn about the forest by walking along a nature trail planned to stimulate interest and observation;
9. *School essay contests* on conservation themes;
10. *A parade* with the theme "The Natural Resources of our Municipality" organized by local teachers in Silva Jardim in 1984 to commemorate the anniversary of the municipality; and;

11. *Visits to local landowners* which still have forested land appropriate for lion tamarins.

In all these activities we attempt to present the Golden Lion Tamarin as a symbol for the conservation of its habitat. Conserving an area of forest for a Golden Lion Tamarin will at the same time conserve nearly all of the elements of that ecosystem.

The final results from our education efforts are not yet known but a large part of the target population now clearly recognizes the Golden Lion Tamarin, knows that it is endangered and why. They also are more aware of the existence of the Poço das Antas Reserve. Many landowners are interested in establishing private wildlife reserves. Also, we currently have more requests for internships, lectures and educational materials than we can fill, and there has been a dramatic increase in the number of Golden Lion Tamarins donated to the Reserve or reported to IBDF as being held illegally in captivity. The challenge now is to make conservation not just something currently in vogue, but a subject of continuing community action.

We hope that the ongoing educational research in Brazil, including the evaluation of different conservation education media in terms of their effect on the attitude of the local population, will lead to the development of a model for conservation education programs using the most efficient and effective techniques.

Reintroduction; Results from 1984

The chronology of the 1984 release (through June 30, 1985) is presented in Table 4.

TABLE 4. GOLDEN LION TAMARIN REINTRODUCTION: CHRONOLOGY OF EVENTS BETWEEN NOVEMBER 1983 AND JUNE 1985

Event	Date	Deaths (or removals)	Births	Wild Born Added	Total Alive
Captive-borns to Brazil	XI 83				15
During quarantine in Rio (CPRJ)	to VII 84	4	2	1	14
After release	to VI 85	11 (incl. inf.)	3	1	7

Causes of Death (or Removal)

Predator	Exposure/ starvation	Snake	Social conflict	Disappear	Medical
1	1	1	1 (remove)	2	5 (viral?)

Fifteen captive-born animals were sent to Brazil in November 1983, of which four died during a six month quarantine and preparation period in the Rio de Janeiro Primate Center (CPRJ). One litter of two was born during quarantine and a wild-born animal was added to the group being prepared for release.

During May and June 1984, the animals were moved from CPRJ to the Poço das Antas Reserve. They were held there in large cages at the release site for 12 to 29 days to acclimate to the local environment. Between May and July 1984, 14 animals were released into the wild, including one family group of eight animals and three adult pairs. The release site contained no Golden Lion Tamarins, although the forest appeared suitable. By June 30, 1985 eleven of the released animals had died or had been removed (rescued).

Causes of death or debilitation included predation, exposure, disease, starvation, snakebite, social conflict and disappearance. Most losses occurred shortly after release. The major cause of mortality was an apparent disease which affected a family group in February, 1985 and resulted in the death of five animals. The symptoms included severe diarrhea, lethargy, and dehydration and may well have been caused by a virus. However, during this same period one female produced a single offspring and another had twins. The twins currently survive.

Starvation could be identified as contributing to a death in only one case. Released animals were provisioned with gradually decreasing amounts of banana, orange and ground meat. Food provisioning was discontinued in March, 1985.

Released animals have been monitored almost daily for a full year to document their adaptation to a wild existence. The long-term, regular monitoring of individuals is unique for a primate release study.

Preparation

The preparation phase has involved differential training in various aspects of foraging and feeding as well as in locomotion. Additionally, in order to choose the best reintroduction candidates in the future, we have studied social behavior and activity to develop personality profiles for individual animals which can later be correlated with differential survivorship of the released tamarins.

Before the first release, we quarantined animals at the Rio de Janeiro Primate Center for six months because the potential for disease transmission, from the captives to the wild population (or the reverse), was a major concern. This also enabled us to observe the process of adaptation as our animals, captive-born in the Northern Hemisphere, responded to the changes in climate, light and diet within Brazil.

FEEDING

We reasoned that the most serious deficit of captive-born tamarins would be in locating and harvesting natural foods. Captives are typically fed finely-cut produce, diced marmoset diet, and immobilized prey—all in a bowl at a predictable place in their cages at a predictable time. Wild tamarins eat whole fruits, and invertebrates and small vertebrates that are cryptic and capable of rapid escape or self-defense. These food items are distributed widely and quite unpredictably in space and time in the forest. Prey is frequently embedded (Parker and Gibson 1977) within crevices, rotten wood, rolled leaves and bromeliads.

We used a training protocol designed gradually to replace the expectation of finding cut foods in a traditional place with the tendency to search for food that is spatially distributed and hidden. Once the animals began to forage for hidden food, we presented likely sites that were empty, thus countering any expectation that all likely sites would contain a pay-off.

Table 5 shows this protocol. "Traditional" is a bowl of cut food at the established site. "Distributed" is a similar bowl at a randomly selected site in the cage. An "Embedded" site is one of a large set of pseudo-naturalistic "puzzle-boxes" that contain the same types and amount of foods as a traditional and distributed site but the food is not visible. Embedded sites were also placed randomly in the cage.

Each condition in the protocol was presented in the morning and afternoon for five days. We scored the animals' use of the feeding sites for the first hour after the morning and afternoon feeding. We noted every time an animal visited a site (defined as touching the container of food) and took food from the site. We also noted which animals first extracted food from an embedded site. This paper documents the performance of the family group from King's Island, Ohio, on the first six conditions of the protocol.

As shown in Table 6, under Condition 1 with just a bowl at a traditional site, each animal in the group makes about 8 "Visits" to the bowl and "Takes" 10.5 pieces of food in the hour following feeding by the keeper.

By adding a distributed site (another bowl at a random place), the numbers of "Visits" and "Takes" increase slightly. Under Condition 3, where we add an embedded site, the number of "Visits" nearly doubles while the number of "Takes" rises only slightly. Adding a second distributed site (Condition 4) makes little difference, but a second embedded site (Condition 5) is accompanied by substantial increases in "Visits" and "Takes". Finally, in Condition 6, we drop a distributed bowl and add an empty site; "Visits" increase even further and "Takes" decrease. Note that the total amount of available food is the same under all conditions: it

TABLE 5. PROTOCOL FOR TRAINING GOLDEN LION TAMARINS TO SEARCH FOR FOOD THAT IS DISTRIBUTED IN SPACE AND TIME AND HIDDEN.

Condition	Traditional	Distributed	Embedded	Empty Embedded	Total sites (with food)
1	1	—	—	—	1
2	1	1	—	—	2
3	1	1	1	—	3
4	1	2	1	—	4
5	1	2	2	—	5
6	1	1	2	1	5 (4)
7	—	1	2	1	4 (3)

simply becomes more distributed and more embedded. By adding extra feeding sites, especially embedded sites, the number of "Visits," a measure of *foraging effort,* increases dramatically.

While the number of "Takes" increases somewhat with the number of feeding sites, the ratio of "Takes" per Visit, a measure of *foraging efficiency,* drops by more than half by Condition 6. The animals are not only expending more foraging energy but are receiving a smaller relative payoff. This would appear to be suitable preparation for life in the wild where foraging efficiency is much lower than in captivity. Parenthetically, the use of distributed and embedded food sites is an effective means to increase the activity of primates and other omnivorous scavenge-hunters (Hamilton 1973) in captivity.

We looked at which animals actually opened and ate first from the embedded sites. The alpha pair of the family opened only 8 percent (6 of 80) of the embedded sites, while the six offspring opened 89 percent (71 of 80; 3 went unopened). There was a non-significant correlation of +0.47 between individual ages and frequency of opening embedded sites by each member of the family, (Spearman Rank Correlation, $n = 8$, $p > 0.05$) but it was clear that adults were much less apt to open embedded sites.

The frequency of opening embedded sites before release is strikingly correlated (+0.86, Spearman Rank Correlation, $n = 6$, $p < 0.05$) with time to death or rescue after release: animals that were more adept at opening embedded sites survived longer.

Once the tamarins had completed our feeding protocol, we introduced whole fruits. We were unable to get natural fruits in sufficient quantity but we chose cultivated analogues when available; and we chose cultigens such as banana and papaya that are found on remnant plantations in the Reserve. We also provided quail eggs in man-made "nests".

Table 7 shows the performance of the adult pairs pooled and of the family group in exploiting these foods. The family group was more successful. One might expect that a group of eight is more likely to accidentally discover and exploit such foods, but the family was housed in twice the space as each adult pair. Further, we biased the results in favor of the faltering adults by hiding the fruits and eggs less well

TABLE 6. FEEDING BEHAVIOR OF A FAMILY GROUP OF GOLDEN LION TAMARINS ON SIX CONDITIONS OF THE TRAINING PROTOCOL.

Condition	$\bar{X}$ Visits/Hr.	$\bar{X}$ Takes/Hr.	Takes/Visits
1 (T)	8.1	10.5	1.30
2 (T+D)	9.9	11.5	1.16
3 (T+D+E)	19.2	12.0	.62
4 (T+D+D+E)	19.0	13.2	.69
5 (T+D+D+E+E)	20.9	15.7	.75
6 (T+D+E+E+EE)	22.7	14.0	.61

and by cutting small windows in the rinds and shells. We even cracked the eggs and added jelly to get some adults to eat eggs.

This exemplifies the dilemma of having to choose between rigorous science and preparation for survival that we encountered frequently in this program. In this case, however, the difference between adult pairs and an age-graded family is still evident.

As additional preparation, we provided as many natural food items and forest features as we could. Our ongoing field study on wild tamarins indicated that bromeliads are important sources of food and water. The captives quickly learned to hunt in and drink from bromeliads, and to explore hollow logs and decaying wood thoroughly. Insects (especially orthopterans), frogs, and lizards were taken readily.

Avoiding Danger

The captives displayed so little selectivity that we wondered how they would avoid dangerous animals and noxious foods. They learned quickly not to seize bees and biting ants, and never sampled mushrooms that grew profusely in their cages. Thorns were negotiated without difficulty. Large over-flying birds and bird-like silhouettes caused our captives to give alarm chirps and escape to the tree core and lower strata; we suspect that this response is genetically hard-wired.

We saw two opportunistic encounters with wild nonvenomous snakes: one of the snakes was eaten and the other successfully defended itself against five mobbing tamarins and escaped. We think that captive tamarins will try to eat small to medium-size reptiles and amphibians and may not discriminate between dangerous and non-dangerous species. One of the reintroductees was killed following an apparent encounter with a snake; we did not see the bite but it occurred during a tamarin intergroup encounter when it was unlikely that the victim was foraging.

We presented a large toad (*Bufo marinus*) to the family group. They approached cautiously at first, but within 2.5 minutes two of the animals had bitten the toad squarely on the parotid sacs. We literally had to wrest the toad from yet a third tamarin. One animal went into convulsions and barely recovered after four hours; another was ataxic for two hours. Both frothed, cried, and vomited while the others watched closely. Nonetheless, they seemed eager to get to the toad on the next day. We placed the toad in a jar and for 30 minutes scored the number of times each

TABLE 7. SUCCESS OF A FAMILY GROUP AND THREE ADULT PAIRS OF GOLDEN LION TAMARINS IN EXPLOITING WHOLE FRUITS AND QUAIL EGGS.

Adult Pairs			
	Fruits	66.7%	(360/540)
	Eggs	63.4%	(104/164)
	Combined	65.9%	(464/704)
Family Groups			
	Fruits	90.3%	(140/155)
	Eggs	71.1%	(32/45)
	Combined	86.0%	(172/200)

tamarin "Visited" the jar and the number of one-minute intervals each animal was at the jar. After 30 minutes, we presented a group of lively grasshoppers, a highly favorite food, in the same jar for 30 minutes, and used the same scoring system. After a break, we again presented the jar full of grasshoppers for 30 minutes and then the toad for 30 minutes.

Table 8 shows each individual's total number of "Visits" to and intervals at the jar for 60 minutes with the toad and 60 minutes with grasshoppers. The affected family members and the observers showed as much interest in the fateful toad as they did to the tasty grasshoppers. Of course, the experiment is flawed since the jar decreased olfactory cues, and olfaction may be more crucial in identifying danger than in finding insects. However, it appears that neither the affected nor the observing animals learned much from this near-fatal encounter. We must entertain the non-adaptationist hypothesis that captive and wild tamarins learn little about reptiles and amphibians: they try to eat the small ones and if they are unlucky they may die. The areas of recognition and avoidance of danger is one where we know little and where we are methodologically handicapped because of wanting to avoid potentially fatal experiments.

Locomotion

During preparation, we induced the tamarins to jump, climb and hang to develop locomotor skills. However, after bringing the tamarins to the "halfway house" enclosures in the forest, we were struck by their reluctance to use natural vegetation of various textures, diameter and flexibility. Older animals, particularly, preferred to stay on the wood frame and wire mesh of the cage. We had to dismantle the cages soon after the release to force some tamarins to enter and use trees.

TABLE 8. RESPONSE OF A FAMILY GROUP OF GOLDEN LION TAMARINDS TO A TOAD AND A FAVORED FOOD (GRASSHOPPERS) 24 HOURS AFTER TWO FAMILY MEMBERS (*) HAD BECOME SERIOUSLY ILL DUE TO BITING THE TOAD.

	Toad		Grasshoppers	
Animal	Visits	Intervals	Visits	Intervals
#1	1	2	1	2
#5	17	18	22	26
#6*	3	6	4	4
#7*	6	5	3	10
#8	9	15	6	10
#9	9	16	15	18
M	4	8	3	6
R	0	0	0	0
	49	70	54	76

Once they moved into natural vegetation, another deficit became obvious: the animals were unable to plot a cognitive route through the forest between themselves and an incentive. Their movements were characterized by false starts, fruitless retracing of pathways to dead ends and, finally, descent to and travel across the ground. At best, travel by the reintroductees was slow and hesitant. At worst they got disoriented and lost. Some simply sat, appearing to give up, and had to be rescued. Two perished on the ground, one taken by a feral hunting dog and one, as noted above, likely killed by a snake.

Our preparation program for 1985 has been amended to include profuse natural cage furnishings, especially small diameter branches and vines. Further, the entire network is knocked down and reassembled twice each week to force the animals to move through a novel 3-dimensional array, as opposed to using familiar routes.

Age

The poorer performance of adults as compared to younger animals in exploiting embedded food sites and whole fruits and eggs, and the adults' apparently greater deficits in locomotor ability, suggested that we look at the relationship between age at reintroduction and survivorship. Using days-to-death or first rescue as the measure of survivorship, this correlation is -0.58 for the 13 captive-born reintroductees. If we use days to actual death (ignoring rescue), it is -0.56. Both negative correlations are statistically significant (Spearman Rank Correlation, $n = 13$, $p < 0.05$). Three of four captive-born adults released as pairs were dead within only 17 days of release.

We interpret these results to mean that young tamarins are more likely to have the vitality and behavioral flexibility to survive the dramatic environmental changes between life in a zoo cage and life in the Brazilian forest.

Future reintroductions will include age-graded family groups, and no adult pairs. Although we believe that our preparation program does confer a post-introduction survival advantage, we will test this belief in 1985 by releasing a group with no formal training. We will rescue and train them if necessary, but this is another systematic step in forging a true cost-effective science of reintroduction which, hopefully, will be applicable to other primates and indeed to a wide variety of vertebrates.

SUMMARY AND CONCLUSIONS

Of an original 15 captive-born animals transported to Brazil and released into the wild, there are currently three individuals still alive. One pair has successfully reproduced and reared offspring; in our minds successful reproduction constitutes successful reintroduction. We not only have begun repopulating suitable but empty tamarin habitat but also have infused new genetic material into the Poço das Antas Reserve.

Although the reintroduction of captive-born animals was a major goal of the Golden Lion Tamarin program in 1984, the methodology which we are developing for reintroduction can eventually be used to translocate wild individuals into established home-ranges and saturated habitats at a time of our choosing. This will eventually lead to a more outbred population.

It is important to state that the long-term conservation of Golden Lion Tamarins was not necessarily dependent upon the release of captive-born animals. If support had been available since the species was identified as endangered for the other elements of the program, (i.e. habitat protection and restoration, public and professional education, field research and censusing of the wild population, and a strong management program for both the captive and wild population,) the reintroduction aspect of this program might not have been pertinent. As it was, the reintroduction of captive-born animals to the wild acted as a springboard for the entire conservation program and as a result, the ultimate chances for the survival of the Golden Lion Tamarin have been dramatically improved.

ACKNOWLEDGEMENTS

This research program has profited tremendously from the support of numerous individuals and institutions, over nearly a 15-year time span.

The following individuals could well be considered co-authors for each of the separate elements of the program: (1) Captive Research and Management: Ron Evans, David Mack, Lynn Rathbun, Robert Hoage, Ken Green, Melissa Ditton, G. Maliniak; (2) Field Studies: Laurenz Pinder, Carlos Peres; (3) Habitat Restoration: Dionizio Pessamilio; (4) Education: Elizabeth Nagagata; (5) Reintroduction: Inês Castro, Beate Rettberg, Vera Cruz, Rosa de Sa.

Additionally, J. Block, M. Bush, L. Phillips and R. Montali of the NZP staff have been incredibly helpful.

Supporting institutions include: Smithsonian Institution International Environmental Sciences Program and Education Outreach Program; World Wildlife Fund—U.S.; National Geographic Society; Friends of the National Zoo; Wildlife Preservation Trust International; Frankfurt Zoological Society; National Institutes of Mental Health (Grant #27 241); Roberto Marinho Foundation; Instituto Brasileiro de Desenvolvimento Florestal, and Fundaçaó Brasileira para a Conservação da Natureza and a host of zoos and zoological societies which have generously given of their time and money.

Finally, the following individuals have provided general support, inspiration, and thoughtful input since the beginnings of the Golden Lion Tamarin research: T.H. Reed, John F. Eisenberg, R.A. Mittermeier, Jeremy Mallinson, George Rabb and Warren Thomas.

REFERENCES

Ballou, J.D. 1985, 1983. International Studbook for The Golden Lion Tamarin *Leontopithecus rosalia*. National Zoological Park, Smithson. Inst., Washington, D.C.

Bridgwater, D.D. (ed.) 1972. Saving the lion marmoset. Wild Animal Propagation Trust, Wheeling, WV. 223 pp.

Brown, K. and Mack, D.S. 1978. Food sharing among captive *Leontopithecus rosalia*. Folia Primat 29:268–290.

Bush, R.M., Montali, R.J., Kleiman, D.G., Randolph, J., Abramovitz, M.D., and Evans, R.F. 1980. Diagnosis and repair of familial diaphragmatic defects in Golden Lion Tamarins. J. Amer. Vet. Med. Assoc. 171:866–869.

Bush, R.M., Custer, R.S., Whitla, J.C., and Smith, E.E. 1982. Haemotologic values of captive Golden Lion Tamarins (*Leontopithecus rosalia*): variations with sex, age and health status. Lab. Anim. Sci. 32:294–297.

Coimbra-Filho, A.F. 1969. Mico-leão *Leontopithecus rosalia* (Linnaeus 1766) situação atual de espécie no Brasil (Callithricidae-Primates) An acad Brasil Cienc 41 (Supl.):29–52.

———. 1977. Natural shelters of *Leontopithecus rosalia* and some ecological implications (Callitrichidae: Primates) Pp. 79–89 *in* The biology and conservation of the Callitrichidae (Kleiman, D.G., ed.) Smithson. Inst. Press, Washington, D.C. 354 pp.

Coimbra-Filho, A.F. and Maia A. de A. 1979a. O processo da muda dos pêlos em *Leontopithecus r. rosalia* (Linnaeus 1766) (Callitrichidae, Primates) Rev. Brasil Biol. 39:83–93.

———. 1979b. A sazonalidade do processo reprodutivo em *Leontopithecus rosalia* (Linnaeus 1766) (Callitrichidae, Primates) Rev. Brasil Biol. 39:643–651.

Coimbra-Filho, A.F. and Mittermeier, R.A. 1973. Distribution and ecology of the genus *Leontopithecus* Lesson, 1840 in Brazil. Primates 14:47–66.

———. 1977. Conservation of the Brazilian Lion Tamarins *Leontopithecus rosalia*. Pp. 59–94 *in* Primate conservation (Prince Rainier and Bourne, G.H., eds.). Academic Press, NY. 658 pp.

———. 1978. Reintroduction and translocation of lion tamarins: A realistic appraisal. Pp. 41–48 *in* Biology and behaviour of marmosets (Rothe, H., Wolters, H.J. and Hearn, J.P., eds.). Eigenverlag H Rothe, Gottingen. 301 pp.

Ferreira, L.M., Poupard, J.P. and Rocha, S.B. 1981. Plano de Manejo Reserva Biologica de Poço das Antas. Technical Document No. 10, Instituto Brasileiro de Desenvolvimento Florestal (IBDF) and Fundação Brasileira Para a Conservação da Natureza (FBCN). Editora Gráfica Brasiliana Ltda, Brasilia. 95 pp.

Forman, L., Kleiman, D.G., Bush, R.M., Dietz, J.M., Ballou, J.D., Phillips, L., Coimbra-Filho, A.F. and O'Brien, S.J. (submitted). Genetic variation within and among lion tamarins.

Green, K.M. (unpublished). An assessment of the Poço das Antas Reserve, Brazil and prospects for survival of the Golden Lion Tamarin *Leontopithecus rosalia rosalia*.

Hamilton, W. 1973. Life's color code. McGraw-Hill, NY.

Hershkovitz, P. 1977. Living New World monkeys (Platyrrhini) with an introduction to primates. Vol. 1. Univ. of Chicago Press, Chicago. 1117 pp.

Hoage, R.J. 1977. Parental care in *Leontopithecus rosalia rosalia:* Sex and age differences in carrying behavior and the role of prior experience. Pp. 293–305 *in* The biology and conservation of the Callitrichidae (Kleiman, D.G. ed.). Smithson. Inst. Press, Washington, D.C. 354 pp.

———. 1982. Social and physical maturation on captive lion tamarins *Leontopithecus rosalia*

rosalia (Primates: Callitrichidae) Smithson. Contribs. Zool. No. 354:1–56.
Jones, M. 1973. International Studbook for the Golden Lion Tamarin, 1972. Unpublished.
Kleiman, D.G. 1977a. Progress and problems in lion tamarin *Leontopithecus rosalia rosalia* reproduction. Internat. Zoo Yearb. 17:92–97.
———. 1977b. Characteristics of reproduction and sociosexual interactions in pairs of lion tamarins (*Leontopithecus rosalia*) during the reproductive cycle. Pp. 181–190 *in* The biology and conservation of the Callitrichidae (Kleiman, D.G. ed.) Smithson. Inst. Press, Washington, D.C. 354 pp.
———. 1978. The development of pair preferences in the lion tamarin (*Leontopithecus rosalia*): Male competition or female choice? Pp. 203–208 *in* Biology and behaviour of marmosets (Rothe, H., Wolters, H.J., and Hearn, J.P., eds.). Eigenverlag H. Rothe, Göttingen. 301 pp.
———. 1979. Parent-offspring conflict and sibling competition in a monogamous primate. Amer. Nat. 114:753–760.
———. 1981. *Leontopithecus rosalia*. Mammalian Species No. 148:1–7.
———. 1983. The behavior and conservation of the golden lion tamarin *Leontopithecus r. rosalia*. Pp. 35–53 *in* Thiago de Mello, M. (ed.). A Primatol Brasil. An 1° Congr. Bras. Primatol; Belo Horizonte.
Kleiman, D.G., Hoage, R.J. and Green K.M. (in press). Behavior of the golden lion tamarin, *Leontopithecus rosalia rosalia in* Coimbra-Filho, A.F. and Mittermeier, R.A. (eds.). Ecology and Behavior of Neotropical Primates, Vol. 2.
Kleiman, D.G. and Jones, M. 1977. The current status of *Leontopithecus rosalia* in captivity with comments on breeding success at the National Zoological Park. Pp. 215–218 *in* The biology and conservation of the Callitrichidae (Kleiman, D.G. ed.). Smithson. Inst. Press, Washington, D.C. 354 pp.
Kleiman, D.G., Ballou, J.D. and Evans, R.F. 1982. An analysis of recent reproductive trends in captive golden lion tamarina *Leontopithecus r. rosalia* with comments on their future demographic management. Int. Zoo. Yearb. 22:94–101.
Konstant, W.R. and Mittermeier, R.A. 1982. Introduction, reintroduction and translocation of Neotropical primates: past experiences and future possibilities. Int. Zoo. Yearb. 22:69–77.
Montali, R.J., Gardiner, C.H., Evans, R.F. and Bush, M. 1983. *Pterygodermatites nycticebi* (Nematoda: Spirurida) in Golden Lion Tamarins. Lab. Anim. Sci. 33:194–197.
Parker, S. and Gibson, K. 1977. Object manipulation, tool use and sensorimetor intelligence as feeding adaptations in cebus monkeys and great apes. J. Hum. Evol. 6:623–641.
Ralls, K. and Ballou, J.D. 1982. Inbreeding and infant mortality in primates. Int. J. Primat. 3:491–505.
Rosenberger, A.L. and Coimbra-Filho, A.F. 1984. Morphology, taxonomic status, and affinities of the lion tamarins, *Leontopithecus* (Callitrichinae, Cebidae). Folia primatol 42:149–179.

CONSERVATION AND REHABILITATION OF THE COMMON BARN OWL

Terry A. Schulz

University of California at Davis
Raptor Center
Davis, CA 95616

INTRODUCTION

The Common Barn Owl, *Tyto alba,* is nearly cosmopolitan in distribution and is considered to be the most widespread land bird in the world (7). It is found in most tropical as well as temperate regions. They breed south of 45° latitude in North America but are often recorded north to 56° latitude as a visitor. The Barn Owl also occurs in South America, Europe, Africa, India, Australia and on many islands but is notably absent from New Zealand (7, 26).

There are 10-11 species and 2 genera in the family *Tytonidae* with only 1 species represented in North America. The family *Tytonidae* differs from the family *Strigidae* in several ways. The inner toe, or third digit, is roughly the same length in the *Tytonidae* with a serrated or comb-like edge on the talon, but much shorter (and lacking the serrated talon) in the *Strigidae*. The *Tytonidae* also has a proportionately longer skull with smaller orbits and a thicker interorbital septum (7, 26).

The general appearance is distinct from most *Strigidae* and is characterized by a well-developed, heart-shaped facial disc with relatively small, dark brown eyes and long legs with short feathers and unfeathered feet.

The Barn Owl favors open prairie grassland and will forage in most non-intensive farmland crops including grain, alfalfa, sugar beets and pasture. In agricultural areas it frequently hunts along roadside weeds and fence rows, especially when cropland is under preparation (1, 52).

There have been numerous studies documenting the Barn Owl's diet (11, 34, 52). Although this species favors microtine rodents, it is also opportunistic and consumes a variety of prey such as rats, moles, gophers, birds, bats and insects, especially the Jerusalem cricket (7, 26, 34, 52). There is also a report of approximately 30 Barn Owls feeding on grunion at a Southern California beach (18).

Because of the Barn Owl's affinity for rodents it was considered to be economically beneficial to humans even when earlier scientists placed bounties on the now endangered Peregrine Falcon.

STATUS IN U.S.

Although the Barn Owl is not rare throughout its range, it appears to be declining in the United States (1, 30).

Stewart (58) used Christmas Count data to determine the population status of the Barn Owl in the U.S. He concluded that the Barn Owl was increasing in some areas and decreasing in others. Based on the percentage of total counts in which the owl was reported in 2 periods, 1952–56 and 1975–77, the Barn Owl has increased along the Pacific Coast (California, Oregon) and has extended its range into Washington. He felt that this was a result of adjustments to habitat changes. The Barn Owl was absent in Montana, Wyoming, North Dakota, South Dakota, Nebraska, Minnesota, Iowa, Wisconsin, Illinois, Maine, Vermont and New Hampshire (58).

The Barn Owl is being considered for the state endangered list in Ohio and is already endangered in Illinois, Indiana, Iowa, Michigan, Missouri and Wisconsin (Fig. 1) (30, 31). In some mid-western states the Barn Owl populations appear to have increased about the turn of the century (31). This increase was thought to be a response to land clearing for agricultural development (60, 62, 63, 65). Barn Owl populations were apparently stable until the late 1940s and then suffered precipitous declines in some states (31, 60).

CAUSES FOR DECLINE

There is probably no single cause for the Barn Owl's decline and the reasons appear to vary geographically. Changing land use such as clean farming which is less conducive to the welfare of the owl, lack of nesting and roosting sites, lack of sufficient prey, cold weather, and pesticides have all been cited as causes for the Barn Owl's decline (11, 23, 30, 31, 52, 54, 63).

- ● Endangered
- ○ Special concern
- ① Not recorded
  Christmas count 1975–1977

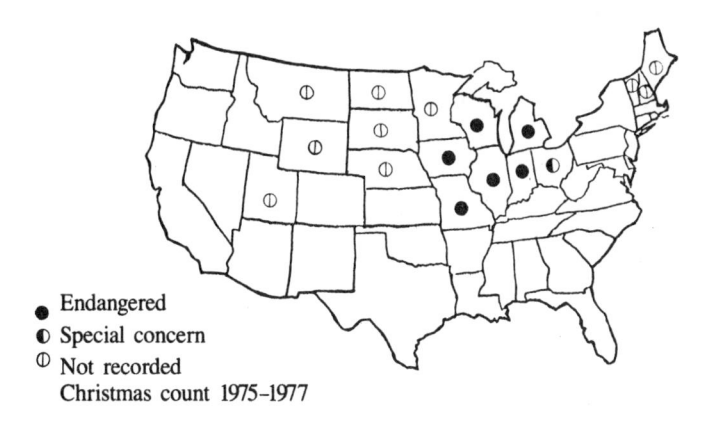

Figure 1. Status of Barn Owls in the U.S.

In Southern California Barn Owl populations are declining due to habitat loss (4). In the California Central Valley, where agricultural lands are predominant and rodent populations are high, the main limiting factor for Barn Owls is the availability and quality of nest sites (52). Since 1970 the number of historical nest sites have decreased locally by approximately 32 percent including destruction of old barns, loss of nest trees, and closing off of former entry sites into buildings (52). Because of the declining number of available good-quality nest sites in the Central Valley the Barn Owl frequently nests in poor-quality sites which often brings it into conflict with humans (Table 1). These poor-quality nest sites usually result in nesting failure (52) and include deep window ledges on buildings, open stairwells, airport hangers, inside large traffic lights, attics, air vents, crevices in stacked, bailed hay and ledges under freeway abutments.

More frequently, Barn Owls have been observed nesting in palm trees, mostly *Washingtonia filifera* and *Phoenix canariensis*. Many of these palm trees were planted in California around farms and in towns for ornamental purposes. They grow to an average height of 60 feet but may reach 100 feet and live more than 100 years (52). Fan palms retain their leaves indefinitely and develop a shag or skirt of old (dead) fronds. Strong winds common in the California Central Valley sometimes cause varying degrees of shag shedding, thus creating space and ledges within the shag. The palm's trunk is soft inside, surrounded by a tough outer layer of hard fibers. In some instances, when an old frond is shed, the tough outer layer may break, thus creating a hollow ledge effect. It is in these dark ledges covered by old overhanging fronds for which Barn Owls have an affinity as their nesting and roost sites.

Observations in Yolo County, California, revealed that over 60 percent of mature, unpruned palms had evidence of Barn Owls nesting or roosting (52). Unfortunately, palm trees lead the list of poor-quality nest sites in which the highest number of nest failure due to falls occurs. Seventy percent of juvenile Barn Owls received at the UC Davis Raptor Center which fell from their nest were found at the base of palm trees. The high rate of nest failure in palm trees can be explained in part

TABLE 1. NEST FAILURE DUE TO CONFLICTS WITH MAN IN COMMON BARN OWLS

Nest type	No. orphans	(%)	% of total nest failures
Attic or vent	42	26.8	11.5
Bailed hay	22	14.3	5.6
Tree cut down	20	12.7	5.1
Farm equipment	19	12.1	4.8
Adult shot	10	6.3	2.5
Hanger	8	5.0	2.0
Bridge/train trestle	7	4.4	1.7
Unknown	29	18.4	7.4
Totals	157	100	40.6

by high winds and lack of adquate space on these ledges as the young grow larger. Over 35 percent of the young which had fallen from palm trees do so during periods of high winds. Unfortunately, there is little data on the number of deaths resulting from falls.

MORTALITY

The Barn Owl's inability to withstand cold climates has been well documented (3, 16, 19, 21, 55, 64). Starvation due to heavy snow depth and cold temperatures are factors which cause death in Barn Owls (21, 36, 57). A breeding population of Barn Owls was eliminated at Martha's Vineyard, Massachusetts, due to cold weather and heavy snow fall (27). Death is probably a result of their inability to locate and catch prey under heavy snow cover (21, 36). Barn Owls also have a low percentage of fat reserves compared to other species of owls (23). According to Kirkwood (29), Barn Owls can lose 25 percent of their body weight in 15 days without food under normal temperatures and thus, would probably lose weight at a faster rate during cold temperatures due to higher energy demands.

Collisions with moving vehicles along roads and freeways have been cited as a mortality factor which may be of greater significance than current data would indicate (31, 52, 54). A survey of road kills in California indicates that it is perhaps the major cause of death in Barn Owls (52). In that survey 912 dead Barn Owls were observed along roads and freeways of the California interior valley between 1981-85 (Table 2).

The cause is probably a function of the owl's behavior and the high rodent density in roadside vegetation. A greater number of dead owls were found during periods of peak agricultural activity (i.e. harvesting of crops and plowing fields). In addition, more dead owls were found along stretches of highways with roadside vegetation (weeds) in the center divider as well as off the road's shoulder. Trapping success in roadside vegetation and frequent observations of diurnal raptors hunting along these areas indicates an abundant food source (Schulz, unpublished).

Roadside vegetation, fence posts and quantity of roads as an "edge habitat complex" were found to be the most important elements for Barn Owl reproductive

TABLE 2. COMMON BARN OWL MORTALITY DUE TO COLLISIONS ON HIGHWAYS IN CALIFORNIA 1980-1985

Year	Dead Owls observed	Total miles	Ave/mile
1980	116	3,530	0.304
1981	202	4,321	.213
1982	261	5,862	.224
1983	110	4,066	.369
1984	127	4,023	.316
1985	96	2,740	.285
Total	912	24,542	.270

success in Oklahoma (2). Barn Owls attracted to roadside vegetation by the presence of rodents become vulnerable to collisions with moving vehicles. When confronted with bright lights while foraging at night, Barn Owls become disoriented, perhaps as a result of temporary blindness. They often move away from the light source continuing in its path, but will occasionally fly directly toward it (Schulz, unpub-

TABLE 3. BARN OWLS RECEIVED AT CALIFORNIA REHABILITATION CENTERS

Cause	A	B	C	D	E	F	G	Total/Category	%
Human conflict[1]		83	79	30	24	157	75*	448	27.40
Confiscated (pet)	4	10	0	12	4	6	9	45	2.70
Shot	3	4	0	0	1	2	0	10	.61
Trauma	35	35	—	48	15	72	39	244	14.90
Collision	2	17	—	—	4	37	—	60	3.60
Fell from nest	1	46	41	67	22	232	74*	483	29.50
Trapped (accidental)	0	8	0	0	5	0	0	13	.79
Disease[2]	5	4	3	10	16	26	8	72	4.40
Starvation	0	3	0	49	0	19	1	72	4.40
Secondary/poisoning[3]	0	0	0	0	17	0	0	17	1.40
Unknown	37	44	47	4	29	29	—	190	11.60
Died/euthanasia	52	94	94	87	50	61	25	463	28.3
Released	49	159	180	141	63	235	178	1005	61.4
Total received	108	253	285	270	114	389	219	1638	

*Approximation
[1] Human conflict includes: nesting in buildings, attics, air vents, farm equipment, airplane hangers, bridges, hay, pipes, signs, tree cut down, etc.
[2] Disease: 56% trichomoniasis, .27% TB, .13% Candidiasis, 43% unknown etiology.
[3] Clinical signs included: seizures, alternating pupillary dilation and constriction, retinal and intestinal hemorrhage, death (anticoagulant rodent control in area).
[4] Key to data sources:
    A Santa Clara Co. Humane Society Wildlife Center (1981–85)
    B Five Mile Creek Raptor Center, Stockton, CA (1981–85)
    C Native Bird Rehabilitation Project, Somis, CA (1981–85)
    D Dr. William Wirtz II, Dept. Biology, Pomona College, Claremont, CA (1973–85)
    E Wildlife Rescue, Inc., Palo Alto, CA (1980–85)
    F UC Davis Raptor Center, Davis, CA (1980–85)
    G Susan Parkes, Raptor Rehabilitator, Orange Co., CA (1978–85)

lished). Another possible factor to consider is the dynamics of high speed air currents created by passing vehicles, especially large trucks. These trucks create strong air currents which could potentially drag or pull owls into their path (66).

Longevity of captive Barn Owls has exceeded 50 years (26) but is greatly reduced in wild birds. The average lifespan of freeliving Barn Owls is 1.5 years (56). Studies of banded Barn Owls revealed that 60 percent died in less than 1 year (56).

ENVIRONMENTAL TOXICITIES

It has been well documented that chemical contamination of ecosystems can effect animal populations, especially those species at the top of the food chain (59). Some investigators have stated that concentration of toxins in the food chain through biomagnification is not a problem for the Barn Owl (31).

A recent study of Barn Owls indicates that secondary poisoning may not be a significant hazard (11). However, there have been a few cases which strongly suggest secondary poisoning in an areas which uses anticoagulant baits for rodent control. Barn Owls exhibited the following clinical signs: alternating pupillary contraction and dilation, seizures, massive intestinal and retinal hemorrhage and massive brain hemorrhage on postmortem (Table 3). Therefore, secondary poisoning is still a potential problem that requires further investigation since there are some studies which have clearly demonstrated the hazard to raptors (22, 38).

DIRECT HUMAN PERSECUTION

Human persecution is probably decreasing due to a greater awareness and changing attitudes toward wildlife. Educational programs associated with rehabilitation efforts have probably contributed significantly to developing more sensitive attitudes. However, some persecution still remains in California as well as in other states (37, 49).

Data collected from 7 rehabilitation centers in California is summarized in Table 3. Out of 1638 Barn owls, only 3.31 percent (confiscated, shot) were brought to centers as a result of direct human persecution. Two major reasons orphaned owls are received are due to nesting in places which conflict with humans (27.40 percent) and falling from nests (29.50 percent). Trauma accounted for 14.9 percent of those received and, although incomplete histories failed to reveal the cause, it is highly likely that the majority were due to collisons. Only 3.60 percent actually documented trauma due to collisions. Other less frequent problems associated with civilization are electrocution, entanglement on telephone wires, kite string, light poles, tar and oil.

DISEASES

The relative effect of disease on Barn Owl populations is unknown due to a paucity of information. Many diseases found in raptors have yet to be reported in

Barn Owls. These include Avian pox, Herpesvirus and Marek's disease (17, 20, 28). Natural infection of Herpesvirus strigis has been observed in several owl species but the Barn Owl proved resistant to massive experimental infection (8).

Serological investigations at Davis, California, revealed no seropositive Barn Owls to the following agents: Toxoplasma gondii, Coxiella burnettii (Q fever), adenovirus, reovirus, infectious bursal disease virus and Newcastle disease virus (44). However, Newcastle disease has been reported in captive Barn Owls (28). Reports of Salmonellosis in Barn Owls are also rare (28). We have diagnosed Tuberculosis on postmortem in two Barn Owls at Davis and one case of Aspergillosis.

Trichomoniasis is one of the most common diseases seen in Barn Owls at rehabilitation centers (Table 3). A total of 40 birds out of 72 classified as diseased were diagnosed with Trichomonas. It is characterized by pseudomembranous lesions of the oral cavity and should be differentiated from other diseases causing similar oral lesions such as Candidiasis (25).

Hemoprotozoal infections are not uncommon in Barn Owls but they usually do not cause debilitating problems (41). Myiasis in juvenile Barn Owls is not uncommon, especially in birds under three weeks of age with poorly-developed facial feathers, but also occurs in older birds. Visualization of the Calliphorid Fly larva in the external ear openings is easy in younger birds. Detection of fly larvae in older birds can often be made by observing the presence of wet and matted feathers around the ear openings. Fly larvae are also found in the mouth of debilitated owls.

An unusual parasitic fly, *Carnus hemapterus,* has been reported previously on other raptors in North America but was found by us for the first time on Barn Owls recently (52). This fly is found on nestling owls and is usually in the apterylae regions including under the wings (axillary), under the legs (femoral), the patagium and abdomen. Although the biology and feeding habits of this fly are not well known, we have observed it feeding on the blood and body fluids of its host. Highly infected individuals had lowered pack cell volumes (Schulz, unpublished).

NUTRITIONAL DISEASE

Young orphaned Barn Owls are often kept by well meaning persons who have little understanding about nutrition. Young owls are fed poor diets including hamburger, steak, liver, beef heart and even cottage cheese. Unfortunately, these diets result in moderate to severe metabolic disease which often require euthanasia. One juvenile Barn Owl removed from a haystack nest had abnormal feather development but was otherwise healthy. The owl was given mice supplemented with bone meal and Vionate. The feathers developed normally by the end of four weeks.

REPRODUCTION

Although the sexes are basically alike, they can be distinguished by subtle dimorphic characteristics. The female is generally slightly larger and darker than the male. The most important characteristic used to determine sexes is the size and quantity of the breast and belly speckling (dark triangular spots). The female has larger and more numerous speckling (1 mm.–3 mm.) and the male has small, sparse speckling (½–1 mm.) (47, 48).

Barn Owls will mate as young as 10 and 11 months old (32, 61). Nesting season varies geographically and is correlated with climate and prey availability (42). In California, nesting occurs throughout the year with peak periods in the spring (March, April) and the summer (July, August). When food is plentiful Barn Owls will produce 2 clutches and rarely 3. They will also renest if they are unsuccessful (52). Clutch size varies between 2 and 10 eggs but the average is 5–6. There is evidence that clutch size as well as fledging success is related to prey availability (11, 42). Eggs are usually laid at 2–3 day intervals. The female incubates as soon as the first egg is laid, resulting in asynchronous hatching which occurs in 28–32 days. When food is scarce the younger, smaller owls are often cannibalized by the older owls (21). According to Henny (21) 44–53 percent of the owl pairs in a population must breed each year and 1.86 to 2.18 young need to be fledged from each nest to maintain the population.

ARTIFICIAL INCUBATION AND HOUSING

Eggs can be successfully incubated in a clean incubator with a temperature of 37°C and relative humidity of 65–80 percent (14, 45). The eggs should be placed in the incubator in an upright position with the air cell up and rotated 45° from the central axis at least 3 to several times a day (14, 45). This provides exercise for the developing embryo and prevents adhesion of membranes (40). Newly-hatched Barn Owls should be kept in a brooder with a temperature of 95–98°F and a relative humidity greater than 60 percent. Observe the birds closely for signs of overheating (panting, wings outstretched) and adjust the temperature accordingly. On the other hand, continuous tremors or shaking may indicate a subnormal temperature.

At 10 days of age the owls can be removed from the brooder and kept in a large cardboard box with clean wood shaving at 80–85°F. Young owls should be housed together as long as they are of similar size and age. Owls kept in groups huddle closely to keep warm. This will also provide a feeling of psychological well being. By 21 days of age the birds are kept at room temperature. At 28 days of age the owls can be placed in outdoor enclosures in mild climates (minimum temperature above 40°F). By 45 days of age the owls will move about more and need room for exercise.

Orphaned Barn Owls should ideally be raised with a surrogate parent or in groups to enhance normal, psychological and social development (37, 51). However, Barn Owls which have been hand-raised by people and are (apparently) "imprinted" should not be considered non-releasable. Two Barn Owls which were hand-raised from hatching until 53–55 days showed pronounced lack of fear toward people. When placed in a chamber with normally imprinted owls of similar ages they displayed threat postures and aggression toward the normal owls. However, the next morning the owls were huddled closely with the normal owls. Within 10 days their behavior toward other owls appeared normal and tameness had diminished but they tolerated human approach. After 3 weeks in a large flight cage (with normal owls) their behavior toward humans had completely reversed (51).

FEEDING AND NUTRITION

The main goal of the rehabilitator should be to provide a natural diet as closely as possible (37, 48). Fresh, wild rodents or laboratory mice are best. However, frozen (thawed) mice are adequate as long as they are not stored over 6 months in the freezer (48). The quantity of food required depends on the size of the bird, age, activity, ambient temperature and season (48). A captive Barn Owl weighing 400 grams requires about 60 kilocalories ME/day for maintenance (33) or 3–4 medium laboratory mice/day.

Observations of a female Barn Owl feeding her young revealed that only small pieces of organ and muscle tissue are fed the first 5 days. Thereafter, the young begin to eat increasingly larger pieces which include bone, skin and fur. Vitamin supplementation is not required in most instances when feeding a whole animal (rodent) diet. However, some rehabilitators feel it is necessary (37, 63). It is important to wait approximately 24 hours prior to feeding newly-hatched owls (37). Captive, hand-raised Barn Owls have developed normally when fed all parts of the mouse except the intestine, bone and fur for the first 5 days. After that they are fed larger pieces of whole, cut-up mice including bone, skin and fur (45).

The young owls are fed with long, blunt-tip forceps until they begin eating on their own. Large numbers of young may be more conveniently fed pre-ground mice from a cone-shaped squeeze tube. Young birds are given food until they refuse to eat. Very young birds may have to be supported manually during feeding. Feeding

TABLE 4. FEEDING SCHEDULE FOR HAND-REARED BARN OWLS

Age (days)	Feeding intervals (hours)	No. times per day
1	1–2	8–10
2	↓	↓
3		
4	↓	↓
5		
6–10	2–3	5–7
11–20	3–4	4
21–50	8	2
50+	24	1

response (mouth opening) can usually be stimulated by touching the corner of the owl's mouth (rectus). Occasionally very young birds require gentle forceful mouth opening followed by careful placement of a small quantity of food in the rear of the mouth. After observation of proper swallowing this can be repeated, being careful not to overfeed. Young birds raised together will stimulate each other's feeding response with their vocalization and behavior (48).

A typical feeding schedule is outlined in Table 4 (45). By the age of 18–21 days the young, rapidly developing Barn Owls will begin swallowing mice whole and will usually eat ad libitum. Enough mice should be made available to young owls housed together so that there are some left over the following day.

HANDLING, RESTRAINT AND TRANSPORT

Barn Owls, like most birds of prey, protect themselves with their feet which are equipped with strong, needle-sharp talons. They are very quick and will either put their head down and spread their wings before lunging forward or lay on their back with talons ready. Barn Owls are capable of inflicting painful injury to the unwary, inexperienced, or careless handler. Knowledge of proper handling techniques and self-confidence by the handler should prevent most injuries. Heavy leather gloves are highly recommended. The safety of the bird being handled is equally important and should not be taken lightly.

If a Barn Owl has a wing fracture and must be transported to a veterinarian or rehabilitation center the wing should be immobilized in order to prevent more serious damage. This can be safely accomplished by placing a 3-inch wide orthopedic stockinette (Tomac tubular stockinettes are distributed by American Hospital) over the head and body (49). The proper sized stockinette is extremely important since a smaller width would be too tight and compromise respiration. Conversely, a width too large would not restrain the bird sufficiently. This method restrains the bird and immobilizes the injured wing and also greatly reduces stress.

The legs can be secured with 1/2–3/4-inch wide, 6-inch long velcro strap (with velcro sewn back-to-back). This is accomplished by first wrapping the velcro securely to one leg just above the feet and securing the other leg firmly by wrapping both legs together. Velcro has the advantage over other materials such as tape in ease of application and quick removal. The bird can then be placed on its back or side on a car seat with the head slightly elevated. This method of restraint is also recommended when routinely weighing owls.

Birds with leg fractures should not be placed in a box while transporting since this would most likely result in further damage. It is advisable to hand-carry a bird with this type of injury, making certain that the uninjured leg is properly restrained and the fractured leg is carefully supported.

Barn Owls with no obvious fractures are best transported in a well-ventilated cardboard box or pet carrier. The use of a wire cage or an airline carrier with metal mesh doors is not recommended. It is not uncommon to see birds which have suffered severe trauma after being transported in these types of crates.

Barn Owls over 3 weeks of age will often react violently toward humans or other disturbances by flailing out with their talons grasping at anything they touch. Therefore, owls should be transported separately to prevent accidental talon injury. One such accident resulted in osteomyelitis with eventual death of a juvenile Barn Owl (46).

A fine mesh or heavy denim cloth net is recommended when capturing Barn Owls in a chamber. The net should not be used in a sweeping fashion while the bird is flying as this could result in injury. When using a net, always approach the bird slowly and quietly, keeping the net below its eye level. If used properly, a net allows the handler to get close enough without causing flight or escape behavior. By using the full length of the net and a 3-6' handle with outstretched arms, one can usually drop the net over a perched owl before it attempts escape.

After netting, the bird is quickly and carefully grasped with both thumbs over the shoulders and the fingers close to the body below the sternum. The hands are then moved carefully in a posterior direction until the legs are felt through the net. After both legs are secured with one hand the other hand regrasps the legs inside the net and the bird is removed. If properly secured, a Barn Owl can be restrained and carried with one hand, allowing the other hand to place a stockinette over the head and body.

REHABILITATION OF INJURED AND SICK OWLS

Most adult Barn Owls received by rehabilitators are sick, starving or suffering from a traumatic injury. Each bird should be carefully examined by a veterinarian and evaluated for signs of shock and dehydration (37, 49). The normal body temperature for Barn Owls should be 103–106°F.

Hematology values are important clinical tools and can reveal valuable information on the patient's condition. Normal blood values for owls are given in Table 5 (53).

A packed cell volume 10–15 percent below normal indicates possible anemia, whereas dehydration is often confirmed with clinical signs of pale, dry oral mucous membranes and an elevated PCV. An elevated white blood count usually means infection. The total protein (TP) is useful in determining the nutritional state or presence of infection. A lowered TP suggests malnutrition and a high TP may indicate chronic infection (53).

Eye damage in trauma cases is common but often inapparent (9). Ophthalmological examination should be standard procedure for all incoming owls. Wild

TABLE 5. NORMAL HEMATOLOGY VALUES FOR OWLS

PCV (%)	41.5 ± 5
RBC (10^6 UL)	2.7 ± .53
WBC (10^3 UL)	15.6 ± 9.5
TP (GM%)	4.2 ± 0.7
MCV (FL)	154 ± 24

From Smith and Bush 1978.

Barn Owls have been observed existing successfully with loss of one eye (Schulz, unpublished). The release of one-eyed Barn Owls is recommended since they depend on hearing to localize their prey more than vision. They should be evaluated for hearing impairment and their ability to catch live prey in a flight chamber prior to release.

After the owl has recovered from its problem the veterinarian and rehabilitator should agree on a program which will return the bird to nature as rapidly as possible. Owls with traumatic injuries will usually require a carefully planned physical therapy program (24). Adults are already experienced catching live prey and, therefore, need less preparation than young, inexperienced owls (37).

GROWTH AND DEVELOPMENT

The Barn Owl does not develop as rapidly as the Short-eared Owl but in 2 months transforms from a small, helpless, uncoordinated chick to a dramatically beautiful, silent-flying, superbly adapted predator.

Table 6 provides an outline of development and behavior in the Barn Owl (7, 45). The eyes open between 7-10 days but do not focus well until approximately

TABLE 6. COMMON BARN OWL: SUMMARY OF DEVELOPMENT

Age (days)	Physical appearance	Behavior
0-1	sparse white down, pink skin	weak, uncoordinated head movements
1-5	sparse white down, pink skin—larger legs and body	sits, crawls on tarsometatarsus, grasps with feet and bill
6-10	2nd buffy cream colored down, eyes opened—blue color	pecks at feet and feathers, begs with wings and neck outstretched
11-15	pin feathers prominent, sparse buffy down developing, pot-bellied	holds head up, reacts to movements, hisses and snaps bill when disturbed
16-24	thick "wooly" down covers body except belly, facial disc developing	stands and walks more frequently, cranes neck and cocks head, focusing, aggressive
25-35	adult feathers unfurling from sheaths of primaries and caudals, facial disc well defined and heart shaped	increasing wing flapping, lays on back and strikes with feet, eating whole mice
36-50	facial feathers well developed, adult feathers appearing on back of head and tarsus, down wearing off, primaries nearly complete	jumps and pounces, defensive posture when disturbed
51-60	patchy down remains on feathers especially belly and top of head	uncoordinated flight, often lands on ground
60-65	adult appearance	flying, catches live prey, exaggerated head movements

a week later. By the 16th day the owl has a "wooly" appearance from the thick, second down which covers the body. The owls are more alert and hiss when disturbed. They are also standing and walking more frequently. On the 25th day the feathers are appearing (unfurling) from the ends of the feather sheaths on the primaries and tail feathers. The facial disc feathers are becoming well defined, giving the owl its typical heart-shaped face. By the 35th day the facial disc is well developed and feathers are appearing on the back of the head. The typical defensive posture with outstretched wings and lowered head is frequently displayed when disturbed. On the 45th day the owl's appearance is more adult-like but down feathers remain. Uncoordinated flight occurs frequently after 50 days and the now well-developed feathers have remnant patches of down on the belly, top of head, wings and back. In 60 days the birds are adult-like in appearance and are now catching live prey and can be distinguished in poor light by their exaggerated head movements (7). Table 7 is a summary of growth data collected from 27 Barn Owls at UCD Raptor Center.

PREPARATION FOR RELEASE OF ORPHANED BARN OWLS

Young Barn Owls aged 60–65 days are placed in a flight chamber (20'W × 40'L × 8–10'H) with perches that are 30' apart and placed a few feet from the walls at each end. In the center of the chamber a rodent-proof arena (10'W × 24'L × 15"D) is provided to prevent mice from escaping. The flight chamber also has an enclosed roosting box (2'W × 3'L × 2'H) in which the owls remain during the day.

Two to four small (20–25 gm.), dark-colored, live laboratory mice per owl are provided in the "arena" each evening. The arena has gravel which is sparsely covered with dry leaves. The number of mice remaining, number of pellets, weekly weights, condition of individual owls, and evaluation of their ability to fly are parameters for judging how well they are doing. Since owls cache or store their food, the chamber must be thoroughly inspected each day for hidden carcasses and then removed (48). A few young owls may be slow but the majority are quick to sharpen their innate hunting and prey-catching abilities (2–3 days).

During the 4-week stay in the flight chamber, young Barn Owls normally lose some weight. Out of 60 birds an average weight loss of 46 grams was observed. When the weight levels off, the birds are usually ready for release. All birds with weight loss were in excellent condition.

We have trained as many as 20 owls in the same chamber simultaneously. Some of the bolder, more aggressive owls will relinquish or feed their mouse to the more timid birds. Sometimes there are aggressive encounters but these are usually harmless and short-lived.

After 3–4 weeks in the flight chamber the owls are banded with USFW aluminum locking bands and released in the evening into nest box-type hack sites which allow the bird to fly out on the first night. Since hunting in the wild will require considerably more skill for the young owl than in a chamber, the hack site allows the young birds a place to roost and be fed if they are reluctant to leave. Mice are placed in the entrance of the nest box each night until they no longer are eaten. A few have returned as long as three weeks but more often the young birds fail to return on the second evening.

RESULTS OF BARN OWL RELEASES

Information concerning the longevity, dispersal and survival of banded, captive-reared Barn Owls is lacking (47, 62). Banding recovery rates for wild, parent-reared Barn Owls are high, from 12.3–14.7 percent (56) perhaps because 1. they often nest in close association with man, 2. their conspicuous size and 3. the fact that they often collide with vehicles along roads (19, 36, 52).

TABLE 7. BARN OWL GROWTH

Age (Days)	Mean Weight (gm)	Weight Range (gm)	Mean Tail Length (mm)	Mean Wing Length (mm)	Tarsus (mm)	Culmen (mm)	Avg. Length 10th 1° (mm)
0	16	14–17	NM	NM	NM	NM	NM
1	20	16–21	NM	NM	NM	NM	NM
2	26	19–28	NM	NM	NM	NM	NM
3	31	23–34	NM	NM	NM	NM	NM
4	35	30–39	NM	NM	NM	NM	NM
5	44	37–48	NM	NM	NM	NM	NM
10	93	87–132	NM	NM	NM	NM	NM
15	236	223–241	NM	NM	NM	NM	NM
20	319	286–349	0	62	65	14	10
25	423	399–434	8	98	77	17	25
30	528	446–557	21	131	89	19	48
35	562	504–612	38	168	92	19	80
40	630	587–649	56	197	95	19	99
45	622	603–641	65	224	96	20	125
50	576	563–595	92	231	96	21	145
55	537	522–556	113	243	96	21	160
60	501	458–523	116	278	96	22	181
65	475	437–505	117	280	96	22	270

($\bar{N}$ 27 UCD Raptor Center Data)

Banding recoveries of wild Barn Owls indicate that long range geographical displacement sometimes occurs (5, 6, 13, 15, 18, 39, 56). Twenty-five band recoveries out of a total of 261 Barn Owls (9.5 percent) banded before 1980 at Davis, California, demonstrated that 50 percent survived more than 100 days and 16 percent survived over 1 year (Table 8). Twelve owls failed to survive over 1 month. Of these, 7 were struck by cars, 3 had severe Trichomoniasis, 1 died from starvation, 1 of unknown cause.

TABLE 8. LONGEVITY OF BANDED BARN OWLS

Days	(0–35)	(36–100)	(101–400)	(401–800)
No. birds recovered	12	5	4	4

The results indicate that our rehabilitation efforts are successful for those owls which survived over 1 month. Two rehabilitated adult owls with repaired wing injuries were recovered after surviving 406 and 755 days and having dispersed a distance of 80 and 90 miles. One owl was recovered within 3 miles of the site it was originally found which was 90 miles from the release site. Each time the owl was hit by a car.

Of the captive-reared owls, 16 (64 percent) remained within 5 miles from the release site and 7 (28 percent) owls were encountered 10–35 miles from the release site (Figure 2). One Barn Owl not included in this data was released in Stockton and recovered 323 days later, 590 miles away.

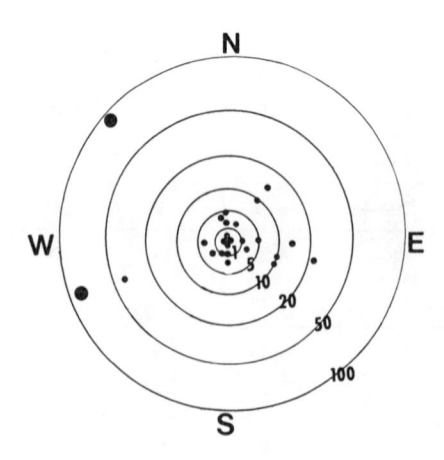

- Rehabilitated adults
- Captive reared (orphaned)

Figure 2. Distance and dispersal direction of banded barn owls.

A summary of the causes of mortality (Table 9) shows that 64 percent of the deaths were a result of highway collisions. These data are no doubt biased since birds along roadsides are more apt to be encountered than those which die elsewhere. However, banding encounters provide valuable data on the success or failure of rehabilitation efforts.

CONSERVATION

Currently there are efforts to reestablish Barn Owls in areas where they are rare or no longer exist in the United States (10, 12, 30, 31, 63). These efforts include captive breeding and release, preservation of existing nest sites, construction and placement of artificial nest boxes, habitat preservation and public education. Nest box management has proved successful, especially in areas with few natural available nest sites (4, 10, 11, 35, 52).

Efforts to reestablish Barn Owls should consider habitat quality and prey availability as the most important pre-requisite for their success. At least one nest box should be available for every 2 birds released within a 5-mile radius. Nest boxes provide known sites for population surveys in areas where the Barn Owl is rare or uncommon. In areas where foraging habitat is limited, design and careful placement of nest boxes is important (10, 11, 12). Since the Barn Owl has difficulty surviving cold weather it is recommended that boxes be placed inside buildings such as barns for greater protection from the elements. Entrances opening to the outside of the building should ideally face open fields (10).

A nest box program begun in 1981 in Davis, California, has proven successful. Our nest box is designed for placement in large trees adjacent to foraging habitat. However, the box can also be placed in and on the side of buildings. The boxes should ideally face the morning sun (east) or away from prevailing winds. The placement height should be 20–40' off the ground. The nest box is constructed out of

TABLE 9. CAUSES OF MORTALITY IN BANDED CAPTIVE-REARED BARN OWLS

Cause	Total number	Percentage
Collisions (Highways)	16	64
Disease	4	16
Starvation	1	4
Collision (Airplane @ Airport)	1	4
Electrocution	1	4
Wing Caught (light pole)	1	4
Unknown	1	4
Totals	25	100

exterior waterproofed, 1/2" plywood. Dimensions are given in Figure 3. This design allows maximum darkness and protection from the elements for the incubating female and subsequent young.

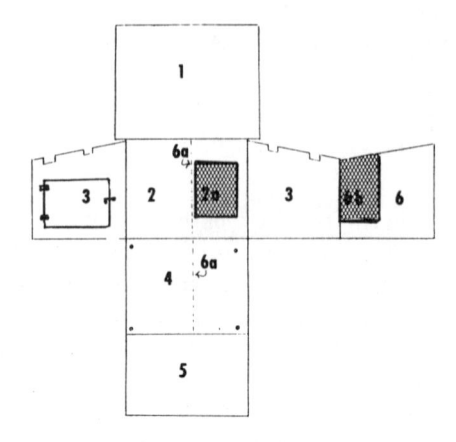

Figure 3. Barn Owl nestbox plans.

1. (Top) 28" x 20".
2. (Front) 24" W x 18" H.
   2a. (Entrance) 6-7" W x 8-10" H.
3. (Side) 18" W x 18" H and slopes to 16" at back. A hinged door opening into the nesting chamber is 13" L x 9" H.
4. (Bottom) 23" x 17".
5. (Back) 24" x 16".
6. (Inside wall) (Baffle) 17" W x 18" H at front and slopes to 16" at rear.
   6a. Placement of inside wall, 9" from wall on entrance side.
   6b. Doorway into nest area, 7" W (cut 4" x above the floor).

Nest boxes used by Barn Owls in Davis increased from 19 percent occupancy in 1981 to 70 percent occupancy in 1985 (Table 10). During that period 95 owls out of 130 eggs (73 percent fledging success) hatched (52) in the 30 clutches monitored. It is noteworthy that nest boxes placed along busy streets, city parks and in heavily vegetated (large mature trees) residential areas were successful. All nest boxes, however, were within 300 yards of open fields.

TABLE 10. NESTBOX USE BY COMMON BARN OWLS 1981–1985

Year	No. nestboxes	No. occupied	%
1981	7	4	19
1982	21	12	48
1983	25	14	50
1984	28	18	55
1985	33	23	70

Occupied nest boxes require annual cleaning to remove large accumulations of pellet and fecal material. Sometimes the boxes may be occupied by unwanted animals such as bees, piegeons and magpies (4, 10).

The Common Barn Owl is a masterpiece of evolutionary design which has both benefited and suffered because of advancing civilization. It is our responsibility as caretakers to gain further insight into its secrets so that we can improve our efforts to protect it.

With continuing environmental changes, the future for the Common Barn Owl and all wildlife depends on carefully planned conservation efforts. One of the most important aspects of these efforts should be a continuing public education program. Public education will help to develop more sensitive attitudes about all wildlife and create the attributes necessary to continue these efforts in the future.

ACKNOWLEDGEMENTS

I would like to thank all the volunteers who gave us their valuable time to help with the Barn Owl project. Although they are too numerous to mention some deserve special recognition.

They are: Bill and C.J. Roertgen, Allen Fish, Dick Schmidt, George Carpenter, Bret Stedman, Dave Phillips, Sally Lewis, Russell Tucker, Tom McNeil, Don Yasuda, Cicely Muldoon and Jon Dunn. Thanks also to the California Conservation Corps for help with the nest box construction.

The following persons graciously offered their data: Dr. Ron Dalzell, Margie Comstock, Dr. William Wirtz II, Liz Beard, Kit Crump and family, and Susan Parkes. Special thanks to my wife Katy whose patience and help with the manuscript made the effort successful.

REFERENCES

1. Arbib, R. 1979. The Blue List for 1980. American Birds 33 (6): 830–835.
2. Ault, J.W. III, 1982. A Quantitative Estimate of Barn Owl Nesting Habitat Quality. M.S. Thesis, Oklahoma State University.
3. Baumgartner, A.M. and Baumgartner, F.M., 1944. Hawks and Owls in Oklahoma, 1939–42: Food Habits and Population Changes. Wilson Bull. 56: 209–215.
4. Bloom, P.H. 1979. Ecological Studies of the Barn Owl in California (Proceedings Nat. Aud. Soc. Symp. Owls of the West, 36–39).
5. Bolen, E.G. 1978. Long-distance Displacement of Two Southern Barn Owls. Bird Banding 49 (1): 78–79.
6. Broun, M. 1954. Long-distance Recovery of Barn Owl. Bird Banding 25: 149.
7. Bunn, D.S. Warburton, A.B. and Wilson, R.O.S. 1982. The Barn Owl. Buteo Books, Vermillion, S.D.
8. Burtscher, H. and Sibalin, M. 1975. Herpesvirus strigis: Host Spectrum and Distribution in Infected Owls. J. Wildl. Dis. 11: 164–169.
9. Buyukmihci, N. 1985. Lesions of the Ocular Posterior Segment of Raptors. Proceed. Amer. College of Vet. Ophthalmologist. Nov. 1985.

10. Colvin, B.A., Hegdal, P.L. and Jackson, W.B. 1984. A Comprehensive Approach to Research and Management of Common Barn Owl Populations. Workshop Management of Nongame Species and Ecological Communities, Lexington, Kentucky, pp. 270–282.
11. Colvin, B.A. 1984. Barn Owl Foraging Behavior and Secondary Poisoning Hazard From Rodenticide Use on Farms. Doctoral Diss. Bowling Green State Univ. 326 pp.
12. ———. 1985. Common Barn Owl Population Decline in Ohio and the Relationship to Agricultural Trends. J. Field Ornithol. 56 (3): 224–235.
13. Cooke, M.T. 1941. Returns from Band Birds; Recoveries of Some Banded Birds of Prey. Bird Banding 12: 150–160.
14. Crawford, W.C. Jr. 1982. Techniques For Artificial Incubation and Hand-Rearing of Raptors. Wildlife Rehabilitation. Proc. Nat. Wild. Rehab. Symp. Vol. 1: 143–152.
15. Dexter, R.W. 1957. Additional Recoveries of Banded Crows, Hawks and Owls. Bird Banding 28: 99.
16. Errington, P.L. 1931. Winter Killing of Barn Owls in Wisconsin. Wilson Bull. 43: 60.
17. Graham, D.L. and Halliwell, W.H. 1978. Virus Disease of Birds of Prey. In Zoo and Wild Animal Medicine Ed. M.E. Fowler. W.B. Saunders, p. 260–265.
18. Gallup, F.N. 1949. Banding Recoveries of *Tyto alba*. Bird Banding 20: 150.
19. Glue, D. 1973. Seasonal Mortality in Four Small Birds of Prey. Ornis. Scand. 4: 97–102.
20. Halliwell, W.H. and Graham, D.L. 1978. Bacterial Diseases of Birds of Prey. In Zoo and Wild Animal Medicine. Ed. M.E. Fowler. W.B. Saunders, p. 265–273.
21. Henny, C.J. 1969. Geographical Variation in Mortality and Production Requirements of the Barn Owl. Bird Banding 40: 277–290.
22. Hill, E.F. and Mendenhall, V.M. 1980. Secondary Poisoning of Barn Owls with Famphur an Organophosphate Insecticide. J. Wildl. Manage. 44 (3): 676–681.
23. Honer, M.R. 1963. Observations on the Barn Owl (*Tyto alba guttata*) in the Netherlands in Relation To Its Ecology and Population Fluctuations. Ardea, 51: 158–195.
24. Horowitz, N., Schulz, T. and Fowler, M. 1983. Physical Therapy and Exercise in Raptor Rehabilitation. Proceedings AAZV Ann. Conf. 153–157.
25. Jessup, D.A. 1980. Trichomoniasis in Great Horned Owls. Mod. Vet. Prac. 61 (7) 601–604.
26. Karalus, K.E. and Eckert, A.W. 1974. The Owls of North America. Doubleday & Co. N.Y. (278 pp.).
27. Keith, A.R. 1964. A Thirty-Year Summary of the Nesting of the Barn Owl on Martha's Vineyard, Massachusetts. Bird Banding 35: 22–31.
28. Keymer, I.F. 1972. Diseases of Birds of Prey. Vet. Rec. 90 (2) 579–594.
29. Kirkwood, J.K. 1981. Maintenance Energy Requirements and Rate of Weight Loss During Starvation in Birds of Prey. p. 153–157. In J.E. Cooper and A.G. Greenwood (Eds.) Recent Advances in the Study of Raptor Diseases. Chiron publishers, West Yorkshire, England.
30. Laycock, G. 1985. Dark Days for Barn Owls. Audubon 87 (6) 28–29.
31. Lerg, J.M. and Maley, A. Status of the Barn Owl in Michigan. 1980. Michigan Dept. of Nat. Res., U.S. Fish & Wildlife Service Endangered and Threatened Species Program. Final Report. Project No. E-1-8 Study No. 605.
32. Maestrelli, J.R. 1973. Propagation of Barn Owls in Captivity. Auk 90: 426–428.
33. Marti, C.D. 1973. Food Consumption and Pellet Formation in Four Owl Species. Wilson Bull. 85: 178–181.
34. ———. 1974. Feeding Ecology of Four Sympatric Owls. Condor 76: 45–61.

35. Marti, C.D., Wagner, P.W. and Denne, K.W. 1979. Nest Boxes for the Management of Barn Owls. Wildl. Sec. Bull. 7 (3): 145–148.
36. Marti, C.D. and Wagner, P.W. 1985. Winter Mortality in Common Barn Owls and Its Effect on Population Density and Reproduction. Condor 87: 111–115.
37. McKeever, K. 1979. Care and Rehabilitation of Injured Owls. W.F. Rannie Pub. Lincoln, Ontario. (112 pp.).
38. Mendelssohn, H. and Paz, U. 1977. Mass Mortality of Birds of Prey Caused by Azodrin, An Organophosphorous Insecticide. Biol. Conserv. 11: 163–170.
39. Mueller, H.C. and Berger, D.D. 1979. Over Water Flights of Barn Owls. Bird Banding 50 (1): 68–69.
40. Olendorff, R. 1971. Special Conference on Captivity Breeding of Raptors A Report. Raptor Res. 6 (B): B7–B34.
41. Olsen, G.H. and Gaunt, S.D. 1985. Effect of Hemoprotozoal Infections on Rehabilitation of Wild Raptors. JAVMA 187 (11) 1204–1205.
42. Otteni, L.C., Bolen, E.G. and Cottam, C. 1972. Predator-Prey Relationship and Reproduction of the Barn Owl in Southern Texas. Wilson Bull. 48: 434–448.
43. Prestt, I. 1965. An Inquiry into the Recent Breeding Status of Some Smaller Birds of Prey and Crows in Britain. Bird Study 12: 196–221.
44. Riemann, H., Behymer, D., Fowler, M., Ley, D., Schulz, T., Ruppanner, R. and King, D. 1977. Serological Investigation of Captive and Free-Living Raptors. Raptor Res. 11 (4): 104–111.
45. Schulz, T. 1975. Artificial Incubation and Rearing of Barn Owls. *Tyto alba*. Ann. Proceedings Amer. Assoc. Zoo Vet. San Diego, CA 197–202.
46. Schulz, T., Silverman, S. and Thilsted, J. 1977. Implant Osteomyelitis in a Barn Owl (*Tyto alba*) J. Zoo Animal Med. 8 (4) 11–15.
47. Schulz, T. 1979. Survival, Dispersal and Longevity of Captive-Reared, Banded Barn Owls. Raptor Res. Foundation Ann. Conf. Oral Report (unpub.).
48. ———. 1979. Captive Husbandry of Owls. American Assoc. of Zoos, Parks and Aquariums. Ann. Proceedings. 309–334.
49. Schulz, T. and Sedgwick, C. 1979. Veterinary Care of Birds of Prey in California. Calif. Vet. 4: 18–24.
50. Schulz, T. 1982. Band Recoveries of Rehabilitated and Captive-Reared Barn Owls. (*Tyto alba*) Raptor Release, Newsletter, UCD Raptor Center 1 (3): 34.
51. ———. 1985. Experiences and Results Using Surrogate Parents to Raise and Rehabilitate Orphaned Raptors. RRF International Symposium on the Management of Birds of Prey. Sacramento, CA. Abstract.
52. Schulz, T. and Yasuda, D. 1985. Ecology & Management of the Common Barn Owl in the California Central Valley. International Symposium on Owls. Annual Raptor Res. Found. Conf. Sacramento, CA. Abstract.
53. Smith, E. and Bush, M. 1978. Hematologic Parameters on Various Species of Strigiformes and Falconiformes. J. Wild. Dis. 14:447–450.
54. Smith, D.G. and Marti, C.D. 1976. Distributional Status and Ecology of Barn Owls in Utah. Raptor Research 10 (2): 33–44.
55. Spiers, J.M. 1940. Mortality of Barn Owls at Champagn, Illinois. Auk 57: 571.
56. Stewart, P.A. 1952. Dispersal, Breeding, Behavior and Longevity of Banded Barn Owls in North America. Auk 69: 227–245.
57. ———. 1952. Winter Mortality of Barn Owls in Central Ohio. Wilson Bull. 64: 164–166.

58. ———. 1980. Population Trends of Barn Owls in North America. Amer. Birds 34 (4): 698–700.
59. Stickel, L.F. 1968. Organochlorine Pesticides in the Environment. U.S. Bureau of Sport Fisheries & Wildlife, Special Sci. Report Wildlife No. 119 (32 pp.).
60. Trautman, M.B. 1940. The Birds of Buckeye Lake, Ohio. Univ. of Michigan Museum of Zoology. Misc. Pub. No. 44.
61. Trollope, J. 1971. Some Aspects of Behavior and Reproduction in Captive Barn Owls. (*Tyto alba*) Avicult. Mag. 77: 117–125.
62. ———. 1973. Release of a Captive-Bred Barn Owl. Avicultural Mag. 79 (1) 7–8.
63. Waddell, W. and Crawford, W.C. Jr. 1982. Barn Owl Recovery Program—Missouri and the Midwest. Wildlife Rehabilitation Vol. 1 Ed. Beaver, p. 74–80.
64. Wallace, G.J. 1966. On the Cause of Death of the Barn Owl. Bird Banding 37: 26–27.
65. Wood, N.A. 1951. Birds of Michigan. Univ. of Mich. Museum of Zoology Misc. Publ. No. 75. Ann Arbor (63 pp.).
66. White, B.R. 1986. Dept. Engineering. U.C. Davis. pers. comm.

Administrative Aspects

THE VALUE OF CENTRALIZED WILDLIFE REHABILITATION

Betsy Lewis

Executive Director
Lifeline for Wildlife, Inc.
Stony Point, NY 10980

INTRODUCTION

Ever since I first began to conceptualize and design Lifeline for Wildlife in 1978, I was convinced that it was a fundamental necessity to create a facility with a central location, a reliable core of staff members, and a strong organizational identity.

In the first hellish years, this grand design was often sorely tested. Lifeline's central location was 75 miles from its veterinarian, clients and supporters; (its reliable core of staff members was me) and its organizational identity was feeble. But each time I made efforts to "decentralize"—by increasing reliance on volunteers and by fostering out more animals—the chaos and confusion increased. It was clear that we were going in the wrong direction.

During a time of wildlife rehabilitation proliferation, when so many people write to tell us about their dream of creating a wildlife rescue center in their community, I think it is time to define three distinct organizational models that are currently used by incorporated wildlife rehabilitation centers.

The first is the network of volunteers, an incorporated organization which operates without any primary base of operations. Volunteers care for distressed wildlife in their homes, transport them to cooperating veterinarians, and give out their home telephone numbers to the public. The organization has a unified public image, and is governed by a board of directors, but the animals are cared for at many different locations.

The second is the rehabilitation center that does have a central location, but relies heavily on volunteers to care for patients in their private homes. Commonly, these facilities are an auxiliary part of a well-established nature or environmental center, humane society or zoo. The funding is ample, the buildings and location can be gorgeous—but rehabilitation itself is *not* the focal point of the larger "parent" organization.

In fact, the annual influx of thousands of tiny, needy creatures is perceived as a massive inconvenience, tolerated because the public demands it, and because substantial donations accrue from animal lovers desiring to make restitution for a baby cottontail eviscerated by their cat! The result is that the majority of the patients are "fostered out" to eager volunteers and well motivated, but worn-out staff members who attempt to care for them on their off time in their own homes.

The third structural model is the facility whose sole purpose is wildlife rehabilitation and rescue (with a Wildlife Rights Education Program, of course!) and which maintains all patients at a single location. There are presumably facilities for intensive care, infant care, medical treatment, surgery, and long-term outdoor rehabilitation. All patients are cared for by a structured team of staff and interns, with volunteers serving an auxiliary role.

It is our belief that this third alternative offers the greatest potential in the design and development of future wildlife centers, both in its advantages in patient care, and its administrative and public relations benefits. We want to stress that such freestanding, funded facilities are not unobtainable!

ADVANTAGES OF A CENTRALIZED PATIENT POPULATION

If I had to condense the advantages of a centralized patient population into one word, that word might be "control." A centralized facility basically gives the rehabilitator increased control over his patients, their caretakers (i.e. staff), and their environment.

Lifeline for Wildlife has not "farmed out" a single patient in 5 years. Fostering out was so counterproductive and inefficient that it was categorically ended in 1981.

I am often questioned about this decision by other rehabilitators and I illustrate my position by pointing out the scene in front of me. My office looks out over what we have (unimaginatively) come to call "The Bird Field"—a large field filled with compounds housing most of our avian patients. I own the field, I employ, with clear contractual obligations, every human being working in that field, and I am legally responsible for the 200+ birds being cared for within my field of vision.

Nevertheless, it is a daily challenge to ensure that each living creature out in that field is optimally fed, optimally housed, living with the maximum degree of comfort, and being evaluated and observed with maximum sensitivity. I am firmly convinced that the challenge would turn into a disaster if our policy were to distribute those same 200+ birds into 10 or more different volunteer households.

The primary goal of any wildlife rehabilitation center is to provide optimal care and comfort for each and every patient admitted into that center. I believe that maintaining all patients at the same location can be the single most important factor in developing a state-of-the-art patient care program. A central location allows the rehabilitator to develop a structure for patient care: a clearly defined hierarchy of responsibility with managers supervising less experienced assistants.

We all recognize that it's easy for any individual to get a little sloppy, a little careless, a little preoccupied—especially in the strenuous, every day routines of wildlife care: lugging all those water buckets and mucking all those compounds!

Last autumn, Shawn, a wonderful young man, who had worked for Lifeline several months, and whose performance had been excellent, fell madly in love. We thought nothing of it until our Patient Care Manager checked a new squirrel compound which Shawn had designed and constructed. He had told her it was ready to house our late-season squirrel babies—and it was—except that Shawn had forgotten to include a door.

My point is that we are all only human, and we all make mistakes. Good intentions are vitally important—but not enough by themselves. An organization needs an unapologetic and effective supervisory structure so that animals do not suffer when a caretaker has a bad day.

At Lifeline, we have a Patient Care Manager; she has no responsibility whatsoever for our budget (or lack thereof!), or any of the myriad of public relations and personnel problems which crop up in any given day. Her sole function is to be an absolute single-minded "terror" in enforcing and enabling the best conceivable care for every living creature on our 34-acre sanctuary. Working under her direction and authority are 5 patient care assistants. The salaried patient care staff is supplemented with 5-10 Interns who commit themselves to 1-3 months of work at the facility. The structure is clear: interns report to the patient care staff, who report to the Patient Care Manager. The Patient Care Manager is directly accountable to me; she and I meet at least once a day.

This personnel structure is strengthened by job descriptions, daily staff meetings, unannounced inspections of work sites, and employee evaluations. I doubt that many volunteers would tolerate these stringent demands, especially unannounced inspections of the rehabilitation they are doing in their homes. But a well-managed and trained staff expects and understands these procedures.

The reason behind, and result of this personnel hierarchy is that it enables the standardization of every aspect of our patients' regimen: diet, medical care, surgical follow-up, housing, psychological and physical development, release and euthanasia criteria. Year after year, we evaluate and improve our medical and release protocols, examine and update our diets, and upgrade our own knowledge of the ethology and captive behavior of the species in our care.

I do not believe that a primarily volunteer facility, housing animals at different locations, can achieve this same continuity of caretakers and consistency of patient care procedures.

If this description makes Lifeline sound like an Army boot camp we cordially invite you to visit the Sanctuary any day from April until October and disabuse yourselves of the notion that we are excessively organized.

One of the most important aspects of patient care is control of the wild patients' environment. By maintaining all patients at one location, far greater control of the environment can occur. Wild animals should not be exposed to children, dogs and cats, friendly neighbors, television and rock and roll. It is extremely hard to regulate 30 or 50 households where volunteers are raising animals. At a centralized facility, those factors are simply eliminated by rigidly enforced rules.

The physical site of the center must be chosen with isolation and remoteness as a prime consideration. If a sufficiently rural piece of land is acquired, with sufficient acreage, patients can be housed outdoors throughout the seasons without ever being exposed to the noise of vehicles, or any sort of human noise, except the necessary daily interruption of the caretakers.

Even though the Lifeline sanctuary is less than 1 hour from Manhattan and totally accessible to major highways, we have utilized our land so that even our permanently disabled city pigeons are located more than 200 feet from the road itself. We have distributed our compounds throughout the acreage, even though this creates hardships for the staff, who must manually transport water and food through rather rough terrain. For the same reason—preservation of an isolated, wild environment—we do not allow labor saving devices such as motorized transportation carts.

Another vital aspect of patient care is pre-release conditioning and patient socialization. Because a centralized facility handles large numbers of each species and presumably has substantial acreage, animals are raised and rehabilitated in outdoor environments with less artificial components and distractions; they can be integrated with peers of their own species rather than being deprived of companionship during vital developmental or recovery stages.

At Lifeline we have rarely had to practice aversion-techniques with our patients. This is because we have stringently followed our belief that a wild animal is intrinsically wild, and will grow up and remain wild, if human intervention is kept to a minimum, and the animal is allowed to relate continuously with its own species. Our patients relate to, compete with, and learn from their own species, and we believe that their behavioral development allows them to compete in the wild. I do not believe the same results can occur when "infant wildlings" are raised in small numbers within suburban split level homes, being the focal point of family and community attention.

A centralized facility allows the staff to develop a unified patient-identification system and consistency of medical record keeping.

We use a computer to record and analyze our data, but this data is worthless if all patients are not identified. We provide each patient with an I.D. tag or band or tatoo as soon as it arrives. At Lifeline, as at other places, we have not yet found a magical solution to the pragmatics of Patient I.D.s: leg bands fall off, fur obscures tattoos, and who wants to remove 50 ear tags from 50 releasable squirrels? But each year, we get a little more accurate and consistent. Medical records are coordinated by only one person, the Patient Care Manager—and it will be a major part of her job to track the 4000+ patients who are admitted to the Center this year. It goes without saying that honest, accurate data is imperative in order to analyze the weakest and strongest areas in patient care, and to make sure that the agency is improving its work each year.

The single most critical factor in any agency is the *human* factor: the people who work within that agency. We believe that people can be recruited, trained, managed, and supervised, best at a centralized facility. Good personnel management is essential, and results in lower staff turnover, higher motivation, and better teamwork. All of this can be more easily obtained with employees who make a clearly defined professional commitment, than with volunteers.

One example of a personnel management problem with many critical ramifications is emotional over-investment by a caretaker in a particular patient. This is not the fault of the individual involved—it is only human for those of us who care deeply about animals to become overly involved in a creature whose life we have spent enormous amounts of energy and time trying to save.

But the results can be disastrous if staff (or volunteers) are allowed, without effective supervision, to pour all of their energy and love into any given patient. Objectivity is lost. Professionalism is lost. Wild animals are over-protected, overly socialized to humans, and infantalized. Euthanasia is avoided even when it is the most humane alternative. Releasable animals are kept as "pets" for years at a time, the justification being that they are "too tame" to release.

At Lifeline, we see patients from all over the state of New York. Each year we are involved in a very significant number of cases in which a wild animal, raised within a private home, bit a member of the family or someone in the community. Usually these animals are living outdoors, in a quasi-tame state, when the incident occurs. Very often, despite our attempts at intervention, the animal is killed for a precautionary rabies test. And more and more often, the family that raised the animal identifies itself as part of a rehabilitation project.

I submit that these problems, and their often dire consequences for the animals, are virtually eliminated in a more professional centralized environment. A disciplined, structured, well-supervised staff understand that they don't make the rules; but in accepting their positions, they have committed themselves to implementing those rules. Obviously, the agency, and its leaders, must be worthy of this level of trust and respect, or the system will not work for very long.

At Lifeline, our staff, even when assigned to a specific species, are systematically rotated among individual patients. Their time is carefully monitored to make sure that they divide their energy equally among all the animals in their care. It is made very clear that no patient "belongs" to anyone, and that their supervisors place the animals welfare ahead of the staff members' job satisfaction! The staff know that if they become deeply attached to an animal, or loose their objectivity, and their overall performance suffers, that they not only risk losing that patient, but their job.

Centralized facilities also ease friction with other professional groups such as the State Department of Environmental Conservation, and with local veterinarians. Representatives of both groups can visit one location and see all aspects of the program: infant care, intensive care, and permanent resident quarters. The entire facility, and every patient in the care of that facility, are available at any given moment. A relatively stable staff with low turnover, builds credibility. It is reassuring to see the same faces and meet with the same staff members, year after year.

I believe that it impresses a state beaurocracy like the D.E.C. to see a disciplined employee hierarchy—rather than a loose volunteer cooperative. As for veterinarians—they demand a lot in return for their donated services: punctuality, professionalism, thorough follow-up. Compliance with these demands can be obtained with fewer headaches from a motivated employee than from a cadre of volunteers.

Another major advantage of a centralized facility is that it increases educational opportunities. At the Lifeline Sanctuary we are trying to teach compassion and empathy, rather than conservation, or ecology. Our primary purpose in our educational efforts is to share our belief that, "Every life is unique; all life is sacred."

Now that we have a 34-acre sanctuary to work with, we are attempting to create an atmosphere of reverence for life, which will hopefully be felt as soon as clients are in the parking lot!

We make it clear that Lifeline is not a nature center, and we emphasize repeatedly that "our animals are not on display." We only allow tours one day of every week so as to ensure our animals their privacy, and all visits are conducted in virtual silence. Our guides speak in whispers. Visitors are not allowed closer than 20 feet to any compound. We are finding that asking families to literally tip-toe through 35 acres of land—so as not to disturb any of the patients living, recuperating and growing up wild—is a very special way to get our message across, much more powerful than a classroom or auditorium.

Perhaps the single most serious handicap plaguing wildlife rehabilitation on both a fund-raising and public relations level, is that wildlife rehabilitation is still perceived by the public as a hobby. And the public is not going to offer substantive financial support to an activity they believe is done by kind people on their back porches, in their spare time, for their own enjoyment. If we want increased funding for our work, it is time to change the image of wildlife rehabilitation, and make it clear that rehabilitation is a vitally needed community service, addressing practical as well as humanitarian concerns.

This is an age of public cynicism about charities. Good promotional material, although invaluable, is not enough. Our members want to be able to say to their friends as well as themselves: "I've been there, I've seen their work with my own eyes, I am satisfied with where my money is going." This is very fundamental. An organization can only thrive for so long on good intentions, promises, and hard luck stories. Sooner or later, it has to produce "something substantive," or the public will lose interest.

One of the best ways to upgrade our image and encourage the public to take our wildlife rehabilitation efforts seriously is to establish a central facility where telephones are answered on a reliable schedule (preferably 24 hours a day), and of which they can get a glimpse (if not a complete tour) when they admit a patient.

The more that an organization appears to be an established entity and the more credibility it has, the less often will a well-intentioned animal lover cling to her nestling starling, stare at you with suspicious eyes, and say, "How do I know what you are going to *do* to my little bird!"

THE MAJOR DISADVANTAGE OF A CENTRALIZED PATIENT POPULATION

The major disadvantage of a centralized rehabilitation facility is disease control.

At Lifeline for Wildlife, our most serious problems are in raising large numbers of raccoons at one time. Raccoons are subject to two major infectious diseases: canine distemper and raccoon parvovirus.

Distemper is endemic in the wild raccoon population in our area of Southern New York. Raccoons showing the characteristic neurological signs of advanced distemper are admitted to Lifeline almost every day. In spite of the prevalence of the virus in our environment, good sanitation, immediate diagnosis and euthanasia in admitted animals—and regular vaccination of unaffected individuals—has enabled us to confine our distemper mortality almost exclusively to animals already infected prior to arrival.

Parvovirus is a much more serious problem. Large numbers of viral particles are shed in the stools of affected animals. The virus is stable in the environment for a year, and is not easily killed by disinfection. Furthermore, currently available vaccines have been extremely unreliable in immunizing raccoons against the disease. We control losses to parvo by raising raccoons in small groups, disinfecting as thoroughly as possible, and by isolating or euthanizing diseased animals. In spite of these precautions, mortality due to parvovirus remains high.

Raccoons also shed the infamous parasite baylisascaris. A normal parasite of raccoons, this roundworm, when eaten by a non-raccoon, has a tendency toward migration into nervous tissue, causing blindness, neurological disturbance, and often death. Species vary in their susceptibility to this visceral larval migrans, but it is a leading cause of death in rodents, and may have even killed several human beings.

We control this problem by routine wormings of all raccoons and regular microscopic monitoring of feces for the characteristic eggs. All animal handlers are advised to wash thoroughly after handling any animal, and to eat in areas away from animal quarters. In addition, cages that have housed raccoons are never subsequently used for other species.

Other contagious diseases have been pigeon and squirrel pox, Newcastle disease, and various bacterial and viral enteridities in many species. These problems are controlled by prompt diagnosis, isolation, and where appropriate, euthanasia.

THE CHALLENGES OF A CENTRALIZED FACILITY

There are three other issues that I'd like to mention briefly. They are: money, business management, and personnel management. All three are absolutely essential in developing a centralized facility. Many people might want to term these, additional "disadvantages"—reasons why it might be easier or better to choose a different method of operation. But I perceive them as challenges rather than disadvantages.

Many people go into non-profit work because they don't want to deal with "business": i.e. profit and loss, hiring and firing. We want to do good deeds and help the world—we don't want to run a business.

Non-profit business is still business. And the business aspects of a non-profit organization cannot be second or third priority. The business end of a non-profit organization must run neck and neck with the charitable work itself. There are 3 fundamental aspects of non-profit business which I'd like to emphasize very briefly:

1. Personnel: Even a 10 or 15 person staff can feel like a fulltime job! There is recruitment, new-employee training, supervision, evaluation, job descriptions, conflict negotiations, discipline, the art of firing. And good management doesn't work very well unless the agency uses creativity and energy in an ongoing recruitment program to find the most exciting, motivated and dynamic people to join the staff.
2. Fund Raising: There is never enough and there never will be enough! An ethical non-profit organization increases its responsibilities commensurate with any budget increases—so the squeeze is always on. The one reminder essential here, is that fund raising is paramount to any center, and that it must be an ongoing, daily task. It cannot be relegated to selected "events" throughout the year; it can't be left for "the slow season".
3. Administration: It is essential that any centralized rehabilitation center develop an administrative staff which is equal in every way to its patient care staff; equal in inspiration, motivation, and deep dedication to the welfare of the animals and the agency. These become two separate, but equal, halves of the organization, united with only *one* purpose: to rescue, rehabilitate and release distressed wildlife.

In conclusion, I want to state that we, the wildlife rehabilitation community, *can* achieve the utopian centers and sanctuaries that we dream of! But a non-profit agency of this size and scope cannot survive without aggressive leadership and a keen instinct for non-profit entrepreneurship! That's a fact that we all have to face. Remember, if the agency fails due to insufficient funding, or poor business management—what happens to the animals it was created to serve?

A NEW APPROACH TO RECORDS ANALYSIS IN A WILD BIRD REHABILITATION CENTER
A Survey of 1,921 Cases Delivered to a Mid-Atlantic Rehabilitation Facility

Lynne Frink and John Frink

Tri-State Bird Rescue and Research, Inc.
P.O. Box 1713
Wilmington, DE 19899

INTRODUCTION

Tri-State Bird Rescue and Research was established in 1977 to examine the effects of oil on birds. The Delaware River was at that time the second-largest oil-carrying waterway in the United States; five major oil spills had occurred in the mid-Atlantic area over a 30-month period, contaminating over 10,000 waterbirds. This early focus on uniting rehabilitation and research resulted in Tri-State's placing a high priority on the development of an accurate and thorough records-keeping system.

Tri-State opened its present clinic in 1982, and currently treats 1,200 to 1,500 birds each year. This paper deals with a broad survey of 1,921 of these birds brought to Tri-State over a 24-month period between 1982 and 1984.

The data encompasses a wide range of information about each bird brought to us. Accurate records are vital to ensure good daily care of the individual animal, but we also view our records in a broader sense, as enabling us to study what is happening outside our clinic, as well as inside. The general survey covers the types of injuries we receive, correlates them with seasonal distribution, and environs, and also takes a look at the relationship between cause of injury and type of injury.

Numerous excellent studies have been done on major causes of mortality in wild birds (Jennings 1961, Cooper and Eley 1979, Fulton 1984, Welty 1979). Oil spills in the North Atlantic around Great Britain account for mortality of over one million waterbirds annually (Cooper and Eley 1979). The use of monofilament gill nets by halibut fishermen in Monterey Bay, California, killed an estimated 17,000 seabirds during the summer of 1981 (Cooper and Eley 1979). Drift nets used in salmon fishing off Greenland annually kill more Thick-billed Murres (500,000) than salmon (Fulton 1984). Between 2 and 3 million wild birds die each year in the United States from lead poisoning (Bellrose 1959).

Not all wildlife mortality is so obvious or well-documented. This paper examines the problem from a different perspective: the types of injuries incurred by birds brought to a mid-Atlantic wildlife rehabilitation facility. This type of regional study has its own place in the scientific literature. There is a need to understand the chronic, long-term pressures on wild birds attempting to survive in increasingly urbanized areas; wildlife rehabilitators may have the best opportunity to record and study trends in this area.

COLLECTING THE DATA

The Tri-State Clinic is located near Wilmington, Delaware, within 10 miles of the states of Pennsylvania, New Jersey, and Maryland. The facility is a converted 100-year-old schoolhouse on 7 acres of county parkland.

Tri-State has received birds representing 135 species, with a wide variety of injuries. The clinic is open during the daylight hours every day of the year. We have three paid staff members, and maintain a trained corps of approximately 100 volunteers who are required to attend 15 hours of training sessions of hands-on workshops and lectures, and who are exepcted to work at the clinic twice per month.

We train veterinary students and graduate students from the life sciences and offer summer work grants to veterinary students, where they can earn up to six credits assisting in rehabilitation efforts or conducting research projects. We have also established a program for training state and federal Fish and Wildlife agents in field stabilization techniques. These training programs are useful not only in improving the treatment our cases receive but also in instructing workers in uniform records-keeping techniques.

A General Records Form is kept on each bird, documenting the location, habitat, and time of retrieval, and pre-delivery care. Also recorded are information obtained from a general physical examination that may include diagnostics such as blood work, radiographs, or parasitology, and immediate treatment. Daily records forms record *every* aspect of the animal's care. Each of the records in this study was reviewed by the authors to ensure accuracy and consistency. The information was then coded onto a Master Data Record and computer-entered. This study utilized an IBM PC with 640K RAM and Lotus 1-2-3 software. For detailed statistical analysis, the data will be uploaded to an IBM 3083 mainframe computer utilizing SAS software.

CASELOAD BY STATE

The 1,921 birds in this study were brought to us from five states, with the majority (72.8%) coming to us from Delaware. At times, birds are brought to us from more distant areas for specialized rehabilitation. Table 1, *Distribution by State*, indicates one such delivery of 28 oiled loons from Virginia. Each year the number of birds brought to us from states other than Delaware increases.

CASELOAD BY HUMAN POPULATION DENSITY

With over 6,084 possible data combinations to examine for each individual bird, we tried to study the information which we felt would give us the broadest initial perspective of our data. We examined the avian caseload in the framework of human population distribution, examining birds brought to us from city, suburban and rural areas (Graph 1). 56% (1,087) of the birds in this study were delivered from suburban areas, where most of our human population resides. While only 16% (304), of our total caseload came from rural areas, 46% (61) of the raptors we received were rural deliveries.

DISTRIBUTION BY LOCATION
1921 CASES — 24 MONTHS 1982-84

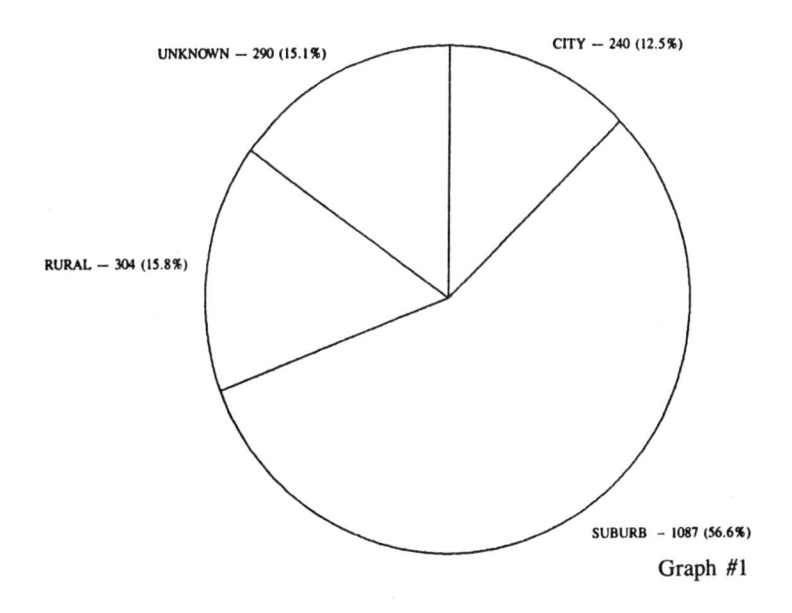

UNKNOWN — 290 (15.1%)
CITY — 240 (12.5%)
RURAL — 304 (15.8%)
SUBURB — 1087 (56.6%)

Graph #1

TABLE 1. DISTRIBUTION BY STATE SOURCE OF REFERRAL (N = 1,921)

State	Number of cases	Percent
Delaware	1399	72.8
Pennsylvania	261	13.6
New Jersey	59	3.1
Virginia	28	1.5
Unknown	132	6.3
Total	1921	100.0

DISTRIBUTION BY CAUSE OF INJURY
1921 CASES — 24 MONTHS 1982-84

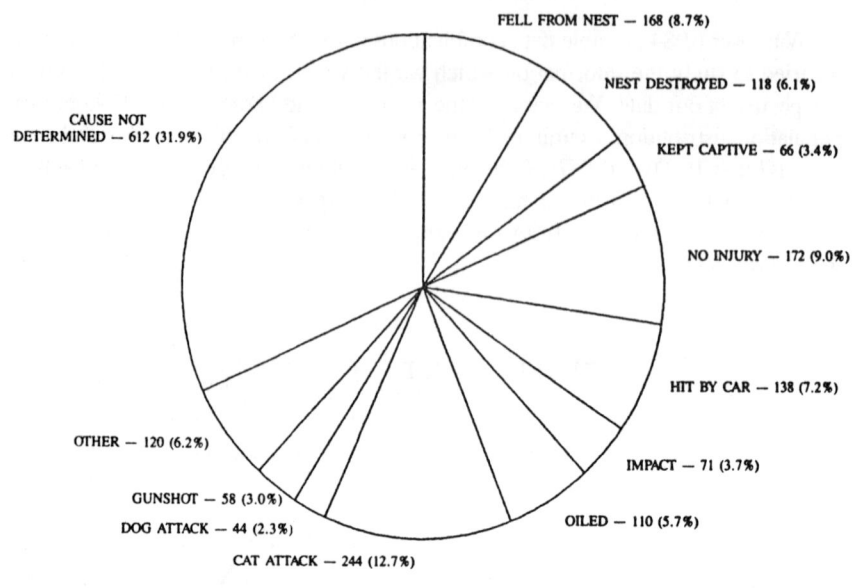

- FELL FROM NEST — 168 (8.7%)
- NEST DESTROYED — 118 (6.1%)
- KEPT CAPTIVE — 66 (3.4%)
- NO INJURY — 172 (9.0%)
- HIT BY CAR — 138 (7.2%)
- IMPACT — 71 (3.7%)
- OILED — 110 (5.7%)
- CAT ATTACK — 244 (12.7%)
- DOG ATTACK — 44 (2.3%)
- GUNSHOT — 58 (3.0%)
- OTHER — 120 (6.2%)
- CAUSE NOT DETERMINED — 612 (31.9%)

Graph #2

TABLE 2. DISTRIBUTION BY REASON FOR REFERRAL BY CITY, SUBURB, AND RURAL LOCATION (N = 1,921)

Referral	City	Suburb	Rural	Total
Cases	240	1088	716	1921
	12.5%	56.6%	15.8%	
Nest problem				
Fell	9.6	9.5	7.3	8.7
Destroyed	7.9	6.3	8.8	6.1
Animal cause				
Dog	—	2.6	3.1	2.3
Cat	7.9	16.5	17.5	12.7
Human cause				
Gunshot	—	1.9	3.4	3.0
Auto hit	9.2	6.3	7.0	7.2
Oil spill	14.6	—	5.2	5.7
Impact	5.0	3.9	3.6	3.7
No injury	6.7	10.0	6.4	9.0
Captive	2.9	3.0	2.4	3.4
Toxicity	2.1	1.6	—	—
Entrapment	1.7	—	—	—
Other	5.4	6.8	5.9	6.2
Unknown	27.1	31.7	29.6	31.9

DISTRIBUTION BY CAUSE OF INJURY

Graph 2, *Distribution by Cause,* was compiled following detailed questioning of every person who delivered a bird. While it is not usually difficult to document *types* of injuries, such as fractured long bones and soft tissue damage, it requires a special effort to determine what caused the problem (cat attack, impact such as flying into a window, etc.)

Table 2 further breaks down the cause of injury by rural, suburb and city areas. If we remove 612 of the cases for which we could not determine cause, and the 172 birds (nestling-fledgling) with no apparent injury, we find that 78% of the birds we received were disabled as a *direct* result of human acitivity.

Hatching year birds account for 55% of our caseload during the study period. However, 93% of the birds presented with "No Apparent Injury" are hatching year birds; many of these were removed from their parents as fledglings by unknowing, concerned citizens. We have made it a priority at Tri-State, through educational handouts and programs, to discourage people from picking up seemingly uninjured fledgling birds.

15% of the birds we receive have suffered traumatic injury as a result of attacks by domestic pets. This is the largest single cause of injury in the birds we received. Welty (Welty 1979) points out that, "Wherever man goes, he takes with him animal satellites whose impact on native birds is almost universally harmful." He includes rats in the same "satellite" category as cats and dogs.

In the Tri-State study, injuries incurred from cat attacks are six times higher than dog attacks. We can speculate on the reasons for this: cats are less likely to be restricted by local pet control ordinances; dog attacks are more violent in nature and may result in immediate mortality; and cats may be better hunters of avian prey. While we understand that it is natural for cats to hunt, we try to point out to the public that high concentrations of well-fed domestic house cats are not a natural predator of wild birds in North America. A special pamphlet, "Songbirds, Your Pets and You" was designed to explain this problem and offer some suggestions to pet owners.

The "Unknown" category was used when direct or primary cause of injury could not be determined, or in cases of general disease conditions of unknown etiology. Miscellaneous and less common problems are listed in "Other," and include abuse at the hands of children and adults, botulism, pox, parasitism, electrocution, lead poisoning and chemical toxicity.

While we suspect that many of our birds suffer from organophosphate and other types of pesticide poisoning, it has in the past been difficult and expensive for us to identify a broad range of toxins, and we have been careful to enter only those cases about which we had a reasonable certainty. We purchased a spectrophotometer cell which will enable us to measure cholinesterase from blood samples in cases where we suspect organophosphate and carbaryl poisoning; 1986 will be our third year of collaborating with the University of Delaware on a set of toxicity studies, and we expect our documented incidence of pesticide poisoning to rise significantly.

DISTRIBUTION BY MONTH
1921 CASES — 24 MONTHS 1982-84

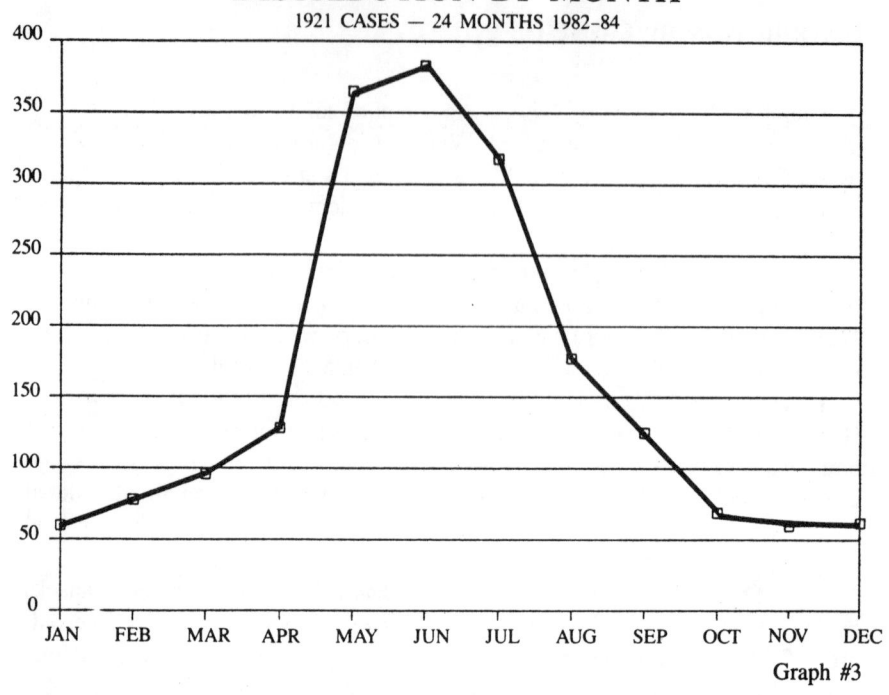

Graph #3

TABLE 3. DISTRIBUTION OF CASELOAD BY REFERRAL BY MONTH IN PERCENT (N = 1,921)

Month	Oil spill (110)	Gun shot (58)	Dog (44)	Cat (244)	Impact (71)	HBC (138)	Total (1921)
JAN	1.8	17.2	11.4	2.0	8.5	5.1	3.1
FEB	2.4	8.6	4.5	.8	4.2	5.1	4.1
MAR	2.5	8.6	6.8	2.9	8.5	.7	5.0
APR	2.7	6.9	9.1	4.9	4.2	8.0	6.7
MAY	2.7	5.2	9.1	17.6	19.1	10.1	19.0
JUN	5.5	—	2.3	28.2	9.9	11.6	19.9
JUL	1.8	—	1.1	18.9	11.3	17.4	16.6
AUG	6.4	5.2	9.1	7.3	5.6	10.9	9.2
SEP	20.9	6.9	4.5	4.9	12.7	10.1	6.5
OCT	7.2	8.6	4.5	6.1	8.5	5.8	3.6
NOV	.1	17.2	4.5	3.2	1.4	4.3	3.1
DEC	.2	15.4	2.3	2.9	5.6	10.8	3.2
							100.0

DISTRIBUTION BY MONTH

Tri-State's caseload peaks dramatically in late spring and summer, emphasizing the fact that nestlings and fledglings comprise almost half of our caseload (Graph 3). At Tri-State, we find that records analysis offers a practical as well as a scientific value. Knowledge of caseload distribution throughout the year is instrumental in planning our budget, staffing our clinic and ordering supplies.

We plotted the distribution by month of different causes of injuries (Table 3). At a busy rehabilitation center it is useful to be able to forecast the types of injuries that are likely to be received during different seasons. A trend is not always apparent. For example, in the distribution of impact injuries (Graph 4) there seems to be no obvious trend. The sharp increase in the number of impact cases in the month of May is interesting, but the number of cases is too low for us to do more than speculate on the reasons for this increase.

The number of birds hit by cars (Graph 5) seems to peak in late summer and winter. We find that many of the summer birds hit by cars are fledglings, and the winter injuries seem to be mostly owls and hawks which we think tend to hunt the roads more when the ground freezes and fields are covered with snow. As our sample size increases over the years, we may be able to demonstrate a statistical correlation here.

Graph 6, which represents gunshot injuries throughout the year, rises sharply during the local hunting season. The overwhelming majority of the birds brought to us with gunshot injuries are species which cannot legally be hunted.

The number of cat and dog injuries peaks in summer along with the overall increase during baby bird season. It is interesting to note, however, that 40% of the individuals injured by domestic pets are adult birds (Graph 7).

The number of oiled birds we receive at Tri-State fluctuates in response to the frequency of oil tanker or heating oil truck mishaps. Line Graph 8 represents a number of small (<25 birds) spills as well as individual oiled birds, such as an Eastern Bluebird in crankcase oil, a Great-horned Owl from an open settling pit, and English Sparrows in doughnut grease. Major oil spills responses, which can bring us 60–200 birds in a three-day period, are the subjects of separate studies. While the major spills tend to occur in the winter when pack ice blocks the river, we don't expect to see any predictable seasonal trends with the small oil spill incidents.

RAPTOR CASELOAD

So far, we have looked mostly at causes of injury, concentrating on the distribution by cause and the seasonal caseload by cause. We can also draw out an entire age group or family of birds to study.

Tri-State received 132 birds of prey during the study period. 46% of these birds came from rural areas. The distribution by cause of injury was plotted for raptors only (Graph 9). 38% came in during the months of April, May and June, and 57% of these were nestlings and fledglings (Graph 10).

14% of the raptors had been shot, compared to 3% of the total caseload. A study of mortality in 1,428 Bald Eagles including gunshot wounds, National Wildlife Health Laboratory, Madison, WI, 1985 (NWHL), and a University of Minnesota study of 1,856 raptors delivered for rehabilitation (Duke 1982) record that 22% and 16%, respectively, of all raptors were delivered due to gunshot (projectile) injuries.

18% of the raptors that came to us had been hit by cars, compared to 7% of the total caseload. In the Bald Eagle study—(NWHL) which combines hit by car and hitting wires under the general category of "Trauma"—20% of the eagle mortalities were placed in this category. (We should point out here, again, that no statistical tests have been run yet to ascertain correlations. For example, there is a possibility that many birds are hit by cars, but birds of prey, generally being larger, are noticed more often, and survive the initial impact better.)

We believe at Tri-State that we only receive a small percentage of the birds of prey which are shot and trapped each year; we agree with Gary Duke in his paper on the University of Minnesota Raptor Research and Rehabilitation Program, that many "trappers will destroy a badly injured bird rather than bring it in for treatment." We likewise agree that trap wounds to legs have a very poor prognosis, and that the many raptors with no *apparent* injury released from the traps have little chance of long-term survival (Duke 1982).

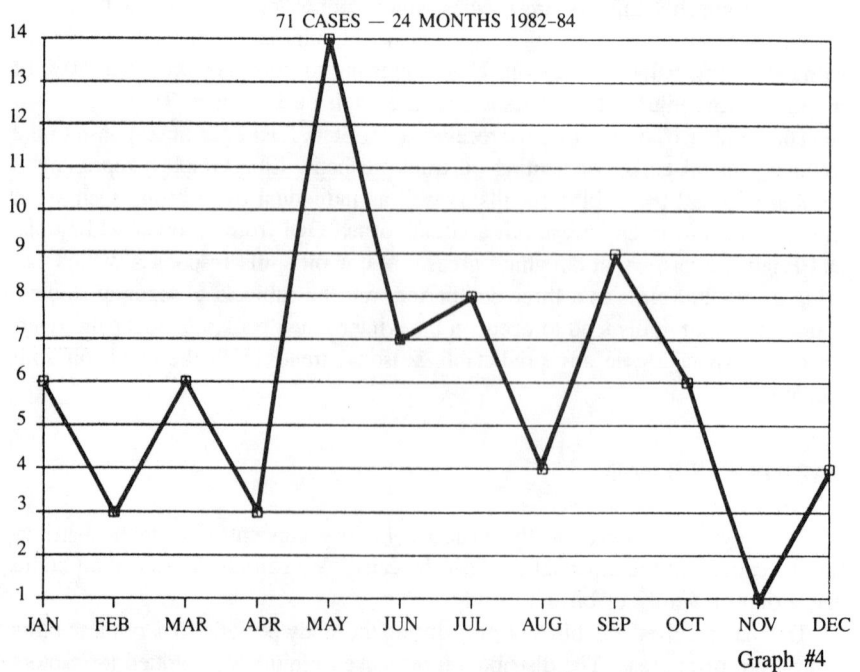

DISTRIBUTION BY MONTH — IMPACT
71 CASES — 24 MONTHS 1982-84

Graph #4

DISTRIBUTION BY MONTH — HIT BY CAR
138 CASES — 24 MONTHS 1982-84

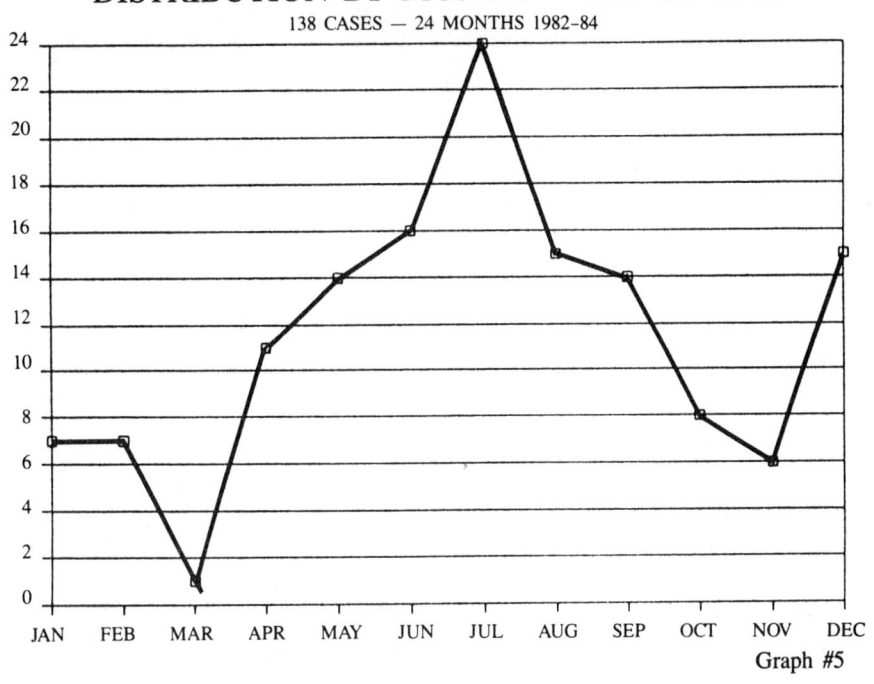

Graph #5

DISTRIBUTION BY MONTH — GUNSHOT
58 CASES — 24 MONTHS 1982-84

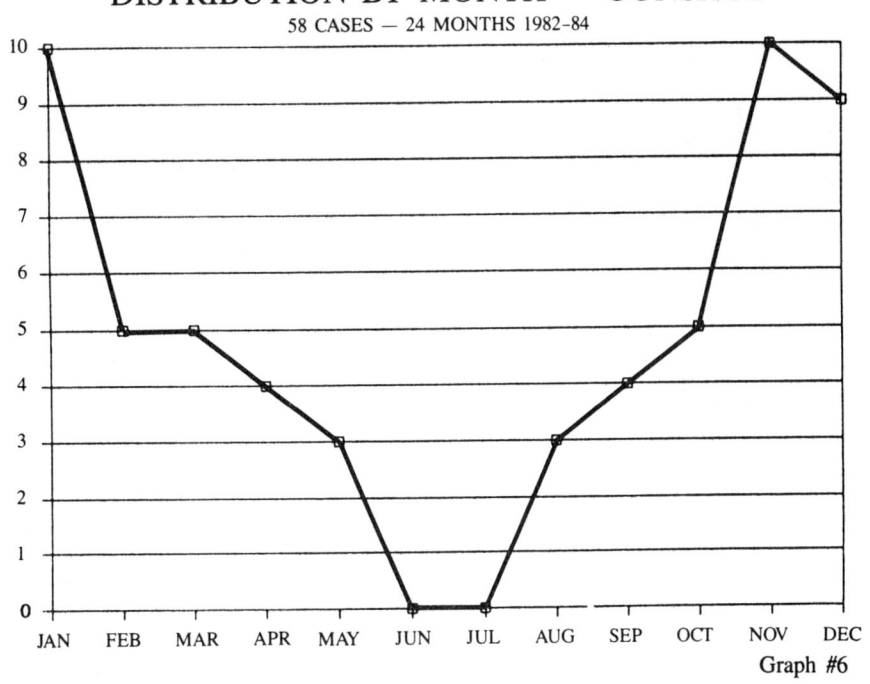

Graph #6

DISTRIBUTION BY MONTH — CAT & DOG
228 CASES — 24 MONTHS 1982-84

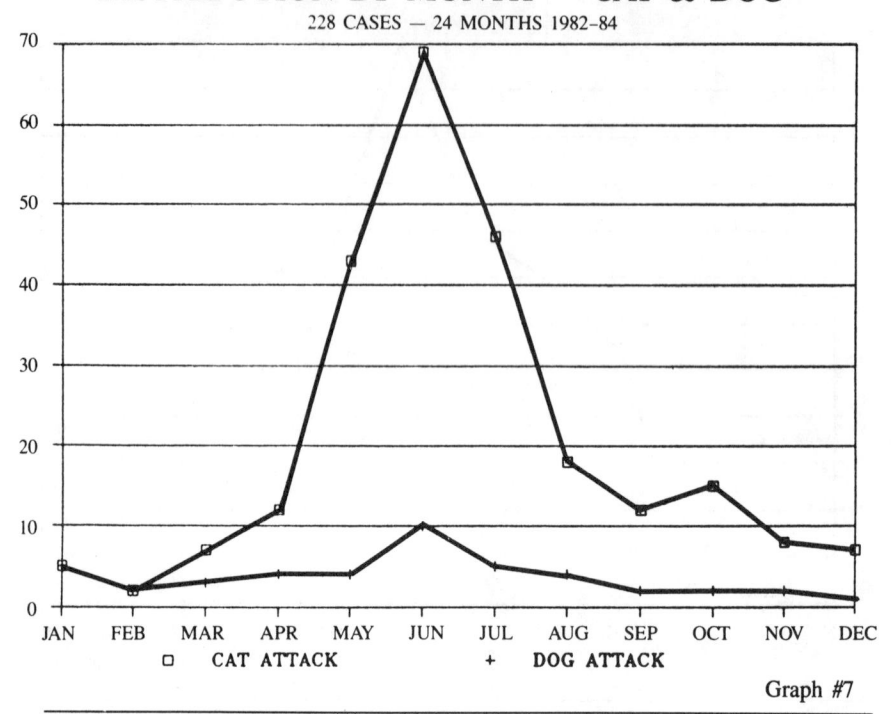

□ CAT ATTACK   + DOG ATTACK

Graph #7

DISTRIBUTION BY MONTH — OILED
100 CASES — 24 MONTHS 1982-84

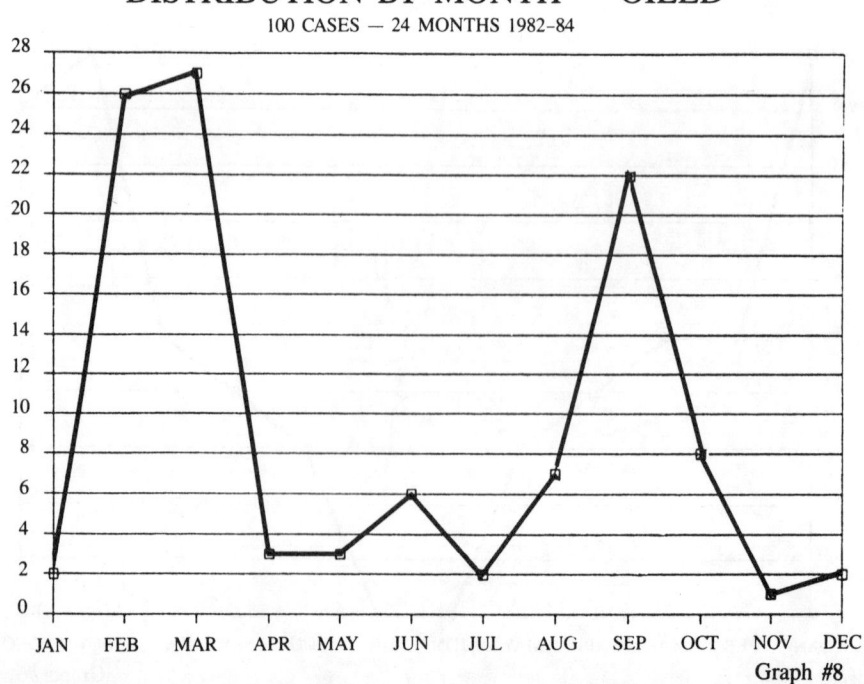

Graph #8

RAPTORS BY CAUSE OF INJURY
132 CASES — 24 MONTHS 1982–84

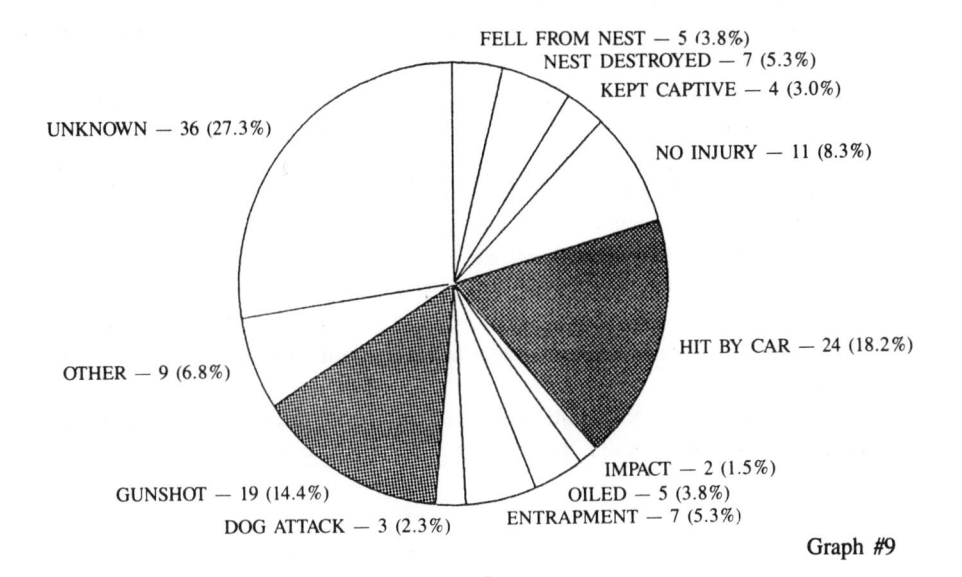

- FELL FROM NEST — 5 (3.8%)
- NEST DESTROYED — 7 (5.3%)
- KEPT CAPTIVE — 4 (3.0%)
- NO INJURY — 11 (8.3%)
- HIT BY CAR — 24 (18.2%)
- IMPACT — 2 (1.5%)
- OILED — 5 (3.8%)
- ENTRAPMENT — 7 (5.3%)
- DOG ATTACK — 3 (2.3%)
- GUNSHOT — 19 (14.4%)
- OTHER — 9 (6.8%)
- UNKNOWN — 36 (27.3%)

Graph #9

RAPTORS BY MONTH
132 CASES — 24 MONTHS 1982–84

Graph #10

INJURY CAUSE AND TYPE

We approached our data (augmenting it to include a total of 30 months of data) seeking relationships between cause of injury and type of injury, and mortality by cause of injury (Graph 11).

We have been able to study the percentage of birds we receive by cause of injury, compared to the number that live and the number that are releasable. With oiled birds, for example, including waterbirds, songbirds, and raptors, 74% of these birds survive, and 71% are released. With gunshot injuries, 57% live, but only 37% are released. One of our lowest success rates during this study period came with cat attacks; only 24% of these birds survived. (During this period we cultured a variety of bacterial organisms, including *Pasturella multocida,* and *Pseudomonas sp.* from a number of the cat bites. Subsequent immediate treatment with an antibiotic effective on gram negative bacteria helped to improve release rates in cat-bite birds.)

We were interested in investigating the relationship between causes of injury and the actual type of injury the bird experienced. Table 4 presents a sample of

SURVIVAL BY CAUSE OF INJURY
689 CASES

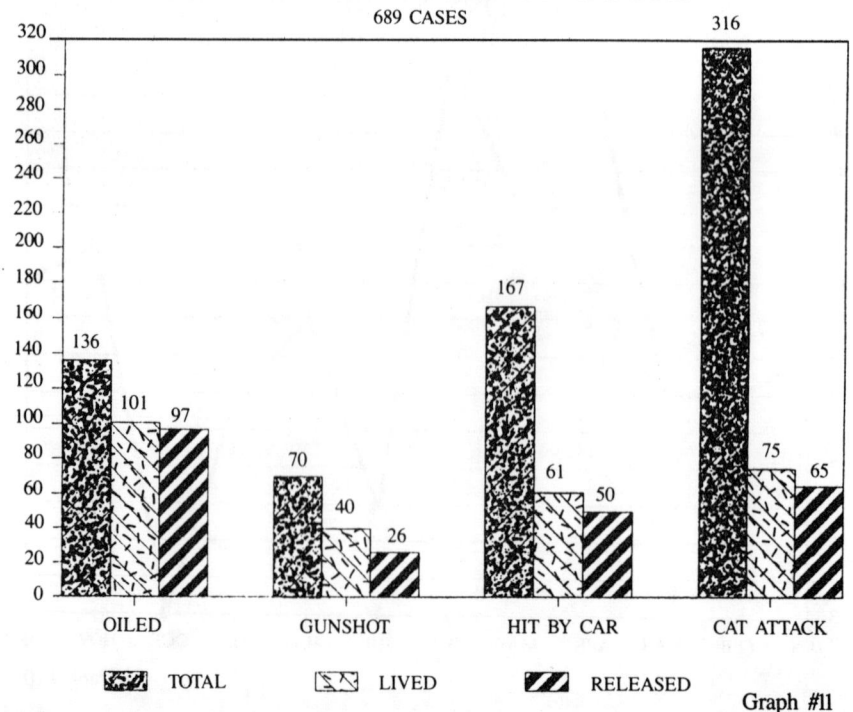

Cause	Total	Lived	Released
OILED	136	101	97
GUNSHOT	70	40	26
HIT BY CAR	167	61	50
CAT ATTACK	316	75	65

Graph #11

this data. These causes of injury: cat bite, gunshot and hit by car usually result in more than one type of injury. This table lists only the major or most debilitating of the injuries incurred. In gunshot injuries, 53% of the major injuries were soft tissue, followed by 36% being orthopedic. In birds that were hit by cars, the damage seems to have been equally distributed between soft tissue, orthopedic and neurologic trauma. While the birds attacked by cats had many injuries, in over 58% of the cases the major injury was to the soft tissue and organs.

FAMILY DISTRIBUTION
AS PERCENT OF TOTAL

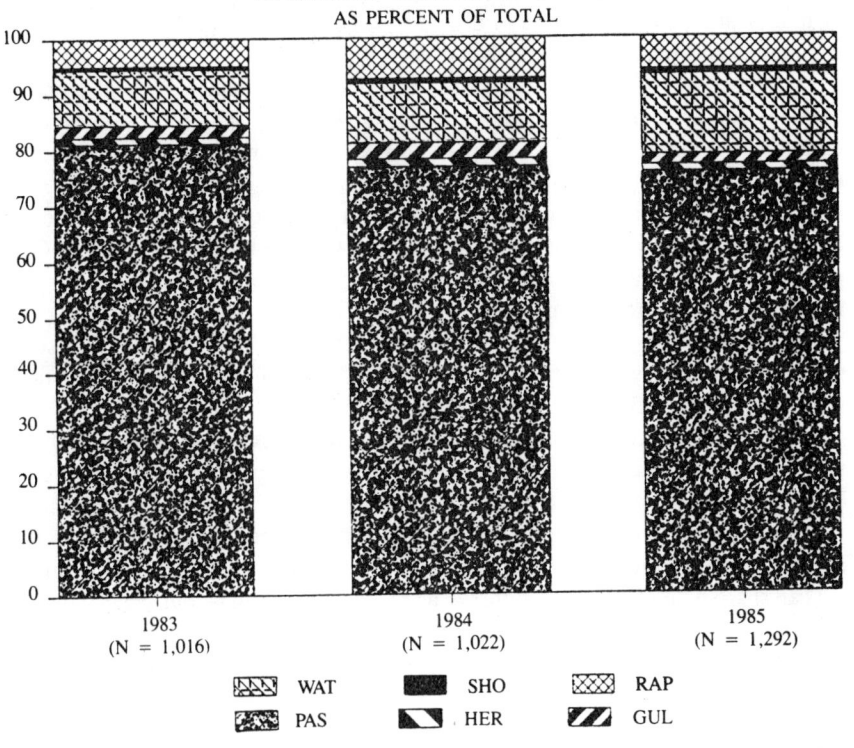

1983 (N = 1,016) 1984 (N = 1,022) 1985 (N = 1,292)

WAT SHO RAP
PAS HER GUL

Graph #12

TABLE 4. DISTRIBUTION OF INJURY TYPE BY CAUSE IN PERCENT: 24 MONTHS 1982–1984 (N = 1,921)

Major type	Gun shot (58)	Hit by car (138)	Cat bite (244)
Orthopedic	36.21	31.88	11.48
Soft Tissue	53.45	31.16	58.20
Neurologic	3.45	32.61	5.70
Other	3.45	2.17	14.34
Unknown	3.45	2.17	10.25

CASELOAD BY BROAD "FAMILY" GROUPING

Analysis of records can also be very useful on a practical level. Before designing new outdoor housing, we examined our caseload. We divided the caseload into very broad "family" groups, and compared three years by types of birds (Graph 12). We received 3,330 birds from 1983 to 1985. In each year, songbirds and woodpeckers (*Passeriformes* and *Piciformes*) made up about 77% of our caseload. The five remaining groups—herons and egrets, gulls and terns, waterbirds, shorebirds, and raptors—were also remarkably consistent from year to year. We will take this and our other findings into consideration as we expend our limited resources of money and people in efforts to design new housing, and determine what new techniques and treatment protocols we need to develop.

This year, we will enter 1,292 more cases into our computer. We will proceed from the survey study presented here to statistical studies using SAS, seeking correlations in a number of areas. We plan to investigate correlations between cause of injury and species; we will investigate the relationship of treatment protocol to release rates; we hope to study parasite burdens and age of avian host, and the effect of such factors as weight, blood values, and parasite burden on survival. Our pathologist has designed a data form to enable us to begin similar studies on histopathology in birds we necropsy.

We are excited about the records work we are doing now. We feel that such analysis makes our rehabilitation efforts more worthwhile and also helps us to understand the factors influencing populations of birds living in our area.

Any conscientious rehabilitator—whether she or he takes care of ten or a thousand animals, can keep accurate, useful records. No special academic training or wealthy donor is needed. Records can be kept by anyone who has a ballpoint pen.

Good records help ensure continuity and quality of care. The better our records are, the more we will learn from our successes and our mistakes, and the more we can share with others. The more we learn, the better will be our understanding of what is happening to the wild creatures who depend on us for their continued survival.

ACKNOWLEDGEMENTS

We extend our appreciation to Kenneth Eckhardt, Bob Lobou, F. Joshua Dein, and Barbara Druding for their assistance in the preparation of this paper.

REFERENCES

Bald Eagle Mortality from Lead Poisoning & Other Causes, 1963–1984. 1985. National Wildlife Health Laboratory, Wisconsin.

Bellrose, Frank C. 1959. Lead Poisoning as a Mortality Factor in Waterfowl Populations. XXVII, #3. Illinois Natural History Survey Bulletin. Urbana, Illinois.

Cooper and Eley. 1979. *Wild Bird Care.*

Duke, Gary E. 1982. Philosophy and Operation of the University of Minnesota Raptor Research and Rehabilitation Program. *Wildlife Rehabilitation: Volume 1.*

Fulton, Carol. 1984. Struggle over the Sea Otter. *Defenders,* Oct., 1984. 10–12.

Jennings, A.R. 1961. An Analysis of 1,000 deaths in wild birds. Proc. Internat'l Ornithological Congr. 353–357.

Welty, Joel Carl. 1979. *The Life of Birds.* Saunder Press, Philadelphia.

Public Education

PRODUCING AN EFFECTIVE PRESENTATION

Stephen L. Barten, D.V.M.

Vernon Hills Animal Hospital
1260 Butterfield Road
Mundelein, IL 60060

When you are asked to deliver a presentation, it is because you have certain knowledge or skills that your audience lacks. Accepting the invitation to speak obligates you to prepare the content, audiovisual, and delivery aspects of your program in order to deliver your message effectively.

ANALYSIS

A. Purpose (content): Do not try to cover too much in too short a time or you will loose the audience. Get your point across without being overly specific or technical. Do not dwell on your area of knowledge or you may earn the reputation of being an expert at being a bore.
B. Form: is your message best delivered as a lecture?
   - Complex subjects are delivered better as written articles in journals.
   - Subjects of limited interest are better when given to smaller groups.
   - Very technical subjects are handled better as workshops, where participants can have a hands-on experience.
C. Audience:
   - Size—can influence whether the talk is formal or conversational, what kinds of AV are used, and whether handouts are needed.
   - Level of education—will determine how much background data is needed and whether technical terms need to be defined.

ORGANIZATION

A. Body:
   - List priorities, consider time limit. Overload the audience and you will lose attention and comprehension.
   - Prepare a summary statement for each priority.
   - Support statements with data and references.
   - Statistics should be clear and not easily misunderstood. Avoid unnecessary numbers. Complex statistics should be available in handout form. State sources.

- Interject and tie appropriate humor to the topic.
- Try to tie your subject in with experiences the audience can relate to.

B. Introduction:
- Capture attention and generate interest.
- If effective, the audience will want to hear the presentation. If not, they will tune you out.
- Foreshadow what you will cover.

C. Conclusion: reinforce the points you have made by summarizing; tie up loose ends, draw implications.

D. Transitions: allow the audience to follow your train of thought. Lack of transition may leave the audience sidetracked.
- Explain why you are moving on to the next point.
- Use an anecdote to relate one point to the next.
- Trigger the next point using AV aids.
- Ask questions to arouse interest before stating what comes next.

AUDIOVISUAL AIDS

These help the audience follow the presentation and keep it on track. They reinforce verbal points, summarize points, and visually clarify concepts. Remember, AV aids are only aids. Visuals should enhance a presentation and not compete with it. Poor visuals cause the audience to become distracted. Using no illustration is better than using a poor one.

A. Do's and Don'ts of Audiovisual Aids
   Do Use Them To:
   - Summarize.
   - Show sequence.
   - Illustrate data with charts and graphs.
   - Add clarity to concepts and ideas.
   - Focus attention on key points.
   - Leave the slide on the screen long enough for the audience to absorb the information.

   Do Not:
   - Project copies of printed text. Instead, summarize information and show key points. If you want the audience to remember what you presented, give them written text.
   - Do not use charts or graphs that contain too much information. The group will not focus on the point you are trying to make.
   - Just read information from slides. The audience will become bored and tune you out.
   - Use copies of slides as handouts. AVs reinforce what you say but don't say it for you.

B. Overhead Transparencies
  1. Each transparency should reflect one idea.
  2. Lettering:
     - 1/4 inch high.
     - Typewriter with Orator typeface.
     - Special overhead lettering system.
     - Rub-off lettering.
     - If it must be handwritten, print; use all capitals, be neat.
     - Add color with ordinary markers, use illustrations and cartoons.
     - Should be able to read the original at a distance of 7 feet.
     - Maximum 6 lines per transparency.
     - Maximum 6-7 words per line.
     - Use horizontal format if possible so image fits the screen.
  3. Number them in case they're dropped.
  4. Clarity:
     - Label all elements on graphs and charts.
     - Use color and shading to stress key points.
     - Title every transparency.
C. Slides Are The Most Commonly Used AV Media
  1. Do not use a slide if:
     - It is too dark, too light, or out of focus.
     - It depicts a complicated graph, table, or printed page with too much data. This detracts from, instead of enriching, a presentation. A printed slide should contain no more than 8 lines and be readable if held 14 inches from the eye.
     - It shows cruel or inhumane restraint.
     - It depicts necropsy done without gloves, radiographs without proper shielding for the takers, or surgery without aseptic technique.
     - The subject is too far from the camera to be clearly seen from the back row of the audience.
     - It does not relate to the topic (except for transition slides).
     - A transition slide is confusing or distracting. Landscapes, sunsets, or flowers work best.
  2. Camera:
     35mm is the most commonly used. The film size is large enough to allow enlargements or projected images to be excellent quality. Smaller negatives limit satisfactory print size.
        Types include:
        (a) Rangefinder cameras: which have an optical viewfinder separate from camera lens. Etched frame outlines subject. Some have automatic parallax correction so the framing shifts as you focus the camera. These cameras are limited in available accessories like lenses.
        (b) Single lens reflex (SLR): looking through the eyepiece you see what the lens sees, no matter what attachments are used. They are available

with manual modes or automatic exposure, in which the camera selects the aperture, shutter speed, or both.
3. Exposure:
A combination of film speed, shutter speed, and lens aperture.
   (a) Film speed is expressed as an ISO/ASA number. The higher the number, the greater the film's sensitivity to light, and the less exposure is needed. However, the higher the number (indicating a faster film), the more grainy the print when enlarged. Film rated 400 and faster can be significantly grainy.
   (b) Shutter speed and aperture present a wide range of equivalent pairs. By doubling the exposure time (say from 1/60 to 1/30 of a second) and halving the aperture (from f5.6 to f8), the same exposure is achieved. Halving the exposure time would require opening the aperture one full stop (i.e. moving to the next lower f-stop number) to maintain the general balance.
   (c) Shutter speed: A moving subject can be frozen on the film with a fast shutter speed, say 1/500 to 1/1000 second. When a flash picture is taken, a setting of 1/60 second is used.
   (d) Aperture controls depth of field, which is the zone of sharp focus in front of and behind the main subject plane.
      1. Shallow zone of sharpness is useful in softening foreground and background details that might clutter the image (i.e. cage bars, fences, unnatural backgrounds, like shopping centers).
      2. Wide depth of field allows more detail in the picture, and is important in landscapes and closeup photography.
      3. Telephoto lenses allow less depth of field than normal or wide angle lenses.
      4. Other things equal, the depth of field increases as the aperture decreases (that is, as the f-stop numbers get larger). Smaller apertures allow less light to enter the camera, so longer exposures or supplemental flash becomes necessary. Most macro work is done at f-22 or f-32 with a flash.
   (e) Bracket your shots. After taking your photograph, take more shots one setting above and one below the first to assure at least one photo turns out just right. This will almost end over/underexposed slides from lectures.
4. Perspective is controlled by the position from which you photograph the subject and is controlled by the lens and the angle of view. Lenses are measured in focal length.
   - 50mm is the standard lens that comes with most cameras and mimics the angle of view of normal human vision.
   - Lenses less than 45mm (many are 28mm) are wide angle lenses. These record more of a given scene at a given distance. These are useful for photographing the inside of rooms and cages as well as landscapes.

Distance and size relationships may appear distorted, especially at close distances.
- Lenses over 55mm are telephoto lenses. These include less subject area than a normal lens and enlarge the subject on the film. Distances between objects appear compressed. Good for bird photography.
- Macro lenses are available in both normal and telephoto focal lengths for closeup work. I like a 100mm macro lens because it allows closeup shots of living subjects from a slight distance, so the subject is not frightened or endangering the photographer.

Inexpensive "closeup lenses" that look like filters, attach to the primary lens and work well. They vary in strengths of magnification (labeled +1, +2, +3) and can be combined for greater magnification.

5. Flash:

More light allows for greater depth of field, highlights the subject, and washes away harsh shadows.
- Automatic flashes have a light sensor that measures light reflected off the subject and cuts the flash off when enough light has hit the subject. Many can be set at three different f-stops.
- If a regular flash is used, bracket 3 shots to ensure at least one good exposure.
- When a camera is focused close up on a small subject, a regular flash in the camera's hot shoe will miss the subject. This can be corrected by using a bracket to redirect the flash or by using ring light that attaches to the front end of the lens.

6. Film:

Pick one brand, one film speed and stick with it, so you know how the film will respond under various conditions. Kodachrome tends to accent the reds; Echtachrome accents the blues; slides are good for lectures; and black and white is good for publications.

7. Useful equipment:

Tripod, cable release, copy stand, rechargeable batteries.

8. Advice:
- Practice by taking many exposures. Become familiar with how your camera will do under various conditions. Discard poor photographs so you are not tempted to use them. Be critical and adjust your technique.
- Bracket: Take several shots of the subject at different exposures.
- Classes: consider a photography class from a local junior college, high school, or photography store. There are many good books available.

D. Video, Film:

More expensive, calls for cautious preparation to produce quality video films. If properly chosen, can have dramatic effects.

E. Audiovisual Check List:
- Check the room layout to locate light switches and dimmers.
- Assure equipment is in good working order. Know how to use it or have

a qualified projectionist present to help. Confirm equipment 24 hours before the meeting, check room before the meeting.
- Confirm slides are in order and facing the right direction.
- Load and advance film to the starting point before the meeting.
- Have a contingency plan if equipment breaks down.

F. Written Handouts:
- Keep as brief as possible but still meaningful whether read a week before the presentation or a year later.
- Clear language—respond to communication biases.
- Relevant. Do not just provide data. Explain what it means.
- Capsulize. Do not repeat entire presentation.
- Specific. Do not give audience reading material they do not need.

DELIVERY

1. Notes are usually necessary.
    - Do not read word-for-word.
    - Effective presenters get into their presentations with eye contact, vocal inflection, facial expression, gestures, and movement.

   What is right for you?
    - Outline with cue words.
    - Major points on transparencies with notes to yourself.
    - Number note cards in case they're dropped.
2. For More Effective Presentation:
    - Indicate structure and sequence of the talk so the audience can follow.
    - Link points to each other and to the experience and needs of the audience.
    - Add support with examples, data, references.
    - Get into the presentation with verbal emphasis, vocal delivery, body language, humor.
3. Rehearsal to an audience, using AV material.
    - Get honest evaluation of content and delivery.
    - Act on suggestions.
    - Or use tape recorder and mirror.
    - *Time it.* Running over is rude and inconsiderate to your audience and the next speaker.

- Vocal delivery: project words. Stress important words. Avoid monotone. *Do Not Rush.*
- Physical delivery: relaxed position—do not fidget. Use hands and body to stress key points but do not gesture aimlessly. Use eye contact with one person for 2–3 seconds then scan group and focus on another.

STAGE FRIGHT

- Do not expect to be perfect. Everyone stumbles, so do not worry, just keep

going. People are willing to accept you as "human" especially if you accept that in yourself.
- You are not an actor alone on stage, you are sharing your knowledge with others.
- Be prepared, know your materials.
- Use deep breathing exercises to help you relax.
- Sit in an armchair and take a deep breath, hold it for a slow count of 5 then slowly exhale to count of 5. Do this 3 times. Now clutch the arms of the chair fiercely. Do 5 count, inhale and exhale 3 times while clutching the arms of the chair. Use whichever method works better for you.

SHARING YOUR NUGGETS OF KNOWLEDGE

Lou Strobhar

Willowbrook Wildlife Haven
Willowbrook Forest Preserve
525 S. Park Boulevard
Glen Ellyn, IL 60137

The Willowbrook Wildlife Haven receives approximately 4,000 wild animals for care annually, and about 10,000 telephone inquiries. Seven thousand of those calls are animal related. In the peak season, it is not unusual to receive 40 to 60 calls a day.

In a previous paper (Strobhar 1984) I suggested that the constantly ringing telephone was an important tool for the rehabilitator—a valuable resource which should not be wasted. It can be used as a means of utilizing public contact for promotion, and for providing educational and helpful information to a public which is increasingly demanding it. We live in an age of fast foods. Why not fast education?

Very few rehabbers have the benefit of a staff naturalist or educator. However, each rehabilitator can be his *own* mini-educator by developing a pattern of replies and a helpful attitude of sharing knowledge. In my first paper, I recommended a list of field guides, nature guides and other literature to keep handy to the phone. If you do not know the answer to an inquiry, look it up and read the information aloud to your caller. In this way, you have assured the person that he has correct and accurate information, and you have learned something you might not have taken the time to look up on your own. The telephone is going to ring anyway. Take advantage of it. Make it a positive, not a negative, experience.

In my seven years at Willowbrook as a volunteer and an employee, I have learned so much; sharing it has been challenging and rewarding—and fun. I would like to share with you some of my callers.

I'm sure all of you have also accumulated a wealth of anecdotes and facts. When we answer our phone or accept animals, we may be the only contact a visitor has with someone who has easy-to-understand and interesting information. We are very privileged to work with these animals, and our knowledge and experiences are unique. This knowledge that we have accumulated should never be taken for granted as commonplace. I have seen that attitude turn into smugness and superiority—and frankly, I have been guilty of it myself.

The most insignificant thing that we know may be a revelation to someone else. I once had a woman caller tell me that the baby squirrel she had just found needed immediate attention, because it was unconscious. When I asked how she knew that, she replied excitedly, "Because it's eyes are closed, but it's still breathing!"

When I explained why the eyes were closed, she was fascinated and wanted to know more. That wasn't ignorance on her part—just a gap in her education. Filling that gap is an important part of our work.

Too often the expression "Public Relations" or "PR"—is only a catch-phrase related to its effect on income, or fund-raising, or appearances. Public relations is exactly what it implies—a relationship with the public. When a person brings us an animal, we have an immediate relationship with that person. We're doing public relations work every time we write out a chart or answer the telephone. And a good job can only take five minutes or less. Even during days when I'm writing out 40 or 50 charts, I can manage a quick, "Thank you for bringing in the animal—we appreciate your caring," before I go on to the next person in line. (And, yes, there are some days when I feel as though we should be giving out numbers!)

Obviously, when you are logging in 40 animals a day with a telephone stuck in your ear, chattiness may have to take a back seat. And my comments are not meant...excuse me, please, while I take this phone call:

"Good Morning, Willowbrook Forest Preserve. Yes? You want some information about bunnies? Of course, how can I help you?... No, no, I promise I won't think it's silly.... You want to know if it's possible for a cat to nurse a baby bunny? Well, I'm not sure, but I would suppose so. There are a lot of stories of female mammals nurturing young of other species.... No, it wouldn't hurt or confuse the bunny. Cottontails are very basic, instinctual animals who do not require any parental investment from their mothers. Once the mother weans them at three weeks, she takes off to get pregnant again and they're completely on their own.... That's right, they don't need a role model to teach them anything.... Do you have a bunny?... Your cat does. Oh, I see. Your cat gave birth to two kittens?... And one died, and yesterday she came home with a baby bunny in her mouth...yes...licked it constantly trying to get it to nurse...and the bunny seems terrified? Well, I suppose it *is* terrified. Tell me, about how long in inches is this baby bunny?... About 5 or 6 inches.... Well, no wonder. That bunny has already been weaned and probably has been on its own for a week.... Yes, that's right, it doesn't need any care.... Well, I'm sorry, and I guess that is too bad for your cat. But really, the bunny won't respond and should be released outside.... Your cat? Well, you'll either have to keep her in for a day or take the bunny several blocks away to release him where there is tall grass or underbrush for hiding.... You're very welcome, and thank you for calling."

As I was saying, my comments are not meant so much for those insane days but for the more even-paced seasons. Now I could have simply and quickly told that woman, "No, the bunny won't nurse and you should let it go." What I did instead was give her confidence she wouldn't be laughed at, give her six quick natural history facts, some acknowledgment of her concern for her cat, and—I hope—the understanding that I cared for both animals involved. It took me about two minutes.

Incidentally, the telephone isn't the only place where this can be done. Filling out acquisition charts has become so automatic for me that while I'm doing that, I try to keep a running banter with people—partly to keep them from telling me *all* the gritty details about how they came across the animal—but mostly to share with them some of the animal's life. The baby season is perfect for that, as most wild babies are not too stressed by the handling.

For instance, as I'm filling in the box marked "sex", I not only tell them what sex the animal is, I demonstrate to them the location of the genitals. I attempt to steer away the "Isn't he cute?" comments to more general comments about the species, i.e. "Yes, he sure is. As a matter of fact, he looks exactly like the other 62 bunnies that are in our nursery, if you'd care to see them through the window in our exhibit room. He'll be one of about 1000 baby bunnies we'll get this year."

I never pass up the opportunity to tell people, "Did you know that if this baby is a female, when she grows up she will have about 30 to 35 babies of her own—every year?!" This usually gets the attention of most mothers. While I'm writing in the date and other automatic information, I explain how long babies nurse and when their eyes open and how long it takes for them to mature. Or how we no longer handle them after they're weaned, or how we isolate them from humans before releasing. Some—of this takes—Excuse me....

"Good Morning, Willowbrook Forest Preserve. Yes, ma'am...you have an unusual problem.... Oh, yes, we hear lots of unusual things, but most of the time to us, they're not so unusual. You were airing out your closets...and left the room windows open...and a Sparrow flew in?...into the closet...and before you could get to the closet a...what?...an owl flew in? After the Sparrow?.... Oh. And you shut the door real quick.... Now they're both in the closet.... Well, you don't want to leave them in there too long.... Oh, my goodness, I see. Your cat saw the whole thing, and is now stationed in front of the closet.... So you want to know how to get them out safely. Well, I suppose it depends on whose safety you're talking about.... You don't want the Sparrow to get hurt. Well, perhaps it would help you deal with the situation if you could keep in mind that nature doesn't operate with human values. It deals with a whole set of different values, and we need to respect that difference. After all, it works, when we don't interfere with it.... Yes, I would assume somebody's going to get the short end of the stick here, and my guess is it's going to be the Sparrow.... Oh, yes, the owl can see very well in the dark—but maybe all those clothes are confusing him.... There's really not too much you can do to control the situation, but I assume you can control the cat by removing him from the room and then open the closet door.... I do know that you're concerned about the Sparrow, but the owl *is* a bird of prey, and sparrows are part of its diet...yes, yes...that's right...and the chase may have ended in your closet—but maybe not. There's nothing you can do to keep him from pursuing the Sparrow again once you let them out...assuming the deed isn't already done.... No, there shouldn't be any carnage in there. He'll eat the whole thing. Then later he will cast up a pellet that has all the bones and feathers and claws in it which don't get digested. That's called casting.... That's right...he'll do that someplace else. Well, I'm sorry I couldn't be of more help to you, but I'm glad you called—you were right, this *is* an unusual one, even for us. You're welcome."

Now about complaints—I'm sure you all deal with them, and are all as tired as I am of defending the wild animal's right to exist. Nuisance wildlife calls became such a problem of repetition at Willowbrook that we finally put it all in a brochure, and we offer to mail it to callers if the situation isn't critical; it does save telephone time. Many people simply cannot grasp the concept of a wild animal existing anywhere else but in...a forest or wilderness.... Excuse me again.

"Good morning, Willowbrook Forest Preserve. Yes, we have wild animals here.... No, sir, we're not missing any. You have an opossum which you've trapped...and you want us to take it...yes...yes, sir...sir...if I may interrupt you for a minute. I don't want to seem rude or uninterested, but I am so swamped with calls today and I *do* want to be able to help you. May I ask you some questions?... Okay. Is there anything wrong with the animal?... It's ugly—for starters...and it doesn't belong in your neighborhood?... You have a lot of children in the area. Well, for one thing, let me try to make you feel a little easier about the safety of the children. This is *not* a dangerous or aggressive animal, although even a little bunny might try to bite you if you attempted to touch it. And they are very common around here...no sir, we would not accept it if you brought it here anyway, because it is a healthy animal and we only accept injured or orphaned animals.... Someone told you it was endangered? Well, no sir, I'm sorry you were given some bad information, although it is possible that the person was confusing the word 'endangered' with 'protected,' and yes, the opossum is protected by conservation laws, the same as raccoons and squirrels and birds. Almost all wild animals are protected by state laws, meaning they cannot be hunted or trapped or killed without a proper license...yes, yes...that's right, that includes the live trap you have. No, no...we're not a law enforcement agency, but we do feel a responsibility to inform people of the laws concerning wildlife.... Yes sir, I *know* you think it is a damned ugly animal with no earthly purpose, and I am sorry you feel that way. But in my view, ugliness is not a justification for a death sentence. You know, many people think the opossum is an interesting animal. It has a pouch, you know...yes, just like a kangaroo...those animals are called marsupials, and it is the only one we have on this continent. The mother is like a walking nest, even after the babies come out of the pouch. They cling to her body wherever she goes. It's a very efficient little system. And really, she *does* have a useful function wherever she lives. Opossums are carrion eaters...carrion, that's dead flesh...yes, dead birds, right, and road-killed squirrels and other animals. Opossums and crows and owls and other species help keep all those dead bodies from going to waste...sure...that's right—a place for everything.... And opossums are not very territorial, either...yes...it will probably move on when you let it go. But not right away, because it may take quite a while before the animal feels safe enough to come out of the trap, so the best time to open it would be at night...yes, they're nocturnal.... No, no—we won't tell anyone on you...well, it's nice you have a sense of humor about it.... Well, thank you, and I'm glad you feel a little better about opossums.... What's that you say?... They're still ugly? Okay, I guess you're entitled. You're welcome. Good-bye."

Now, where was I? I say that a lot during the year. In addition to logging in animals and answering the phones and directing visitors and groups, and record keeping, I am the secretary to the manager and four staff members, and I write a monthly newsletter. Interruptions are a way of life for me. Excuse me.

"Good morning, Willowbrook Forest Preserve. Yes ma'am...it's so cold outside. Yes it certainly is today...and you want to know what to feed the poor squirrels. Well, we want to thank you for calling for information—a lot of people wouldn't bother to do that, so we're glad you care enough to get information. The squirrels, fortunately, really do not need us to provide food for them. Nature has it all out there for them. And as far as the weather goes, they're quite used to it otherwise they wouldn't remain here all winter...yes, they do find adequate shelter in trees and hollow logs and such...yes.... What *do* they eat out there? Quite a variety of things which *we* certainly would not recognize as food—acorns, of course, and buds from twigs and branches, different fungus growths, insect eggs and larvae that are in the bark of trees—even the bark itself.... Do you have trees?... Well, then, every time you start feeling sorry for the squirrels, think of those trees as big squirrel supermarkets. They provide all the food and shelter that squirrels need to survive.... Right...sure...you're very welcome, and we would love to have you come visit our center some day. Good-bye."

It helps to be able to read the mood of your caller. Humor goes a long way, but if the caller is angry, you don't want to seem flippant. If the caller is distressed, your levity may seem insulting. Reassure the caller that he has called the right place for information, and by asking a few simple lead questions such as, "How long has it been there?", or, "When did you first notice it?". You can get...a feel for your caller's attitude.... Excuse me again.

"Good Morning, Willowbrook Forest Preserve.... Yes, this is the animal place.... No, no, that's okay...you wouldn't be the first caller with a silly situation. And they're usually not silly to us. You have a skunk...hanging around your garden.... Really? Well, you're unusual because most people I talk to *don't* like them.... Oh, of course, I know the odor is terrible. You can mist your rooms with a mixture of white vinegar and water to help neutralize the odor.... Oh, your real problem is that he sprayed your tomatoes...and you want to know...if you eat them, can you get rabies? Okay—well, for starters no, rabies is carried through the saliva of the carrier, which has to be injected into open tissue—like a bite, yes—but it can also be contracted from other body fluids which come into contact with a scratch or cut, or the eyes...yes, that's right. So there's no need to worry about your tomatoes. As a matter of fact, there is really no need to be overly concerned about rabies in our county, as we fortunately do not have a problem. There was only one case reported last year. And that was a bat.... That's right.... You're very welcome. Good-bye."

As I said before, interruptions are a way of life through much of the busy season. Granted, I'm doing basically secretarial work (when I'm not running in to help the keeper restrain a raccoon, or feeding baby squirrels at my desk because the volunteers didn't show up). My point is that I, too, have schedules that must be met and work that is unending and demanding.

Two years ago when I delivered my paper on telephone techniques, a rehabilitator wanted a copy to give to her supervisor who had told her she was wasting too much time with callers. Believe me, it is *not* time wasted. As the person "up front," I can testify to the effectiveness of this kind of public relations and good will. People have thanked me profusely for the information, delighted they could pass it along to their children or neighbors. Others have been genuinely grateful for the helpful information about a nuisance wild animal, saying, "It's good to know you're here."

Visitors have remarked, "I spoke with you on the phone a few weeks ago, and we thought we'd drop by and see what it was like." And they drop some bucks in the donation box. Or they refer us to their neighbor's Boy Scout den, or to their children's teacher for a possible field trip. One couple I spent twenty minutes with were so grateful for the information and my patience they sent us a check for $200...and have remained annual contributors.... Excuse me.

"Good Morning, Willowbrook Forest Preserve. You wanted some information about Mallard ducks? How can I help you?... You have a boat docked on Lake Michigan...and you came back from vacation and went down to check out the boat...went on board...and found a Mallard in the hatch? And she flew away...and left 14 eggs! And you want to know how long it will take for them to hatch. Well, they probably won't without the female to incubate them, and we don't encourage people to artificially hatch duck eggs.... You won't have to? Oh.... I see...she came back...and stays there...and every weekend when you get on board you knock on the deck.... I see...she takes off and you get on board.... And then you and your husband cruise around the lake for a few hours...with the eggs. Then when you return, she's waiting on the dock.... You leave and she hops back on board. How long has this been going on?... About two weeks? Well, the Mallard will lay one egg a day and won't incubate until she's laid them all, which could be anywhere between 6 and 16. Then it takes 28 days for hatching.... Yes, that's right.... What if they hatch in the hatch?...during the week while you're gone? Yes, the babies will be trapped down there. They don't climb very well, although they can hop some...steps are too high...might be there for days before you get there. Well, all I can suggest is for you to get a calendar and start estimating the first possible date she could have laid the 14th egg, calculate 28 days from that, and make sure somebody gets over there to check the boat—maybe the marina personnel might be willing...yes, just gather them up and drop them overboard...yes, they can swim 24 hours after hatching—just make sure their down is dry and fluffy. The mother will probably get all excited and maybe fly off, but she won't go far.... Oh, you're welcome—Bon voyage!"

To repeat myself, filling in all those little information gaps *is* an important part of our work. If you can't—or don't want to interact with the public, find yourself a volunteer who does. Train that person to handle your telephone inquiries, because without the good will of an informed public, our work with wildlife is merely wheel-spinning. We work for the benefit of wildlife. We can't realistically do it alone. We need people. We need to nurture them, also. We need for them to understand these animals and their needs before we can expect people to support the wildlife cause.

REFERENCE

Strobhar, Lou. 1984. The Telephone as An Educational Tool. Wildlife Rehabilitation Vol. 3.